MW01000172

The Neighborhoods of New York City

KENNETH T. JACKSON, GENERAL EDITOR

ADVISORY BOARD

Osborn Elliott Founding

Chairman, Citizens Committee

for New York City

Henry Cornell Chairman,

Citizens Committee

for New York City

Peter H. Kostmayer President,

Citizens Committee

for New York City

Thomas H. Guinzburg

Director Emeritus,

Citizens Committee

for New York City

Although outsiders often regard New York City as an undifferentiated mass of 8 million rude, indifferent people, Gotham is in fact a collection of more than 400 individual neighborhoods, each containing its fill of involved and friendly residents and each cherishing a unique sense of identity and place. Here, as elsewhere in America, locally owned haberdasheries, hardware stores, delicatessens, greengroceries, and bakeries along main streets compete with shopping centers and malls, but it is still a fact that New York is almost the last place in the nation where neighbors routinely pass one another on the sidewalk or exchange greetings at a corner store, in the local park, or at a community center. From stoops and front porches they discuss news of their block, or of the world. Indeed, New York has become the best place in the United States to experience what was once the essence of small-town America.

THE NEIGHBORHOODS OF

Queens

Claudia Gryvatz Copquin

Introduction by Kenneth T. Jackson

CITIZENS COMMITTEE
FOR NEW YORK CITY

Yale University Press ■ New Haven and London

PROJECT STAFF

Sonia S. Estreich,
  Managing Editor
Michelle LeMay-Santiago,
  Development
Jemilah Magnusson,
  Project Coordinator

Mary Jane Peluso, Publisher
Lauren Shapiro,
  Sponsoring Editor
Vadim Staklo, Sponsoring Editor
Julie Carlson,
  Development Editor
Susan Laity, Manuscript Editor
Steve Colca, Assistant Editor
Laura Robb, Editorial Assistant

Ray Anastas, Photographer
William L. Nelson, Cartographer
Colette Nelson, Cartographer
Timothy Calabrese, Demographer
Kaleila Pu-Folkes, Mapping and Pro-
  files Coordinator
Ana C. Diaz, Survey Coordinator

Christina Coffin,
  Production Director
Karen Stickler,
  Production Controller

Copyright © 2007 by Citizens Committee for New York City. All rights reserved. This book may not be reproduced, in whole or in part, including illustrations, in any form (beyond that copying permitted by Sections 107 and 108 of the U.S. Copyright Law and except by reviewers for the public press), without written permission from the publishers.

Photographs by Ray Anastas unless otherwise identified.

Photographs, p. ii: see p. 34; p. vi: Adam Coglianese, NYRA track photographer

Set in Bodoni type by Technologies 'N Typography, Inc. Printed in the United States of America.

Library of Congress Cataloging-in-Publication Data

Copquin, Claudia Gryvatz, 1961–
  The neighborhoods of Queens / Claudia Gryvatz Copquin ; introduction by Kenneth T. Jackson.
    p. cm.—(The neighborhoods of New York City)
  Includes bibliographical references and index.
  ISBN 978-0-300-11299-3 (alk. paper)
    1. Queens (New York, N.Y.)—Description and travel.   2. New York (N.Y.)—Description and travel.   3. Neighborhood—New York (State)—New York.   4. Queens (New York, N.Y.)—History.   5. New York (N.Y.)—History.   6. Queens (New York, N.Y.)—Biography.   7. New York (N.Y.)—Biography.   8. Historic buildings—New York (State)—New York.   9. Queens (New York, N.Y.)—Buildings, structures, etc.   10. New York (N.Y.)—Buildings, structures, etc.   I. Title.
  F128.68.Q4C67 2007
  917.47′243—dc22   2007013716

A catalogue record for this book is available from the British Library.

The paper in this book meets the guidelines for permanence and durability of the Committee on Production Guidelines for Book Longevity of the Council on Library Resources.

10 9 8 7 6 5 4 3 2 1

Major support for *The Neighborhoods of Queens* was provided by JPMorgan Chase

Additional support was provided by

- Furthermore, a program of the J.M. Kaplan Fund
- Ben-Ness Photos & Digital

Contents

Foreword

Long before we became the United States of America, one of this nation's earliest and most significant human rights struggles took place right here in Queens. The Flushing Remonstrance, dated December 27, 1657, was a written protest by English colonists on behalf of Quakers who were being persecuted by their Dutch rulers under Peter Stuyvesant, the governor of New Netherland.

This forerunner to the Bill of Rights is just one of the many firsts in Queens's rich history. Did you know that the United Nations was originally headquartered here or that the first commercial nursery opened in what is now Downtown Flushing? Long before there was a La Guardia Airport, thousands of people flocked to East Elmhurst in warm weather to enjoy a massive amusement complex, complete with beer halls and water rides. We have hosted two World's Fairs, one in 1939–40 and another in 1964–65, which drew millions of people from all over the world to our borough's famous Flushing Meadows–Corona Park.

In fact, Queens boasts miles of lush parkland, walking trails, playgrounds, and athletic fields. But it's also a dynamic place to conduct business, as witnessed by the many industrial and office complexes that dot our landscape, along with hospitals, colleges and universities, galleries and museums, and every kind of retail business you could hope to find. And its unique neighborhoods offer a welcome to immigrants and visitors from around the world.

In the most diverse county in the United States, everyone can find a neighborhood to call home. From Astoria to the Rockaways, people from every continent have brought their own cultures and made them part of the vibrant mix that is Queens. Now, with *The Neighborhoods of Queens*, residents and visitors alike can take an insightful, informative walk around America's most diverse borough.

In these intimate profiles, readers can find out more about the people of Queens, its many neighborhoods, and the qualities that make it unique: community solidarity, excellent housing, lots of open space and parks, every kind of cultural attraction, and world-class sporting events. With two of the world's busiest airports, we offer a haven for newcomers in the beloved borough we call "the Gateway to America."

Enjoy *The Neighborhoods of Queens* and the fascinating facts and figures that Claudia Gryvatz Copquin has gathered for your enjoyment. I hope that they inspire those of you who live here to venture out of your own neighborhood and learn more about the areas around you. You will surely be happily surprised at your discoveries. And if you don't live in Queens, come and visit us! As I tell everyone, "Visit Queens and see the world."

Helen Marshall
President, Borough of Queens

Preface

When Norman Lear created the ground-breaking 1970s television situation comedy *All in the Family,* he was trying to show how cultural change, particularly racial change, was affecting the country. To typify working-class America, Lear chose the borough of Queens. At a pivotal moment in late-twentieth-century history, blue-collar worker Archie Bunker and his family were fictional witnesses to change that was transforming the country. It is no accident that Lear chose Queens as a microcosm: at the time Queens was on its way to becoming the most populated and most diverse borough in the city. In fact, in 1992 the U.S. Census Bureau declared Queens, which is also a county, the most diverse county in the country.

This diversity is visible on the streets of every one of Queens's 99 neighborhoods and subneighborhoods. People come here from all parts of the world and join those who came before them to create social, cultural, ethnic, and religious communities—neighborhoods.

People define themselves by the neighborhoods they live in—residents of Jackson Heights take pride in their myriad languages and the diverse cuisines offered on Roosevelt Avenue; those in Hollis brag about the talents of native music moguls Russell Simmons and LL Cool J. Richmond Hill boasts historical architecture, and Astoria a thriving film and television industry. Long Island City is experiencing a renaissance of art galleries and new luxury development. And the Rockaways, which for years attracted surfers to its shores, are booming, offering a new generation of homeowners affordable housing near the beach.

Citizens Committee for New York City has an intimate connection with neighborhood residents throughout the borough of Queens. Its mission since 1975 has been to support and encourage neighborhood volunteer organizations throughout the city, working with them to improve the quality of life in every neighborhood.

In 1996, Citizens Committee for New York City joined forces with Kenneth T. Jackson and Yale University Press, editor and publisher of the highly acclaimed *Encyclopedia of New York City,* to create a series that will celebrate the history and spirit of every neighborhood in the city. These volumes, organized by borough, will tell the story of the world's greatest city from an intimate and unique perspective.

We began our research by surveying the myriad neighborhood and civic associations we serve. In interviews and questionnaires, we asked residents to tell us about their neighborhood: what its boundaries are, who their neighbors are, and how they spend their time. These neighborhood groups spend thousands of hours every year on local initiatives, coming together for meetings, festivals, and community improvement projects. Their understanding of, their pride and investment in these neighborhoods uniquely qualified them to introduce us to their homes. With their help, we began to construct neighborhood portraits.

The 45 chapters of this book tell the stories of 56 neighborhoods. They also identify 43 smaller areas that we call subneighborhoods—areas that are now merged within the larger entities, which provide various services, but that still exhibit distinct features such as architectural similarities or a shared history or ethnic background. Flushing, for example, encompasses ten subneighborhoods; Long Island City has six. Each neighborhood portrait seeks to convey the "feel" of the area through an examination of its people, history, architecture, landmarks, points of interest, curiosities, and vital statistics. Each chapter contains a street map.

A word about the maps. Other than in *The Neighborhoods of Brooklyn*, the first book in this series, no one has ever before attempted to map all 400-plus of the city's neighborhoods, although local maps have identified a number of the largest. This caution is understandable. There are no official government boundaries, and not every boundary is agreed upon by every resident of a particular area. Yet neighborhoods are "real" social entities. We identified boundaries on the basis of hundreds of hours of research and consultation with local civic and neighborhood associations. In the course of these interviews, we were delighted to discover strong agreement among resident groups concerning their own neighborhood's boundaries as well as those of the neighborhoods around them. The maps are therefore meant as tools in understanding each neighborhood in its current social and political context. A composite map on page xxix situates each neighborhood geographically within the borough.

We are very pleased to include 2000 census numbers, compiled by Timothy Calabrese, Geographer for the Population Division of the New York City Department of City Planning. The Neighborhood Profiles found within each chapter provide quick reference to essential places and services. Because some services, like fire departments and hospitals, cross neighborhood boundaries, we have generally listed only those that actually sit in the neighborhood. Similarly, a comprehensive list of schools or services like senior or day-care centers provided difficulties both in terms of length and because new entities are constantly springing up to accommodate growing communities and changing populations. Famous schools and longstanding neighborhood associations are discussed in the text of the chapter.

This has been a rewarding and highly satisfying journey, and there are a number of people who helped us along the way who deserve our thanks. Michael Clark, former president of Citizens Committee for New York City, Tina Weiner of

Yale University Press, and their mutual friend Thomas H. Guinzburg envisioned **xv** the project, which would not have been possible without the generous support of our funders: JPMorgan Chase and Furthermore, a program of the J.M. Kaplan Fund. Ben Ness Photos & Digital donated a portion of the photo processing. Development Director Michelle LeMay-Santiago spearheaded the fundraising.

Kenneth T. Jackson, the renowned New York City historian, general editor of the series, and editor of the *Encyclopedia of New York City*—an invaluable source of information on the neighborhoods of Queens—vetted the manuscript and wrote the introduction, which gives an overview of the borough. James Driscoll, president of the Queens Historical Society, who himself has an encyclopedic knowledge of the borough, was always on hand to answer questions and offer guidance. In addition, he created the lively timeline at the back of this volume. Stanley Cogan, Queens Borough Historian, was an early supporter of the project and has cheered us on every step of the way. The historian and prolific author Vincent Seyfried is another Queens expert to whom we are grateful for advice and support.

At the Long Island Room of the Queens Library in Jamaica, we dove into an enormous pool of files containing historical documents and archival photographs—a fascinating experience facilitated by John Hyslop, assistant manager of the Long Island Division. Other libraries throughout the Queens County system helped us with our extensive research, as did the experts at the main branch of the New York Public Library.

The various Queens neighborhood historical societies were a tremendous source of information in researching this book, and we offer our thanks to them for documenting the fascinating details of their communities. For statistics and current data, we called upon a number of Borough District Offices, which provided us with essential information. The list is long, but we would like to thank them all: 112th Precinct Community Council, Forest Hills; 118th Avenue Block Association, St. Albans; 149th Street Civic Association, Inc., South Ozone Park; 207th Street Block Association of Bayside, Inc., Bayside; 6300 Wetherole Street Homeowners Association, Rego Park; 68th Street Block Association, Maspeth; 96-97-98-99-100-104th Street Block Association, Corona; 97th Place Block Association, Corona; Academy of Aeronautics, East Elmhurst; Adoptive Families of Older Children, Flushing; American Littoral Society–Northeast Chapter, Broad Channel; American-Bangladesh Friendship Association, Jamaica; Arverne Neighborhood Organization, Arverne; Asian American Association, Corona; Astoria Local Development Corporation, Astoria; Astoria Restoration Association, Astoria; Baisley Park Community League, Jamaica; Bayside Hills Civic Association, Bayside; Bayswater Security Patrol, Far Rockaway; Be Counted For, Inc., Hollis; Bellaire/Bell-Vill Civic Association, Hollis; Bellerose Commonwealth

Civic Association, Bellerose/Bellerose Manor; Botanical Society of Sunnyside, Sunnyside; Boundary Civic Association of Little Neck, Little Neck; Bowne Park Civic Association, Flushing; The Brathwaite Group, Jamaica; Briarwood Community Association, Briarwood; Brinkerhoff Action Association, Inc., St. Albans; Brookfield Civic Association, Inc., Springfield Gardens; Bukharian Jewish Museum, Rego Park; Cambria Heights Civic Association, Cambria Heights; Catholic Charities of Brooklyn and Queens, Long Island City; Manuel Caughman; Cedar Grove Civic Homeowners Association of Queensboro Hill, Inc., Flushing; Center for American Muslim Research and Information, Inc., Richmond Hill; Central Astoria Local Development Coalition, Astoria; Central Queens Partnership/ Q.C.G.C., Flushing; Cherokee Language and Cultural Circle, Rosedale; Cherry Office Products, Richmond Hill; Church of Holy Child Jesus, Richmond Hill; Citizens Against Recidivism, Inc., Arverne; City Councilman Peter Vallone, Astoria; Civic Association of Utopia Estates, Fresh Meadows; Clearview Civic Association, Bayside; College Point Civic Association, College Point; College Point Civic/Taxpayers Association, College Point; Communities of Maspeth Elmhurst Together, Inc., Maspeth; Community Board 8, Jamaica; Community Board 1, Astoria; Community Board 13, Springfield Gardens; Community Board 7, Flushing; Community Board 9, Kew Gardens; Community Board 9, Ozone Park; Community Conciliation Network, Corona; The Cornucopia Society, Inc., Springfield Gardens; Council for Unity, Jamaica/Briarwood; Creedmoor Civic Association, Bellerose/Bellerose Manor; Cultural Awareness Council, Jackson Heights; Cultural Collaborative Jamaica, Jamaica; Douglaston Bay Manor Civic Association, Douglaston; Douglaston Civic Association, Douglaston; Dunton Block Civic Association, Jamaica; Dutch Kills Civic Association, Long Island City; East Bayside Homeowners Association, Inc., Bayside; East Elmhurst Civic Association, East Elmhurst; Editorial Historian, Community Newspaper, Bayside; Elmira, Dunlop and Liberty Avenues Neighborhood Association, St. Albans; Family Learning Project, Inc., Briarwood; Federated Blocks of Laurelton, Laurelton; Federation of Italian American Organizations of Queens, Astoria; Flushing Heights Civic Association, Fresh Meadows/Flushing; Forest Hills Action League, Forest Hills; Forest Hills Chamber of Commerce, Forest Hills; Forest Hills Community and Civic Association, Inc., Forest Hills; Forest Hills Garden Corporation, Forest Hills; Forest Hills-Van Court Association, Forest Hills; Forest Hills Volunteer Ambulance Corps, Inc., Forest Hills; Forest Park Senior Citizens Center, Woodhaven; Fresh Meadows Tenant Association, Fresh Meadows; Friendly Block Association, Springfield Gardens; Friends of Baisley Pond Park, Jamaica; Friends of Crocheron Park, Bayside; Garden Club of Laurelton, Laurelton; Girl Scouts no. 6484, Springfield Gardens; Glendale Civilian Observation Patrol, Glendale; Glendale Property Owners' Association, Inc., Glendale; Goodwill Industries of Greater NY

& NJ, Astoria; The Greater Astoria Historical Society, Astoria; Greater Ridge-wood Restoration Corporation, Ridgewood; Greater Woodhaven Development Corporation, Woodhaven; Haitian Americans United for Progress (HAUP Inc.), Cambria Heights; Hanover Court Mutual Housing Cooperative, Inc., Elmhurst; Arthur Hill, St. Albans; Hillcrest Estates Civic Association, Jamaica; Hispanic Society, Flushing; Holliswood Civic Association, Holliswood; The Hope United Methodist Church of New York, Corona; Hour Children, Long Island City; Hunt-ers Point Community Coalition, Long Island City; Hunters Point Community De-velopment Corporation, Long Island City; Ilion Area Block Association, Inc., St. Albans; Islamic Circle of North America, Jamaica; Ivanhoe Park Civic Associa-tion, Glendale; Jackie Robinson School, Springfield Gardens; Jackson Heights Beautification Group, Jackson Heights; Jackson Heights Neighborhood Associa-tion, Inc., Jackson Heights; Jamaica Hill Community Association, Jamaica; J-Cap, South Ozone Park; Jewish Community Council of the Rockaway Peninsula, Far Rockaway; Juniper Park Civic Association, Middle Village; Kew Gardens Civic Association, Inc., Kew Gardens; Kew Gardens Hills Civic Association, Inc., Kew Gardens Hills; Kissena Park Civic Association, Flushing; Korean-American Senior Citizens Counseling Center, Flushing; La Asociasion Benefica, Corona; Lama Meadows Civic Association, Fresh Meadows; Laurelton Associa-tion, Laurelton; Little Sisters of the Poor Convent, Queens Village; Long Island City Business Development Corporation, Long Island City; Long Island City In-terblock Association, Long Island City; Margert Community Corporation, Far Rockaway; Maspeth Chamber of Commerce, Maspeth; Materials for the Arts, Long Island City; Merrick Boulevard Local Development Corporation, St. Albans; Montibellier Park Warriors, Inc., Laurelton; Nankama International, Jamaica; National Action Network, Flushing; New York City Outward Bound Center, Long Island City; North Bellerose Civic Association, Bellerose; North Hills Estates Civic Association, Little Neck; North Queens Home Owners Civic Association, Jackson Heights; North Star Civic Association, Jamaica; Nu Image Family Cen-ter, Jamaica; Our Savior Lutheran Church, Jamaica; Ozone Tudor Civic Associa-tion, Ozone Park; P.S. 80Q, Jamaica; Parkside Civic Association, Inc., Queens Village; Parkway Village Historical Society, Kew Gardens Hills; Partnership for Parks; Polonians Organized to Minister to Our Community (POMOC), Maspeth; The Property Civic Association, Bayside; Pomonok Neighborhood Center, Inc., Flushing; Property Owners/Resident Association, Middle Village; PS 101Q, For-est Hills; Queens Borough President; Queens Civic Congress, Inc., Flushing; Queens County Farm Museum, Bellerose; Queens Sickle Cell Advocacy Network, Inc., St. Albans; Queens Village Civic Association, Queens Village; Queens-bridge Community In Action, Long Island City; Queensbridge Tenant Council, Long Island City; Queensbridge Tenants Association, Long Island City; Rachel L.

Carson Intermediate School 237Q, Flushing; Ravenswood Resident Association Inc., Long Island City; Remsen Park Coalition, Forest Hills; Richmond Hill Association, Richmond Hill; Richmond Hill Hall Corporation, Richmond Hill; Ridgewood Historical Society, Ridgewood; Rockaway Artists Alliance, Rockaway Park; Rockaway Beach Civic Association, Inc., Rockaway Beach; Rockaway Development and Revitalization Corporation, Far Rockaway; Rocky Hill Civic Association, Bellerose Manor; Rosedale Civic Association, Inc., Rosedale; Rosedale Civilian Patrol, Rosedale; Saint Johns University, Jamaica Estates; The Salvation Army, Long Island City; Silvercup Studios, Long Island City; Socrates Sculpture Park, Long Island City; South Asian Youth Action (SAYA), Elmhurst; South Ozone Park Community Development Corporation, South Ozone Park; Spring Park Civic Association, Howard Beach; Springfield Rosedale Community Action Association, Springfield Gardens; Spring-Gar Community Civic Association, Springfield Gardens; St. Michael's Church, Flushing; Steinway Child and Family Services, Long Island City; Summerfield Block Association, Ridgewood; Sunnyside Chamber of Commerce, Sunnyside; Sunnyside Community Services, Sunnyside; Sunnyside Foundation for Community Planning and Preservation, Sunnyside; Sutphin Boulevard Local Development Corporation, South Ozone Park; Theatrical and Artistic Women of NY (TAWNY), Jamaica; Times Ledger, Queens; Tri-Block Association, Jackson Heights; Two Coves Community Redevelopment and Business Advisory Councils, Astoria; United Forties Civic Association, Woodside; Utopia Improvement Association, Fresh Meadows; Wayanda Civic Association, Inc., Queens Village; West Cunningham Park Civic Association, Fresh Meadows; West Lawrence Civic Association, Far Rockaway; West Maspeth Local Development Corporation, Maspeth; The Whitestone Boosters Civic Association, Whitestone; The William Simmons Community Garden Club, Jamaica; Win-Wood Neighbors, Woodside; Women of Faith, Inc., Jamaica; Woodhaven Business Improvement District, Woodhaven; Woodhull Civic Association, Hollis; Woodside on the Move, Woodside; YMCA-NYC Flushing Branch, Flushing.

The talented professionals at Yale University Press provided endless support and advice; this project could not have happened without them. Julie Carlson ensured that the chapters had a certain flair; Susan Laity meticulously edited every chapter; and Mary Jane Peluso, Lauren Shapiro, and Steve Colca led the team through the first stages of the project, while Vadim Staklo and Laura Robb brought us to the finish line.

There is no one who took this project more to heart than photographer Ray Anastas, who donated his time and huge talent to capturing the essence and spirit of Queens in visual detail. He rode his bicycle, red helmet on his head, camera dangling from his shoulder, and covered hundreds of miles in both warm and cold weather to get the right shot.

Kaleila Pu-Folkes did an enormous amount of work, from mapping neighborhood boundaries and researching area profiles to assisting in sorting through the archival photography. She is a gem. Others were critical to this project: Delia Valladares-Perez, Ana Diaz, Melissa Rodriguez, Thelma Leemans, and Jesse Eng. They each played an important part in gathering vital information. Project Coordinator Jemilah Magnusson entered the project at a late stage, but she plunged right into things, deftly handling the myriad details connected with the final stages.

Special thanks to John Aerni and Ann Marie Donohue of LeBoeuf, Lamb, Greene & MacRae for their brilliant legal advice and to literary agent Robert Lescher, whose wisdom and guidance were indispensable.

This project would not have been possible without the serendipitous reunion of two women who grew up as friends in Jackson Heights and found each other as adults: Sonia S. Estreich, from Citizens Committee for New York City, and Claudia Gryvatz Copquin, the author of this book. Sonia has been the driving force of this project from the beginning and was involved in every aspect, from raising funds and recruiting the team to overseeing the mapping and researching and editing the entries. Claudia, a South American immigrant who settled in Queens as a child with her family in the late 1960s, is an award-winning freelance journalist and editor who writes extensively for *Newsday* and other publications. Having spent thousands of hours researching and writing about Queens's culture, history, people, and neighborhoods, she has happily discovered how extraordinary the borough she grew up in really is.

Last, we thank the people who live in this dynamic borough—they are the ones who make Queens such an intriguing place. For a glimpse into their lives and their neighborhoods, take a stroll through these pages. It's a fascinating trip.

Osborn Elliott   Henry Cornell   Peter H. Kostmayer
Founding Chairman   Chairman   President

Citizens Committee for New York City

Introduction

Kenneth T. Jackson, Director of the Herbert Lehman Center for
American History and Jacques Barzun Professor of History
and the Social Sciences, Columbia University

If Queens had been an independent municipality in 2000, when the United States officially counted its citizens, it would have been the fourth-largest city in the nation, trailing only New York, Los Angeles, and Chicago, and a bit ahead of Houston. At that time, it was half again as large as Philadelphia, twice as big as Detroit, and approximately as populous as Atlanta, Baltimore, Boston, Buffalo, and St. Louis combined. Within New York City, Queens is the largest of the five boroughs in area (110 square miles) and second only to Brooklyn in population.

But Queens is more distinctive for diversity than for size. Indeed, by most measures, Queens is the most heterogeneous place in the world. Although London had 2.2 million foreign-born citizens in 2000 (second only to New York City with 2.9 million), and although Miami had a larger proportion (more than 60 percent) of international residents, Queens has a larger proportion of foreign-born than London and a larger number of foreign-born than Miami.

The diversity of Queens can best be appreciated at the neighborhood level. Elmhurst, for example, counted immigrants from 110 countries in 2000, while Flushing had almost 100,000 Asian residents, most of them from China or Korea. Astoria has the largest Greek population outside the Mediterranean, Jamaica is mostly African American and Caribbean, and Richmond Hill has the largest population of Sikhs outside of India. Jews predominate in Forest Hills and Kew Gardens, while Italians give Howard Beach and Middle Village a distinctive character. And the 7 subway line passes through so many ethnic communities that it has been officially recognized as the "international express."

Why then, if Queens is so populous, so large, and so diverse, is it so little known and understood even among those who live relatively close to it? In part, this circumstance derives from the fact that Queens is just one borough among the five that make up the city of New York. Moreover, all of the outer boroughs—Brooklyn, the Bronx, Staten Island, and Queens—are overshadowed by the skyscrapers, corporate headquarters, spectacular apartments, famous museums, and glamour and glitz of tiny Manhattan Island, the self-styled capital of capitalism and the world.

Second, the relative anonymity of Queens is a function of a quirk in U.S. Postal Service operations. In St. Louis, for example, a central post office handles

Carpenter's Tavern (1710) at Jamaica Avenue and 195th Street, Hollis, as it appeared in the late nineteenth century (Queens Library, Long Island Division, Illustrations Collection)

In 1949, Bell Boulevard in Bayside was a quiet road on which elegant homes were interspersed with small businesses like the Candy, Soda and Ice Cream Shack (Consolidated Edison Company of New York, courtesy Queens Library, Long Island Division, Illustrations Collection)

mail for both the city and many of its suburbs, so that a St. Louis address does not imply residence within the city. In New York City and Queens the opposite is true. New York, N.Y., means the island of Manhattan. And Brooklyn, the Bronx, and Staten Island also have a singular address for the entire borough.

Not so with Queens. The Postal Service divides the borough into five "towns" based roughly on governmental organizations that were in place in 1898 when the five boroughs came together as New York City. In Queens those five towns and the neighborhoods around them use as addresses those places—Long Island City, Jamaica, Flushing, Far Rockaway, and Floral Park—or, in some cases, the neighborhood name.

Thus, in a peculiar twist, Queens is not really a place in the usual American sense. It is not politically independent, it does not have a distinctive personality, it does not have a single post office address, and its sports teams are known by another moniker—the New York Mets rather than the Queens Mets, for example. Revealingly, Queens even has two of the most important airports in the world—John F. Kennedy International and La Guardia—but neither uses Queens in its name.

Moreover, perhaps more than in other places, residents of Queens identify with their neighborhood rather than with their borough or with the city as a whole. For decades, for example, the U.S. Open Tennis Championships were held in Forest Hills, New York, not in Queens or in Gotham.

This is not a big book. But it does have a big objective—to remind both residents and visitors that Queens is in fact one of the most exciting, most diverse, most American, and most promising places on earth. Fortunately, this is easy to do, especially because it has been written from the point of view of neighborhood residents. And their insights are enhanced by the clear and careful maps of cartographers William L. and Colette Nelson.

History Before the Consolidation of 1898

Before 1524, when Giovanni da Verrazano became the first known white man to sail up the narrows in the lower bay, the place now known as Queens was home to various groups of American Indians, who lived near the bays and along the coast in what are now Flushing Bay, Douglaston, Jamaica Bay, and Little Neck Bay. None of these local Indian groups was as advanced as the Mayans, Incas, or Aztecs, who lived farther south in the Western Hemisphere. But these early inhabitants of Queens did cultivate wheat, maize, beans, and squash, which they combined with fish and assorted animals to provide a varied diet. Instead of tee-pees, they constructed long bark houses, replete with thatched domes of substantial size, to house many families at once.

In 1624 these original Americans were perhaps startled when the Dutch West India Company established a permanent settlement of European white people on Governors Island in the harbor. In 1625 the Dutch moved their tiny community to the southern tip of Manhattan, and in 1626 they presumably "bought" the island from the Indians.

Between 1636 and 1639 they turned their attention to Queens and made several land purchases from the natives, who probably did not understand that to Europeans land once bought could not be used again by the former owners. In any event, Dutch settlers began farming along the East River in what became the Hallets Cove and Dutch Kills areas. And after a series of military skirmishes with the native inhabitants in 1643, the Europeans had forced out the Indians by the middle of the seventeenth century. All that remains in the twenty-first century

The Weeping Beech, ca. 1930 (Courtesy of the Queens Library, Long Island Division, Postcard Collection)

of more than a millennium of Indian settlement are a few place names and trails that later became wagon roads and major automotive thoroughfares.

Although the Dutch were in control and gave the various Queens settlements their initial names, English settlers were more numerous in the area, and they resented the authority of the various Dutch governors, especially Peter Stuyvesant, who ruled New Netherland from 1647 to 1664. When Stuyvesant ordered the residents of Vlissingen (now Flushing) to deny to Quakers the opportunity to worship as they wished, he infuriated the local inhabitants and gave rise to the strongest statement of religious tolerance in all of American history—the Flushing Remonstrance of 1657. That document, now a precious treasure in the archives of the state of New York, formally protested against the ability of the government to interfere with the religious beliefs of citizens. Governor Stuyvesant arrested and fined several petitioners, prompting John Bowne to allow Quakers to worship in his home. When Bowne was subsequently imprisoned and then banished from the colony, he took his complaint to company headquarters in Amsterdam. They decided in favor of Bowne and ordered Stuyvesant to offer religious freedom in the colony. Bowne returned to America, and his home on Bowne Street is now a national landmark. And the Flushing Remonstrance of 1657 remains the most eloquent defense of religious freedom in all of American history.

In 1664, soon after Bowne's triumphant return, an English fleet, accompanied by 500 professional soldiers, appeared in the harbor. Stuyvesant, ornery to the last, wanted to fight the invaders. But his citizens could see the powerful guns of the Royal Navy, and they knew that their little town could be blown to pieces in a military showdown. So, on September 8, 1664, with drums beating and flags flying, Stuyvesant surrendered Fort Amsterdam and the entire colony to the English. They immediately renamed the community New York, after the duke of York, who later became King James II of England. The city then gave its name to the entire colony, which after independence became the "Empire State," as George Washington had foreseen.

In 1683, Queens became one of ten administrative subdivisions, or counties, in the province of New York. Queens took its name from Catherine of Braganza, the Portuguese wife of King Charles II of England, and it originally included not only everything within its current boundaries but all of what is now Nassau County.

The Pennsylvania Drug store, located on the corner of Queens Boulevard and Continental Avenue, 1951 (Queens Library, Long Island Division, Illustrations Collection)

The century of English rule between 1664 and 1776 affected Queens only slightly. There were a few towns—Newtown, Flushing, and Jamaica prominent among them—but the population was mostly rural and the economy based on farming. Some families experimented with specialty crops. The Newtown Pippin apple, for example, became available after 1730, and this first American-grown apple soon became a luxury item suitable for export. And William Prince opened in Flushing the first commercial nursery for trees and plants in what would become the United States.

When revolutionary fervor swept the thirteen colonies in the 1770s, Queens remained mostly outside the debate, and if anything, its white population favored the British. New York City soon became the pivot for both royalist and revolutionary strategy, and Brooklyn was accordingly the scene, in August 1776, of the largest and most horrific battle of the entire Revolution. Queens did not play an important role in the contest, except that under the parliamentary Quartering Act, British soldiers could occupy private homes more or less as they pleased. Meanwhile, the Redcoats requisitioned livestock, stole produce, and used fence posts for fires. And when they left for good in 1783, they used Queens as a staging ground for the evacuation of Loyalists from all over America for resettlement in Nova Scotia, Newfoundland, and England.

After independence from George III was won in 1783, Queens remained a quiet district of small villages and isolated farms, and before 1830 the population of the entire county never reached as much as 10,000, even as neighboring Manhattan was passing Mexico City to become the largest metropolis in the Western Hemisphere, and rival Brooklyn was itself becoming one of the important cities in a growing nation.

The situation changed between 1830 and 1860, however, as the population of Queens quadrupled to more than 30,000. For one thing, railroads began arriving in 1836 and accelerated their coverage and service in the coming decades. For another, Queens became a place of suburban escape and urban recreation as new communities like Ravenswood developed after 1848, and as new racetracks and cemeteries gave New Yorkers reason to venture away from the congested city. Far Rockaway had even become a seaside resort for the affluent by the 1850s. Finally, Whitestone, Woodhaven, and College Point began attracting factories by 1860. And after the Civil War, three-mile long Newtown Creek, which divided Brooklyn and Queens, became one of the nation's busiest waterways as factories and warehouses lined its banks.

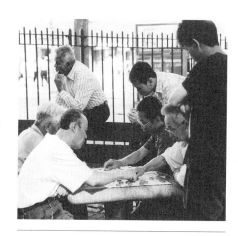

Playing checkers in Clement Clarke Moore Homestead Park, Elmhurst

History Since Consolidation with New York City

In 1894 the residents of Queens County took part in a nonbinding referendum on whether to consolidate with the city of New York, which was then composed only of the island of Manhattan and a small part of Westchester County that was known as the Annexed District and which is now the South Bronx. Jamaica, New-town, and Long Island City voted to be part of the greater city; Flushing, Hemp-stead, and other parts of eastern Queens were opposed. Overall, however, the consolidation measure passed, and on January 1, 1898, Queens became a borough within the city of New York. The easternmost towns became part of a new juris-diction outside the city—Nassau County.

As a result of the consolidation of the five boroughs into one municipality, New York became the second-largest city in the world, after London, as well as the richest, most heterogeneous, and most dynamic human agglomeration on earth. Queens at the time was smaller and less important than either Manhattan or Brooklyn, but its population surged in the first two decades of the twentieth cen-tury, primarily because a series of transportation improvements gave it better connections to the giant metropolis across the East River. The Pennsylvania Railroad bought the Long Island Rail Road in 1900 and promptly electrified the tracks through Queens and opened new commuter tunnels under the river. Mean-while, the new Queensboro Bridge opened in 1909 and gave access to Manhattan via automobile and trolley.

Most important, New York's vast, efficient, and relatively cheap (five cents) subway system reached Hunters Point, Ozone Park, Woodhaven, and Richmond Hill in 1915 and Astoria, Corona, and Jamaica in 1917. With such easy access to the city, the population of Queens surged from 153,000 in 1900 to 469,000 in 1920.

But the most rapid growth was yet to come. During the 1920s, Queens was among the fastest-growing counties in the United States, and by 1930 the borough counted well over one million residents, or already more than Cleveland, Balti-more, Boston, Pittsburgh, St. Louis, or San Francisco would ever have. And along with more people, Queens spawned rich employment and recreational opportuni-ties. It was the national center of production for the film industry, with about twenty studios there before the shift to Hollywood in the 1920s. It also had four airports and eighteen golf courses.

The Great Depression, which began with the stock market crash on Wall Street in October 1929, was as devastating to the city as to the nation as a whole. But huge public works projects, many of them directed by the greatest builder in American history, Robert Moses, added new transportation facilities, not to men-tion many thousands of jobs to the Queens economy. (In fact, it could be argued that Queens, more than any of the other New York boroughs, owes its current built topography to Moses.) The vast Triborough Bridge complex, together with the Grand Central Parkway from the bridge to Kew Gardens, opened in 1936, fol-lowed three years later by the Bronx-Whitestone Bridge and La Guardia Airport. And additions to the commuter rail and subway systems in Queens further solidi-

The Bronx-Whitestone Bridge

fied its status as a place of increasing importance.

Probably the most important, and undoubtedly the most exciting, event of the decade was the World's Fair of 1939–40. Located on a former ash and rubbish heap in what was later transformed into Flushing Meadows–Corona Park, the great exposition ultimately attracted 45 million patrons and was the largest such event ever held up until that time.

During World War II, Queens sent tens of thousands of its sons to the bat-

Forest Hills Gardens

tlefields of North Africa, Europe, and the Pacific. After the Japanese surrender on September 2, 1945, the borough returned to the tasks it had always done so well, which were to provide homes, schools, parks, religious institutions, and economic opportunities for families that were linked by the desire to be happy, healthy, and successful. The Throgs Neck Bridge and the Long Island Express-way opened, blocks of four- and five-story apartment houses went up in Flushing, and single-family houses sprouted on former farms and golf courses. In 1964 Shea Stadium opened as well as the largest world's fair of the postwar period. This time more than 50 million people passed through the gates during its run. By 2000, well over two million people lived in the borough, which was unusual among urban political jurisdictions in the Middle West or Northeast in that the Queens population was larger at the turn of the millennium than it had been in 1950, even though its boundaries had changed not at all.

With maturity came important educational, artistic, and sports institutions. St. John's University, founded in 1870 by the Venetian Fathers, became one of the nation's largest and most prominent Catholic institutions after World War II, opening its major campus in Queens in 1955, while Queens College, established in 1937, similarly advanced in the postwar decades to become one of the elite colleges in the City University of New York system. Meanwhile, the borough gained notice as an artistic hub, with the American Museum of the Moving Image, the Socrates Sculpture Park, the Isamu Noguchi Museum, the Queens Museum of Art (which features the Panorama of New York City, created for the 1964 World's Fair), and the Museum for African Art receiving particular attention. Also impressive is the fact that since 1987 the Queens Library has maintained the highest circulation of any library in the United States.

Diversity and the Future of Queens

But the most important fact about Queens is not its size or its cultural institutions or its library circulation statistics, although all are significant by any measure. Rather, the borough is distinguished by the fact that 44 percent of its population is officially foreign born. (No one knows how many undocumented immigrants live within its boundaries.)

More than other American places, Queens has been transformed by the Immigration Act of 1965, which overturned the more restrictive legislation that had prevailed since 1924. The borough, which had had the highest population of native-born in New York City as late as 1930, soon saw an influx of Asians and Latin Americans, with the largest number of newcomers from China, Guyana, the Dominican Republic, Colombia, Jamaica, Korea, India, Haiti, and Ecuador.

The future of Queens is tied to the energy and aspirations of its people. For generations, the borough has offered newcomers opportunity, tolerance, and relative peace, which is all they have needed to establish a solid foothold. It is worth noting, for example, that Queens annually has fewer homicides than places like Atlanta, Memphis, New Orleans, Washington, and Baltimore, none of which is even a third as large as the underappreciated jewel of New York. To celebrate the history and meaning of Queens, then, is to celebrate the history and meaning of the United States. This book is only an introduction to its history, its treasures, and its people.

The fifty-story Citicorp building in Queens Plaza, the tallest building on Long Island

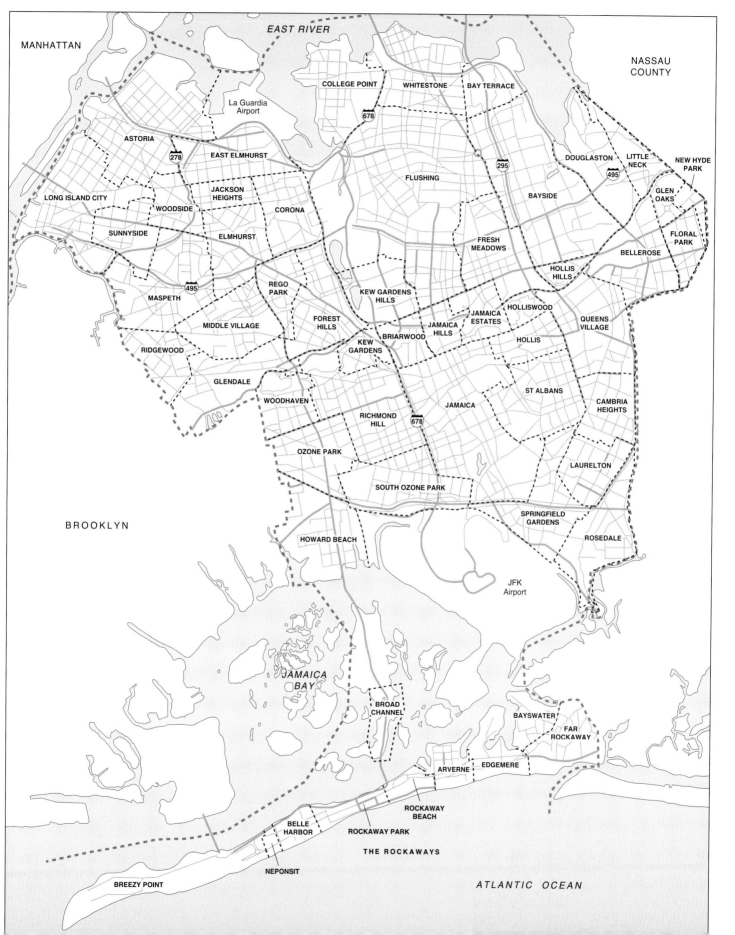

Astoria

Steinway Street and Broadway (Sonia S. Estreich)

The gorgeous, regal sound of a just-finished Steinway piano. The dreamy smells of a shisha (water pipe) café wafting onto the street. The hubbub of a bustling shopping district, with friends chatting in many languages. In Astoria, multilingual residents and unique cultural elements come together in a wonderfully diverse neighborhood.

Astoria was perhaps destined to become trendy. With its affordable rent, cosmopolitan flavor, and close proximity to Manhattan—via the Triborough Bridge; the N, R, and V trains; and the Q101 bus—Astoria is now a highly desirable home for commuters with downtown jobs.

Astoria is a welcoming place to come home to, but it's also an exciting place to live. History buffs will enjoy discovering one of the oldest parts of the neighborhood, **Hallets Cove,** named for a family who settled in this northern waterfront section in the 1600s. Before the Civil War, wealthy merchant Stephen A. Halsey purchased real estate there and with associates began laying out lots. In 1839 he had the area chartered by the state as the incorporated village of Astoria, after millionaire John Jacob Astor, Halsey's acquaintance, who had made a minor financial contribution to a local girls' seminary. Astoria remained a distinctive village until 1898, when it officially became part of New York City.

Successive and overlapping migrations of people into the area have led to a wide array of international offerings for visitors and residents alike: delis, grocery stores, cafés, and restaurants throughout the neighborhood offer foods and other goods from Greece, Italy, Brazil, Ecuador, Thailand, Mexico, the Czech Republic, Hungary, India, Pakistan, Israel, Argentina, Ireland, and Romania. Steinway Street, which cuts across Astoria in a northerly direction, is a shoppers' paradise, with more than 300 stores in a small,

2 walkable area. The street, dubbed the "World's Largest Department Store," features familiar chain stores as well as independent, one-of-a-kind shops. Several blocks on Steinway are unofficially known as Little Middle East, with Arabic signs for cafés, bookstores, delis, barbershops, and other stores.

Two other hotspots for those hoping to discover an eclectic mix of stores and foods are 30th Avenue and Broadway, which run parallel in an east-west direction. Ditmars Boulevard, situated farther north, is quieter but offers its own sampling of international shopping and cuisine. Theater lovers can indulge their passion at the Astoria Performing Arts Center (APAC) on 33rd Street, a not-for-profit organization presenting original and classic theatrical works.

View of Triborough Bridge from Astoria Park

NEIGHBORHOOD FACTS

■ The Riker-Lent Homestead, a private home, is considered by many to be the oldest dwelling in America, dating back in part to around 1655. Located at 78-03 19th Road, its address is easily mistaken for East Elmhurst, or even Jackson Heights, but the structure is actually within Ditmars, bordering Steinway. The Dutch Colonial farmhouse was built by Abraham Lent, a descendant of Abraham Rycken Van Lent, a prominent farmer and one of the early Dutch immigrants. (The family name went through various incarnations over the years—Rycken, Ryker, Ricker, Riker, and Lent.) Rikers Island, home to New York City's main jail—and the world's largest penal colony, with 15,000 inmates—was once part of the Riker-Lent Homestead. Although it is now part of the Bronx, Rikers Island can be accessed only through Ditmars via the Rikers Island Bridge, which passes by the Homestead.
■ The tiny industrial and residential area known as Two Coves, near Hallets Cove, is home to the headquarters of the Goodwill Industries of Greater New York and Astoria Houses, a public housing project built between 1944 and 1951.
■ The Queens Rainbow Community Center, located at 30-74 Steinway Street, was the first lesbian, gay, bisexual, and transgendered community center in Queens. The center is a multiservice social hub that seeks to promote "multicultural understanding and positive community relations" among people of all sexual orientations. Events organized there include youth pride dances and outreach, police sensitivity trainings, and an annual interfaith AIDS memorial service.
■ Celebrities from Astoria include singers Tony Bennett and Ethel Merman and actor Christopher Walken.

The Greater Astoria Historical Society holds walking tours of Old Astoria, where restored pre–Civil War mansions, charming cottages, old churches, and colonial family cemeteries dot the streets as testaments to the past. Farther north is an area some residents refer to as **Ditmars,** the core of Greek Astoria. New York City has the largest Greek population outside of Athens, and those Greeks who don't live in Astoria flock to the neighborhood for the culture, most evident in Ditmars. Greek may be heard as often as English along Ditmars Boulevard, and Greek banks, newspapers, radio and television stations, restaurants, and Orthodox churches contribute to this area's special flavor. Even the MetroCard vending machines in some stations have instructions in Greek.

3

QUEENS COUNTY
NY COUNTY

BRONX COUNTY

EAST RIVER

RIKERS ISLAND

CON EDISON

EAST RIVER

HELL GATE

NY COUNTY

HELL GATE BRIDGE

TRIBOROUGH BRIDGE

278

SHORE BLVD

ASTORIA PARK

ASTORIA PARK SOUTH

TRIBORO PLAZA

NY COUNTY

DITMARS

DITMARS BLVD

STEINWAY PL

BERRIAN BLVD

RIKERS ISLAND BRIDGE

RIKER-LENT HOMESTEAD

STEINWAY

2 ST
3 ST
26 AVE
8 ST
9 ST
12 ST
14 PL
14 ST
26 AVE PL
25 RD

1 ST
27 AVE
18 RD
26 RD
28 AVE

ASTORIA BLVD

MAIN AVE

WELLING CT

HALLETS COVE

28 AVE
30 AVE
30 RD
30 DR
31 AVE
31 RD
31 DR

VERNON BLVD

TWENTY-FIRST ST

CRESCENT ST

NEWTOWN AVE

HOYT AVE

ASTORIA BLVD SOUTH

ASTORIA BLVD NORTH

ASTORIA

BROADWAY

33 AVE

THIRTY-FIRST ST

STEINWAY ST

NEWTOWN RD

25 AVE

28 AVE

30 PL

26 AVE

27 AVE
28 AVE

BROOKLYN-QUEENS EXPWY WEST

BOROUGH PL

HOBART ST
56 PL
57 ST
60 ST

31 AVE

STRIPOLL SQ

KAUFMAN ASTORIA STUDIOS

THIRTY-FOURTH AVE

35 AVE

36 AVE

MUSEUM OF THE MOVING IMAGE

ASTORIA PERFORMING ARTS CENTER

NORTHERN BLVD

Saloon at what was the corner of Astoria Boulevard and Newtown Road (now Newtown Avenue), ca. 1885 (Queens Library, Long Island Division, Illustrations Collection)

Ditmars was named after Abram Ditmars, who became the first mayor of Long Island City in 1870, and it is home to the 66-acre Astoria Park, with a solar-heated bathhouse and a pool in which the Olympic swimming trials were held in 1936. Founded in 1913 (and expanded twice) in a prescient effort to save some of the East River shoreline for the public, Astoria Park offers breathtaking views of the Triborough Bridge and the Manhattan skyline. Ditmars also boasts the last surviving outdoor beer garden in New York City: Bohemian Hall and Beer Garden on 24th Avenue. Construction of the landmark began in 1910, funded by the Bohemian Citizens' Benevolent Society, a Czech-Slovak organization formed in 1892.

Nestled within Ditmars is a small but distinct area known as **Steinway.** The German Steinway family, famous for its piano manufacturing company Steinway & Sons, developed this part of Astoria beginning in 1877. They built a company town, consisting of a factory complex, homes for employees, a post office, a library, and other amenities—and along the waterfront, an enclosed dock and basin for keeping wet the logs that were needed to make their famous pianos. Today the company employs more than 500 people within its 11-acre site, and remnants of the original Steinway Village can be found throughout the area. One intact example is the Steinway Reformed Church on 41st Street and Ditmars Boulevard. On 20th Avenue and 41st Street is a group of two-story neo-Greco- and Italianate-style brick houses, built before 1880 for company employees. The Steinway family mansion, still standing today, was built in 1856 to resemble an Italian villa. Also in Steinway is the Lawrence Cemetery, a New York City landmark on 20th Road and 35th Street, which has ninety-one monuments, some dating as far back as 1751.

On the outskirts of Astoria, at 34-12 36th Street, is Kaufman Astoria Studios, built in 1920 to serve the new film industry. This 14-acre complex of sound stages and production offices is today headquarters for Lifetime Television and WFAN Radio. The Museum of the Moving Image, which screens films and other works from its collection of film, television, and other moving image–related artifacts as well as offering educational and interpretive programs, is situated nearby. But for an authentic cultural treat, there's nothing like street theater. People-watching is a wonderful source of entertainment while sipping a cup of coffee at Omonia Café on Broadway or any other local café or bakery—there are plenty to choose from in this lively neighborhood.

An important geographic feature of

N E I G H B O R H O O D
P R O F I L E

Boundaries: Astoria: north border: Bronx County line; east border: Rikers Island Bridge to 19th Avenue to 81st Street to Astoria Boulevard North to Brooklyn-Queens Expressway West to 31st Avenue to 49th Street; south border: Northern Boulevard to 34th Avenue to Steinway Street to 36th Avenue to 31st Street to Broadway to Vernon Boulevard to 31st Avenue; west border: New York County line; Hallets Cove: north border: Astoria Park South; east border: 21st Street; south border: Broadway to Vernon Boulevard to 31st Avenue; west border: New York County Line; Ditmars: north border: Bronx County line; east border: Rikers Island Bridge to 19th Avenue to 81st Street; south border: Astoria Boulevard North to Hoyt Avenue to 21st Street to Astoria Park South; west border: New York county line; Steinway: north border: East River; east border: Hazen Street; south border: Ditmars Boulevard; west border: 31st Street to 20th Avenue to 37th Street to 19th Avenue

Subway and Train: N,W trains: 36th Avenue, Broadway, 30th Avenue, Astoria Boulevard, Ditmars Boulevard; R, G, V, trains: 36th Street, Steinway Street

Bus: Q18: 30th Avenue; Q66: 35th Avenue; Q101: Steinway Street; Q102: 31st Street; Q103: Vernon Boulevard; Q104: Broadway; Q19A: 21st Street/Ditmars Boulevard; Q101A: 21st Street/20th Avenue; M60: Astoria Boulevard

Libraries: Queens Library, Astoria Branch (14-01 Astoria Boulevard), Broadway Branch (40-20 Broadway), Steinway Branch (21-45 31st Street)

Museums: American Museum of the Moving Image (35th Avenue at 36th Street); Greek Cultural Center (27-18 Hoyt Avenue)

Theaters: Astoria Performing Arts Center (31-60 33rd Street), Rilkis Theater at the American Museum of the Moving Image (34-12 36th Street)

Community Board: No.1

Police Precinct: 114th Precinct (34-16 Astoria Boulevard)

Fire Departments: Engine 262 (30-89 21st Street); Engine 263, Ladder 117 (42-06 Astoria Boulevard); Engine 312, Battalion 49 (22-63 35th Street)

Hospitals and Clinics: Mount Sinai Hospital of Queens–Astoria General Hospital (25-10 30th Avenue); Creedmoor Psychiatric Center, Steinway Out-Patient Clinic (38-11 Broadway); Queens Surgical Community Center (46-04 31st Avenue); Medisys Family Center (4-21 27th Avenue)

which was said to have carried a freight of gold and silver. The strait is also the site of the worst single disaster in New York City's history before September 11, 2001, and one of the worst maritime disasters ever. On June 15, 1904, the steamer *General Slocum* caught fire, and at least 1,021 passengers of the 1,300 aboard, many of them women and children and most of them members of St. Mark's German Lutheran Church, burned to death on the ship or drowned in the turbulent waters of the East River before the ship ran aground on North Brother Island.

The treacherous strait is spanned by two major bridges: the motor-vehicle Triborough (see the Bridges photo spread) and the Hell Gate, a railroad

Brick homes built before 1880 on 20th Avenue and 41st Street

the area is Hell Gate, the narrow strait between Astoria and Ward's Island connecting the East River and the Long Island Sound. For years the waterway (whose name means "beautiful strait" in Dutch) was extremely hazardous for navigation, because of its powerful tides and rocky outcroppings. Before 1876, when the Army Corps of Engineers began blasting most of the dangerous underwater rocks, hundreds of ships sank there, among them the British frigate *Hussar*,

bridge. The Hell Gate was designed by Gustav Lindenthal, who also designed New York City's Williamsburg, Manhattan, and Queensboro Bridges. Chief engineer for the project was Othmar Ammann, the designer of six major New York City bridges, including the Triborough, the George Washington, and the Verrazano-Narrows. When it opened in 1917, the Hell Gate was the longest steel-arch bridge in the world, with an arch of 1,017 feet—a title it lost in 1931 to Ammann's Bayonne Bridge, linking Staten Island and New Jersey.

Since the twenty-eight-gun British navy frigate HMS *Hussar* sank in Hell Gate on November 23, 1780, it has been a source of interest to residents, historians, and perhaps especially treasure hunters because it was rumored to have hundreds of thousands of pounds of gold and silver aboard. (The ship may have been carrying the payroll for British soldiers fighting in the colonies, along with perhaps extra plunder from American and French ships in the area.) But the location of the ship and whether there is indeed treasure aboard are a source of continued debate. In his day, Thomas Jefferson made an attempt to find the vessel, but came up empty-handed; others too have tried and failed. One man, actor and

When Hell Gate Bridge opened in 1917 it was the longest steel-arch bridge in the world

Little Middle East on Steinway Street

• Kaufman Astoria Studios

In 1920, Astoria became home to a major Hollywood-style film production company. Originally called Famous Players–Lasky, the studio became a key player in the fledgling American motion picture industry. Stars of the day such as Gloria Swanson, W. C. Fields, Tallulah Bankhead, the Marx Brothers, and countless others acted in more than a hundred films produced at the studio during that era—films that drew from the vast pool of actors, screenwriters, and other talented theatrical and literary figures conveniently found just across the East River in Manhattan.

Later called Paramount Pictures, the studio was purchased by the U.S. government in 1942 and renamed the Signal Corps Photographic Center. The army produced wartime films there and actually retained the facility until 1970, long after the war ended. Six years later, Astoria Studios was designated a national historic landmark by the federal government. In 1982 the real estate developer George S. Kaufman, in partnership with the late comic Alan King and the late talk-show host Johnny Carson, undertook a $50 million expansion of the facility. Today the studio is headquarters for Lifetime Television and WFAN Radio.

Many will be familiar with shows and films produced at the studio. HBO's *Sex and the City* was filmed here. *Sesame Street* has been produced at these studios since 1993. And *Picture Perfect*, *First Wives Club*, *Scent of a Woman*, *Age of Innocence*, and *Hollywood Ending* are just a few of the feature films produced at Kaufman Astoria Studios.

diver Joe Governali, has recently stumbled upon documents that he thinks identify the ship's location, and his dives have unearthed ballast and an earthenware pitcher from the period. But are these relics truly from the *Hussar?* And could the treasure have survived the canal-opening efforts of the U.S. Army Corps of Engineers in 1876, when it "blew the worst features of Hell Gate straight back to hell" with 56,000 pounds of dynamite? One thing is sure: the mystery of the shipwreck and the potential treasure it holds will continue to captivate those interested in Astoria's historic waterway.

Bayside and

Bell Boulevard bustles with diverse businesses, large and small

Residents of Bayside and Bay Terrace enjoy the upscale neighborhoods' excellent schools and prime waterfront on Little and Little Neck Bays. But they are also justly proud of their history of preserving and enhancing their neighborhoods' open spaces, even when challenged. The result: uniquely beautiful parks and a historic fort that enchant residents and visitors alike.

Bayside was settled in the late seventeenth century by the English, who displaced the Matinecoc Indians. In 1644 rights to the area were given by Charles I to William Lawrence, and the prominent Lawrence family retained a large portion of Bayside until after the Civil War. Around that time, in 1866, the Flushing and North Shore Rail Road arrived, and a building boom began.

Some of the most colorful history of the neighborhood is told through its magnificent parks. Overlooking the bay in the heart of Bayside are the John Golden and Crocheron Parks, located next to each other between 32nd Avenue and Corbett Road and offering athletic fields, picnic grounds, playground equipment, and hiking trails. John Golden was a Broadway producer and one of the founders of the American Society of Composers, Authors and Publishers (ASCAP). After he and his wife moved into a 20-acre estate in 1920, they opened their grounds to community residents, who often held Little League baseball games there. Golfers, too, could frequently be seen practicing their swings. When Golden died in 1955, he left his estate to the city so that it could become a neighborhood recreational area.

NEIGHBORHOOD FACTS

■ Queensborough Community College (QCC), one of six community colleges of the City University of New York, opened in 1958; a new 34-acre campus was completed in 1978 at 56th Avenue and Springfield Boulevard. The college currently enrolls more than 12,000 students in associate degree or certificate programs, while another 10,000 students participate in programs offered by the Department of Continuing Education. In addition to an observatory, a recording studio, an art gallery, the Queensborough Performing Arts Center, and photography and digital art laboratories, QCC is home to the Harriet and Kenneth Kupferberg Holocaust Resource Center and Archives, which sponsors programs, exhibitions, and resources to commemorate the victims and families of the Holocaust and to educate the public.

■ Bayside's Lawrence Cemetery is designated a New York City landmark, with headstones dating back to 1842, including many from the Lawrence family, among them governors, judges, statesmen, mayors, and naval heroes. Judge Effingham Lawrence has been credited with giving Bayside its name.

■ The Cord Meyer Development Company, founded by Cord Meyer, Jr., who developed Forest Hills, has been a family-owned business since its founding in the nineteenth century. The company holds title to the Bay Terrace shopping center as well as many other residential and commercial properties throughout Queens.

■ Former notable residents of Bayside include Pearl White, one of the first great silent film stars, and star pitcher Tom Seaver.

As One Champ to Another

"As One Champ to Another": heavyweight boxing champion and Bayside resident "Gentleman Jim" Corbett with Jack Meshirer, New York City marble champion, around the turn of the century (Queens Library, Long Island Division, Illustrations Collection)

Crocheron Park is named after the Crocheron Hotel, which was reportedly a popular hangout for the likes of Boss Tweed, who reigned over city politics from 1866 to 1871. Tweed and his Tammany Hall crew held picnics on the grounds of the hotel, and it's possible that Tweed hid there after he escaped from prison in 1875, before fleeing to Cuba. Twenty years after the hotel burned down in 1907, the city of New York purchased the property and by 1936 had converted it into a park.

Bay Terrace

10 Just south of Crocheron Park is Corbett Road, named for the heavyweight boxing champion James J. "Gentleman Jim" Corbett, who held the title from 1892 to 1897. After retiring from the sport, Corbett became an actor, and the road named after him became known to many as Actor's Row because movie stars like W. C. Fields and Gloria Swanson made their homes here, commuting to Astoria Studios (now Kaufman Astoria Studios), where they worked. Other famous people who called Bayside home include Buster Keaton, John Barrymore, Irving Berlin, Norma Talmadge, and Rudolph Valentino.

Among the prominent names associated with Bayside's development are John Rodman, a Quaker who settled there during the American Revolution, and Thomas Hicks, a Flushing resident who owned a 246-acre Bayside farm, "The Oaks," that spread from what is now 46th Avenue to today's Long Island Expressway. The farm was purchased by Abraham Bell in 1824. Bell Boulevard, which crosses all of Bayside in a north-south direction, was named after this shipping merchant, who erected a mansion (razed for development in 1971) on Bell Boulevard and 39th Avenue.

Hicks's farmland later belonged to John H. Taylor, one of the founders of the 110-acre Oakland Golf Club in 1896; other land was developed during the late nineteenth century and, especially, following World War II, when single-family housing and apartment

complexes went up. In the early 1960s the city purchased the Golf Club, and the land is now the site of a housing development, Benjamin N. Cardozo High School, P.S. 203, and Queensborough Community College. (The college's art gallery is housed in the 1920s Oakland Building, the former club house.)

South of the original farmland lies the area known as **Oakland Gardens,** which extends from the Long Island Expressway to Hollis Hills, bordered by Alley Pond Park to the east and Cunningham Park to the west. Some single-family ranch and Colonial homes can be found here, but most residents live in garden apartments, condominiums, and co-ops.

The overall character of Bayside was transformed after 1930, when the politically powerful Robert Moses, New York City Parks Commissioner and head of the Triborough Bridge and Tunnel Authority, designed the Belt Parkway system, and in particular the Cross Island Parkway, opened in 1940, which cut off access from Bayside and Bay Terrace to Little Neck Bay. Thereafter, the Throgs Neck Bridge, opened in 1961 to connect Bayside and the Bronx, and the Clearview Expressway, completed in 1963 and designed to link the Throgs Neck Bridge with the major east-west arteries of Queens and Long Island, were also built to accommodate motorists.

Today, train commuters into Manhattan have a half-hour direct ride on the Long Island Rail Road, beginning at the gambrel-roofed station built in 1923 at 213th Street and 41st Avenue. A large section of this area, from 41st Avenue to

Aerial view of Bayside area in 1923, before Bay Terrace was built (Queens Library, Long Island Division, Illustrations Collection)

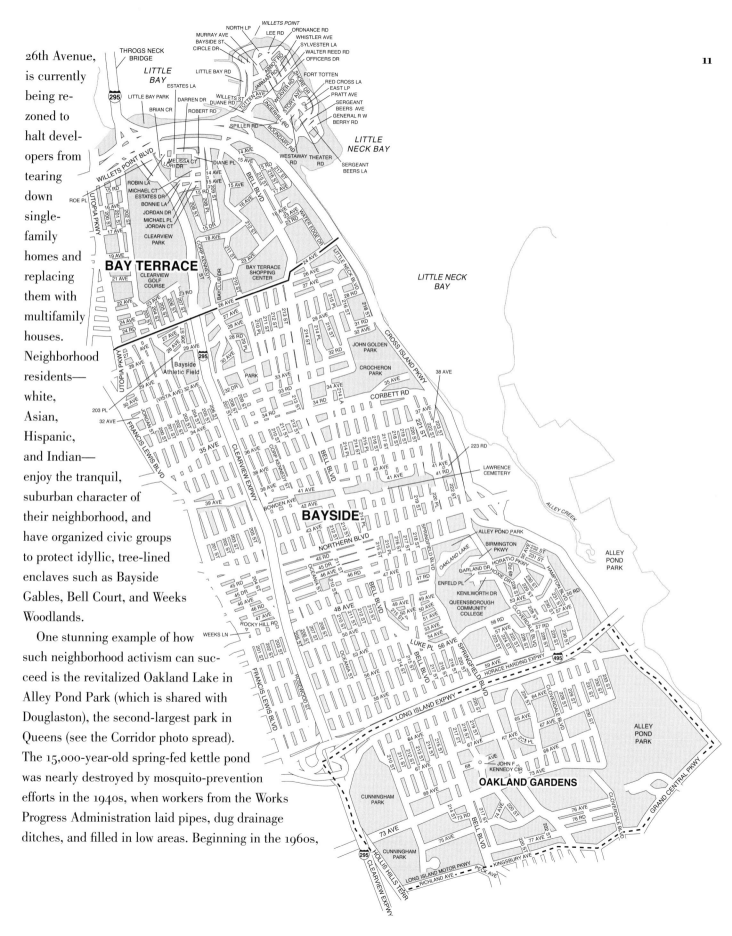

26th Avenue, is currently being re-zoned to halt developers from tearing down single-family homes and replacing them with multifamily houses. Neighborhood residents—white, Asian, Hispanic, and Indian—enjoy the tranquil, suburban character of their neighborhood, and have organized civic groups to protect idyllic, tree-lined enclaves such as Bayside Gables, Bell Court, and Weeks Woodlands.

One stunning example of how such neighborhood activism can succeed is the revitalized Oakland Lake in Alley Pond Park (which is shared with Douglaston), the second-largest park in Queens (see the Corridor photo spread). The 15,000-year-old spring-fed kettle pond was nearly destroyed by mosquito-prevention efforts in the 1940s, when workers from the Works Progress Administration laid pipes, dug drainage ditches, and filled in low areas. Beginning in the 1960s, however, under the spirited leadership of Dr. John O. Riedl and the Alley Restoration Committee, and continuing into the 1970s and 1980s with the efforts of Gertrude Waldeyer and the Oakland Lake and Ravine Conservation Committee, the lake experienced a dramatic turnaround. Today's lake is stocked with several varieties of fish and supports many bird species. Part of the original forest remains, and many other mature trees now offer shade around the lake's natural shoreline.

Single-family homes on 50th Avenue near Bell Boulevard

NEIGHBORHOOD PROFILE

Boundaries: <u>Bayside:</u> <u>north border:</u> 26th Avenue to Bell Boulevard to 24th Avenue; <u>east border:</u> Cross Island Parkway; <u>south border:</u> Grand Central Parkway to Kingsbury Avenue to Richland Avenue (running path/old Long Island Motor Parkway); <u>west border:</u> Hollis Hills Terrace to Clearview Expressway to Long Island Expressway to Francis Lewis Boulevard to Utopia Parkway; <u>Oakland Gardens:</u> <u>north border:</u> Long Island Expressway; <u>east border:</u> Cross Island Parkway; <u>south border:</u> Grand Central Parkway to Kingsbury Avenue to Richland Avenue (running path/old Long Island Motor Parkway); <u>west border:</u> Hollis Hills Terrace to Clearview Expressway; <u>Bay Terrace:</u> <u>north border:</u> Little Bay (including Little Bay Park); <u>east border:</u> Little Neck Bay (including Fort Totten and Cross Island Parkway); <u>south border:</u> 24th Avenue to Bell Boulevard to 26th Avenue; <u>west border:</u> Utopia Parkway
Subway and Train: <u>LIRR:</u> Bayside
Bus: <u>Q88, x32:</u> 73rd Avenue to Springfield Boulevard; <u>Q27:</u> Springfield Boulevard to 48th Avenue; <u>Q75:</u> 73rd Avenue; <u>Q76:</u> Francis Lewis Boulevard; <u>Q30:</u> Horace Harding Expressway; <u>Q12, N21, N20:</u> Northern Boulevard; <u>Q31:</u> 48th Avenue to Bell Boulevard; <u>Q28:</u> Francis Lewis Boulevard to 32nd Avenue to Corporal Kennedy Street; <u>x32:</u> 32nd Avenue to Corporal Kennedy Street; <u>Q13:</u> Northern Boulevard to Bell Boulevard
Libraries: Queens Library, Bayside Branch (214-20 Northern Boulevard); Bay Terrace Branch (18-36 Bell Boulevard)
Museums: Holocaust Resource Center and Archives at Queensborough Community College (222-05 56th Avenue), Queensborough Community College Art Gallery (222-05 56th Avenue)
Theaters: Queensborough Community College Performing Arts Center (56th Avenue and Springfield Boulevard)
Community Board: Nos. 7 and 11
Police Precinct: 111th Precinct (45-06 215th Street); 109th Precinct (37-05 Union Street, Flushing)
Fire Department: Engine 326, Ladder 160 (64-04 Springfield Boulevard); Engine 306 (40-18 214th Place)

On the opposite end of Bayside, starting at 26th Avenue, lies Bay Terrace, an upscale neighborhood of townhouses, condominiums, and cooperative apartments whose proudest achievement may be the preservation of Fort Totten, which opened as a New York City park in June 2005. Area residents, along with the Bay Terrace Community Alliance, Friends of Fort Totten Parks, the Fort Totten Conservancy, the Bay Terrace Community Organization, the Bayside Historical Society, and the Citizens Action Committee, devoted years of planning, negotiations, and paper-pushing to preserve the 49.5-acre park. And while some express concern about lack of sufficient parking at the fort and the effects of additional traffic on quiet Bay Terrace, most feel relieved that the historic landmark will not fall into the hands of developers.

Fort Totten was built on Willets Point (to the east of the Throgs Neck Bridge) during the Civil War, but it never engaged in battle. Named after

Bayside Marina on Little Neck Bay

Brig. Gen. Joseph G. Totten, the 136-acre site includes more than a hundred buildings, among them the former officers' club, a beautiful Gothic Revival structure that is now home to the Bayside Historical Society. In the past, the fort served as the Army Engineering School and performed other military functions. It will continue to be home base for the 77th Army Reserve Support Command, as it has been since 1967. But to many in the area the famous fort is best known for its Civil War–era battery, eleven historic buildings, a 13-acre parade ground with soccer fields, and amazing views of the Long Island Sound.

Another important green space is the Clearview Park and Golf Course, founded in 1925 on the western part of Bay Terrace. New York State governor Alfred E. Smith (1873–1944) was just one of the prestigious members of the originally private Clearview Golf and Yacht Club. The eighteen-hole golf course is now owned by the city of New York.

While some savor the panoramic views of the bay, others prefer the convenience of the single-family homes overlooking the expansive Bay Terrace shopping center on Bell Boulevard and 26th Avenue. This center features virtually every national chain imaginable, as well as independent retailers, a multiplex theater, a supermarket, a post office, and abundant dining options, making it an attraction for residents throughout the borough.

Bellerose

Meticulously kept brick homes line Bellerose streets

In Bellerose, residents have a strong tradition of caring for their neighborhood. Every year neighbors support and cheer on junior baseball players, celebrate and raise money for a community school, accept those who need treatment at their well-known mental health centers, and work together to preserve their unique heritage.

A lovely, peaceful neighborhood, Bellerose, which includes the **Bellerose Manor** community, bears the same name as a neighborhood in Nassau County that borders it to the south—because the two now-distinct neighborhoods were developed by the same enterprising woman. At the turn of the twentieth century, Helen Marsh, a real estate agent based in Massachusetts, formed the United Holding Company and constructed houses in the Nassau County section.

The Queens area was developed for residential use starting in 1910. Legend has it that Bellerose was named after an original farming family named Rose, who had a daughter named Belle, although historians have disputed this theory. One- and two-family Capes and Tudors still dominate this mostly white, upscale community—one that has managed to maintain its quiet character even after the busy Cross Island Parkway opened in 1940.

While Bellerose is predominantly a residential neighborhood, with ample shopping on Hillside Avenue and farther south along Jamaica Avenue (which becomes Jericho Turnpike farther east), the neighborhood is also well known for its mental health treatment facilities. The Queens Children's Psychiatric Center at 74-03 Commonwealth Boulevard serves seriously emotionally disturbed children and adolescents between the ages of five and eighteen with both inpatient and outpatient services.

Nearby, on Winchester Boulevard, is Creedmoor Psychiatric Center, named after the Creed family, original titleholders of the property. Long ago this site housed the National Rifle Association, but the rifle range closed down in

NEIGHBORHOOD PROFILE

Boundaries: <u>Bellerose</u>: <u>north border</u>: Grand Central Parkway; <u>east border</u>: Little Neck Parkway; <u>south border</u>: Jamaica Avenue; <u>west border</u>: Gettysburg Street to Braddock Avenue to Springfield Boulevard; <u>Bellerose Manor</u>: <u>north border</u>: Union Turnpike; <u>east border</u>: Winchester Boulevard to Hillside Avenue to 235th Court to Moline Street; <u>south border</u>: Braddock Avenue to Springfield Boulevard; <u>west border</u>: Grand Central Parkway
Bus: <u>Q27, Q88</u>: Springfield Boulevard; <u>Q1</u>: Springfield Boulevard to Braddock Avenue; <u>Q43, x68, N22A, N22, N26</u>: Hillside Avenue; <u>Q79</u>: Little Neck Parkway; <u>Q36, N24</u>: Jamaica Avenue; <u>Q46</u>: Union Turnpike
Libraries: Queens Library, Bellerose Branch (250-06 Hillside Avenue)
Theaters: Queens Children's Theater/Queens Family Theater (85-05 249th Street)
Community Board: No. 13
Police Precinct: 105th Precinct (92-08 222nd Street, Queens Village)
Fire Department: Ladder 160, Battalion 53 (64-04 Springfield Boulevard, Queens Village); Engine 304, Ladder 162, Battalion 53 (218-44 97th Avenue, Queens Village); Engine 251, Battalion 53 (254-20 Union Turnpike, Glen Oaks)
Hospitals and Clinics: Creedmoor Psychiatric Center (80-45 Winchester Boulevard); Queens Children's Psychiatric Center (74-03 Commonwealth Boulevard)

1908, owing primarily to complaints about stray bullets from neighborhood residents. Creedmoor opened in 1912 as part of the Brooklyn Psychiatric Center. In order to cater to a growing population in need of mental health services, numerous buildings were constructed in the late 1920s, and by 1933 the center had become a separate state hospital with over fifty buildings on

Long Island Rail Road steam locomotive pulling two passenger cars through the fields at Bellerose in 1900 (Queens Library, Long Island Division, Illustrations Collection)

16

In 1930 a row of brick buildings was moved back to widen Jamaica Avenue at 246th Street (Queens Library, Long Island Division, Illustrations Collection)

Creed Farmhouse, now part of the Queens County Farm Museum, 1927 (Queens Library, Long Island Division, Eugene Armbruster Collection)

more than 300 acres. In the 1940s and thereafter various new treatments for dealing with mental illness were introduced at Creedmoor, including hydrotherapy, insulin therapy, electroshock, and lobotomy. But it was the newly developing antidepressants and tranquilizers that transformed the facility and that paved the way for patients to manage daily living outside, as part of the community and as workers on a community farm owned by the center.

NEIGHBORHOOD FACTS

■ Founded in 1983, the 40,000-square-foot Living Museum at Creedmoor Psychiatric Center is the nation's only museum featuring art—murals, sculptures, paintings, poems—created by people with mental illness. It is open to the public by appointment.
■ Since 1980 residents of Bellerose have hosted their annual Gregorian Festival, an eleven-night event featuring live music, rides, games, dancing, and homemade cuisine. The festival attracts 75,000 people each year and raises tuition funds for St. Gregory the Great Church.
■ The Hollis–Bellaire–Queens Village–Bellerose Athletic Association, a Babe Ruth–sanctioned league based on Hillside Avenue, has been offering baseball and softball to children for almost fifty years. The stadium complex is maintained by volunteer parents and includes nine playing fields.

This farm, at 73-50 Little Neck Parkway, offered patients a chance to work outside, raising livestock and growing fruit and vegetables both for consumption and for the therapeutic value of working the land. But in 1973 this vital piece of Queens history was in danger of being lost to development when New York State declared the property excess land. A band of neighborhood activists formed the Colonial Farmhouse Restoration Society of Bellerose to save the land's historic structures. Thanks to their determination, the Dutch-style Jacob Adriance Farmhouse, built circa 1772, and the farm it sits on are today a national and New York City landmark known as the Queens County Farm Museum, run by the New York City Department of Parks and Recreation. The longest continuously farmed site in New York State, it encompasses 47 acres (7 of which are landmarked) that include farm buildings, a greenhouse complex, livestock, farm vehicles and tools, fields for crops, an orchard, and an herb garden. It is open to the public for tours, educational activities, and special events.

Under Governor George Pataki in 2001, just over 32 acres on the northern end of this property were designated for a different use: public education. The Glen Oaks School Campus, completed in time for the 2003–4 school year, serves some 3,000 students in three new public schools. The new campus includes playgrounds, athletic fields, and open space.

Community activism has helped Bellerose retain and revitalize its unique features. The Joint Bellerose Business District Development Corporation, founded in 1995 by local merchants, residents, and civic groups in both Bellerose, Queens, and the incorporated village of Bellerose in Nassau County, works to increase business in the area and enhance residents' quality of life. In addition, a proliferation of groups such as the Creedmoor Civic Association, the North Bellerose Civic Association, and the Bellerose Commonwealth Civic Association have been instrumental in improving the neighborhood while retaining its one-of-a-kind character.

Briarwood

NEIGHBORHOOD FACTS

■ Here since 1957, Archbishop Molloy High School at 83-53 Manton Street is run by the Marist order. It has built a reputation of academic excellence, religious studies, service to others, and athletic achievement. One of its well-known alumni is Kenny Anderson, formerly of the Boston Celtics, who honed his basketball skills on the campus.

■ Famous former Briarwood residents include civil rights leader Roy Wilkins and feminist Betty Friedan.

Modest homes on 86th Avenue near 143rd Street grace the quiet, residential community of Briarwood

Those who seek a tranquil haven in central Queens will feel right at home in Briarwood. Relaxed living and entertainment attract many families to this quiet community, which is surrounded on four sides by major arteries—Union Turnpike, Parsons Boulevard, Hillside Avenue, and the Van Wyck Expressway—and by its neighbors Kew Gardens Hills, Kew Gardens, Jamaica Hills, and, to the south, Jamaica. Shopping and other amenities can be found along Queens Boulevard,

on Union Turnpike, and on Parsons Boulevard. And for outdoor fun, residents head to Hoover Park, which boasts a playground, handball courts, basketball courts, and benches.

Briarwood was referred to as northern Jamaica for years before it developed its own identity as a middle-class residential community with its own library (opened in 1975) and post office (opened in 1997). Just nine miles from Manhattan, locals can commute via a variety of nearby subway stops or the Long Island Rail Road, which picks up passengers in Jamaica or Kew Gardens.

The neighborhood was a late bloomer compared to other areas of Queens. After the 1907 Briarwood Land Company went into bankruptcy, not much was built until 1936, when the development firm Briarwood Estates began selling off lots at auction. The Parkway Village garden apartment complex was built in the late 1940s on Union Turnpike between Main Street and Parsons Boulevard. Back then, the United Nations had its headquarters in Flushing Meadows–Corona Park; Parkway was built initially as housing for diplomats. The United Nations relocated to its permanent home in Manhattan in 1952, and much later, in 1983, Parkway became a 670-unit cooperative, housing residents of various ethnicities and nationalities, among them African Americans, Asians, and Hispanics.

Other housing in Briarwood includes apartment buildings erected in the 1950s. Throughout that decade, residents experienced a neighborhood under development as empty, muddy lots were transformed into six- and seven-story apartment buildings—today co-ops and rentals—that surrounded the modest single-family Tudors and Colonials already situated along the neighborhood's winding streets.

In 1987 an architect at the Queens office of the Department of City Planning raved, "The Briarwood community has many examples of New York craftsmanship at its best." But in 2001 Briarwood, along with neighboring Jamaica Hills, faced one of its more challenging housing issues when a number of these homes had to be evacuated because of cracking foundations. Residents claimed that the shifting was caused by the fact that houses had been built on loose soil.

Another housing issue that upset the Briarwood community was the announcement that the Salvation Army intended to build a homeless shelter in this neighborhood. Despite opposition by homeowners, the plan went ahead, and in 1992 the red-brick Briarwood Family Residence, a transitional housing program at 80-20 134th Street, opened its doors to the needy, not far from the Queens branch of the American Red Cross on Queens Boulevard. Today the structure blends in seamlessly with the area, and Briarwood residents have learned to

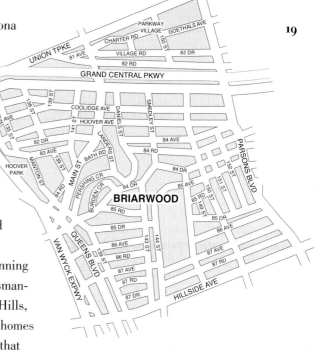

welcome the facility. In 2003 one of the shelter's residents, Eli Couvertier, became a neighborhood hero of sorts when he found an abandoned newborn baby girl on his way to a construction job. He discovered the little bundle at 134th Street, and promptly rushed her to the shelter—his own shelter, just two blocks away.

NEIGHBORHOOD PROFILE

Boundaries: <u>North border:</u> Union Turnpike; <u>east border:</u> Parsons Boulevard; <u>south border:</u> Hillside Avenue; <u>west border:</u> Van Wyck Expressway

Subway and Train: <u>E, F trains:</u> Briarwood/Van Wyck Boulevard; <u>F train:</u> Sutphin Boulevard, Parsons Boulevard

Bus: Q44: Main Street; Q20A, Q20B: Main Street; Q25: Parsons Boulevard; Q34: Parsons Boulevard; Q43, Q44: Hillside Avenue; x68: Hillside Avenue

Libraries: Queens Library, Briarwood Branch (85-12 Main Street)

Community Board: No. 8

Police Precinct: 107th Precinct (71-01 Parsons Boulevard, Flushing)

Fire Department: Engine 315, Battalion 50 (159-06 Union Turnpike, Jamaica Hills)

On 84th Drive apartment buildings rub shoulders with single-family homes.

Cambria

NEIGHBORHOOD FACTS

■ The only remaining evidence of Cambria Heights's once-thriving Jewish community is Montefiore Cemetery at 121-83 Springfield Boulevard, resting place of the revered Lubavitcher rebbe, Rabbi Menachem Schneerson. Schneerson, the leader of the Hasidic movement based in Crown Heights, Brooklyn, died at age ninety-two in 1994. Every year, tens of thousands of Jews from around the world, who claim Schneerson as the messiah, visit his gravesite, entering from the Ohel Chabad Lubavich Center on Francis Lewis Boulevard and 121st Avenue. The Chabad house, open twenty-four hours a day, six days a week, offers a private walkway through a rear door. Men and women enter the area separately, and it is customary to walk backward upon exiting the gravesite.
■ Jazz legend Chick Corea once lived in Cambria Heights.

Visitors to Cambria Heights will delight in the Caribbean sounds and flavors of this vibrant neighborhood. But the many residents from Haiti, Jamaica, and Trinidad and Tobago are only the most recent migrants to make this appealing area their home.

Until its purchase in 1923 by real estate agent Oliver B. LaFreniere, the area known as Cambria Heights was largely lush farmland and pristine woods, perched 50 feet above sea level—one of the highest elevations in Queens. Later known as Kerosene Hill (before it was set up with piped gas lines), Cambria Heights may have been named after a coal company in Cambria County, Pennsyl-

Wide, tree-lined streets such as 222nd Street typify Cambria Heights

Heights

vania. (The source of the name may also have been the Cambria Title Savings and Trust Company, a bank from the same county that may have funded early home construction in the neighborhood.) But as the neighborhood was developed, its history became defined by the various peoples who came to the area looking for a new start.

The first settlers were predominantly Italian, German, and Irish families moving from over-crowded neighborhoods in Brooklyn and Man-hattan. In his memoir *Paperboy* (2002), Henry Petroski, the engineer and author of *The Pencil, The Evolution of Useful Things,* and other popular books, describes the Cambria Heights he moved to from Brooklyn in 1954. For a twelve-year-old white boy desiring nothing but a bike and a paper route, this Queens neighborhood, with its wide, tree-lined streets and modest Cape, Colonial, and Tudor houses, proved idyllic. By contrast, when William Durham, with his wife and seven-year-old daughter, relocated from Brooklyn to a house on 235th Street just six years later, he experienced an entirely different Cambria Heights.

In 1960 blacks were not welcome in this pre-dominantly white neighborhood, and Dur-ham, the first African American to move into Cambria Heights (and today fondly known as "the Mayor"), recalls having a cross burned on his lawn and rocks thrown at his windows many times by residents who didn't want him there. That was be-fore the "white flight" of the late 1960s and 1970s, when numerous neighborhoods, particularly those in southeastern Queens, experienced an

Afro-Caribbean businesses lining Linden Boulevard

exodus of white, middle-class residents to the suburbs. During that time, Cambria Heights's ethnic composition changed, and the pioneer Durham saw his neighborhood become predominantly black.

Today it is not uncommon to come across Afro-Caribbean–owned businesses along the main shopping street, Linden Boulevard, which crosses Cambria Heights in a roughly east-west direction. Nearly every establishment between 221st and 223rd Streets—including a restaurant that features fried goat on the menu—is Haitian-owned, while the headquarters for the Haitian Americans United for Progress, a nonprofit social services agency providing immigration assistance, ESL courses, and other services, is located at 221-07 Linden Boulevard.

Families of all backgrounds enjoy gathering at Frederick Cabbell Park, named

The Cambria Heights Civic Association is one of the oldest in Queens

for a longtime New York City police officer and Cambria Heights resident who devoted his life to the community, directing the Cambria Heights Little League for twenty-two years and leading a popular Boy Scout troop. The 4.5-acre park was recently refurbished with the addition of new baseball fields, basketball courts, and a playground.

Although residents worry that the neighborhood has become so desirable to outsiders that newcomers are illegally converting single-family homes to multiple dwellings, organizations like the Cambria Heights Civic Association, founded in 1932 and one of the oldest civic associations in Queens, continue to work to keep the neighborhood, in the words of one longtime resident, "a beautiful place to live."

NEIGHBORHOOD PROFILE

Boundaries: <u>North border</u>: Murdock Avenue; <u>east border</u>: Nassau County border (includes Hook Creek Boulevard); <u>south border</u>: 121st Avenue to Francis Lewis Boulevard around Montefiore Cemetery; <u>west border</u>: Springfield Boulevard around Old Springfield Cemetery to Springfield Boulevard to Francis Lewis Boulevard

Bus: <u>Q83</u>: Murdock Avenue to 113th Drive; <u>Q27</u>: Springfield Boulevard; <u>Q84</u>: 120th Avenue; <u>Q4, x64</u>: Linden Boulevard; <u>Q77</u>: Springfield Boulevard

Libraries: Queens Library, Cambria Heights Branch (220-20 Linden Boulevard)

Community Board: No. 13

Police Precinct: 105th Precinct (92-08 222nd Street, Queens Village)

Fire Department: Engine 317, Ladder 165, Battalion 54 (117-11 196th Street, St. Albans); Engine 314, Battalion 54 (142-04 Brookville Boulevard, St. Albans)

Cambria Heights Community Church, established in 1928, was the first church in the neighborhood

College

Elliott's Hardware in the late 1800s on what is now 14th Road (Queens Library, Long Island Division, Illustrations Collection)

Visitors to the 28-acre Hermon A. MacNeil Park, on the original grounds of St. Paul's College in northern College Point, are treated to a spectacular view of the East River and Flushing Bay, whose waters surround this neighborhood on three sides. An area rich in architectural history and dotted with lush green spaces, College Park boasts abundant landmarks—a wonderfully vibrant historical legacy that survives in large part because of active, preservation-minded community groups that have resisted overdevelopment.

Early names for this area were Lawrence Neck, after members of the Lawrence family, who helped shape borough history, and Tew's Neck. In 1645 a grant for 900 acres near Flushing was given by the Dutch to family patriarch William Lawrence. In 1839 Rev. William Muhlenberg of St. George Episcopal Church in nearby Flushing opened St. Paul's College near the tip of the peninsula, giving College Point its name, even though St. Paul's closed down before it reached its tenth anniversary. In 1867 the communities of Flammersburg and Strattonport (named for other early settlers) became part of College Point proper.

The area remained small and rural until 1854, when German entrepreneur Conrad Poppenhusen opened Enterprise Rubber Works, a factory that created household goods based on Charles Goodyear's 1839 patent. One of the first large-scale manufacturing plants to open in Queens, the factory required hundreds of laborers, so Poppenhusen built for his mostly German immigrant

Fishing at College Point overlooking Flushing Bay and the Bronx.

Point

workers and their families a community complete with schools, water and sewage systems, and a railroad (the Steinway family would shortly follow suit with their own factory town in Astoria). The plant flourished during the Civil War as orders poured in for hard rubber flasks, cups, and buttons. Even so, Poppenhusen went bankrupt in 1877. College Point, however, continued to thrive, not only as a minor industrial center but also as a summer resort, with restaurants, sporting facilities, and bathing areas. (A bust of Poppenhusen by sculptor Henry Baerer was commissioned by residents in 1884 and still stands today where College Place, College Point Boulevard, and 11th Avenue meet.)

There are many culturally or historically significant structures in College Point, and a number of these have been honored by the Queens Historical Society with a Queensmark award, which recognizes the same high standards of architectural beauty and importance as official New York City landmark designations (although the same legal sanctions are not imposed). One example is the Poppenhusen branch of the Queens Library, at 121-23 14th Avenue. Built in 1904 by renowned architects Heins and LaFarge

The Classical Revival–style Poppenhusen branch of the Queens Library (1904) is a New York City landmark

NEIGHBORHOOD PROFILE

Boundaries: <u>North border:</u> Queens–Bronx county border and East River; <u>east border:</u> Powell's Cove to 138th Street to 13th Avenue to 143rd Place to 14th Avenue to Whitestone Expressway; <u>south border:</u> Flushing Bay; <u>west border:</u> Flushing Bay and East River
Bus: <u>Q65:</u> College Point Boulevard; <u>Q25:</u> 127th Street to Ulmer Street; <u>Q20B:</u> 14th Avenue; <u>Q20A:</u> 20th Avenue; <u>Q76:</u> 20th Avenue; <u>QBx1:</u> Whitestone Expressway
Libraries: Queens Library, Poppenhusen Branch (121-23 14th Avenue)
Community Board: No. 7
Police Precinct: 109th Precinct (37-05 Union Street, Flushing)
Fire Department: Engine 297, Ladder 130 (119-11 14th Road)

The magnificent French Second Empire Poppenhusen Institute (1868)

and only one of five remaining Carnegie libraries in the Queens system, this Classical Revival jewel was designated an official New York City landmark in 2000.

The Poppenhusen Institute, located at 114-04 14th Road, is a magnificent French Second Empire structure built in 1868. A designated New York City landmark (1970) and listed on the National Register of Historic Places (1973), the institute was originally a vocational school and starting in 1870 housed the first free kindergarten in the United States. It also served as the village hall, a firehouse, and even a jail. Despite its historic significance, in 1980 the institute was threatened with demolition. In response, neighbors formed the Concerned Citizens for the Poppenhusen Institute, whose efforts, including three years of court battles, saved the building, which today is a community cultural center offering

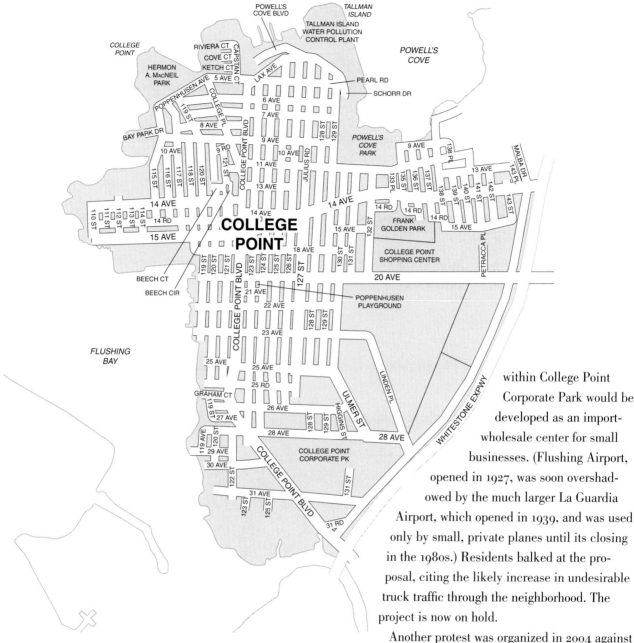

within College Point Corporate Park would be developed as an import-wholesale center for small businesses. (Flushing Airport, opened in 1927, was soon overshadowed by the much larger La Guardia Airport, which opened in 1939, and was used only by small, private planes until its closing in the 1980s.) Residents balked at the proposal, citing the likely increase in undesirable truck traffic through the neighborhood. The project is now on hold.

Another protest was organized in 2004 against a developer's plan to erect more than eighty-five houses near College Place and 5th Avenue, just east of the lovely Hermon A. MacNeil Park and atop a toxic landfill. To allay concerns about potential health hazards cited by locals, some environmental experts, and the Northeastern Queens Nature and Historical Preserve Commission, the developer spent millions of dollars to clean up the land in accordance

programs for all ages, including group piano lessons, karate for children and adults, acting classes, lectures, and exhibits.

Community activism continues to play a large role in this otherwise quiet residential area. In February 2004 residents picketed when Mayor Michael Bloomberg announced that a 26-acre site on the former grounds of Flushing Airport

with Department of Environmental Conservation regulations, and Sound-view Pointe opened for sales in 2006. Designed using feng shui principles to appeal to the neighborhood's growing Asian population, the complex offers residents peaceful views of both water and parkland.

Parks have an important place in the layout of College Point. Among notable parks in the neighborhood are Frank Golden Park and Poppenhusen Playground. One of the more unusual parks is Powell's Cove Park, an environmentally beneficial waterfront recreation area completed in 1999. Only about 7 acres of the 24.4-acre Powell's Cove Park are above ground—the rest are submerged marshlands, one more way water shapes the character of this elegant, secluded neighborhood.

NEIGHBORHOOD FACTS

■ The first law signed by Mayor John V. Lindsay was legislation changing the name of Chisholm Park (also called College Point Shore Front Park) to Hermon A. MacNeil Park, in honor of the well-known sculptor, a local resident. Among MacNeil's best-known sculptures in New York are the statue of George Washington at the base of Manhattan's Washington Square Arch and the War Memorial in Flushing. MacNeil sometimes used his College Point neighbors as models for his sculptures.

■ The Chisolm mansion, situated within what is today Hermon A. MacNeil Park, was used in 1937 as a summer city hall by Mayor Fiorello La Guardia. The mansion was subsequently torn down; only a flagpole marks the area today.

■ College Point Corporate Park, on the Whitestone Expressway, boasts some unusual businesses. Crystal Window and Door Systems is also home to an Asian art gallery, featuring a collection of ancient Chinese art, while the Center for Automotive Education & Training, run by the Greater New York Automobile Dealers Association, is the first facility in the nation designed to teach the latest in automotive technology.

■ Roesch's Tavern, at 20th Avenue and College Point Boulevard, was a neighborhood institution for more than a century until it closed its doors in 2003. Business had declined dramatically after the city banned smoking in bars and restaurants.

The Lepine family butchers have been in the neighborhood since 1921 at 14-26 College Point Boulevard

Corona

Corona moves to a Latin beat. With its unique combination of Spanish-speaking, Italian, and African American influences, this community knows something about diversity, and it celebrates it every year with popular summer festivals and closely held, unique traditions.

Corona was transformed from a rural community to the densely settled neighborhood it is today after the Long Island Rail Road arrived in 1854, opening a station on National Street, named after the National Race Course, which opened in the same year. The course, set along 97th and 105th Streets and 34th and 37th Avenues, was renamed Fashion Race Track (see Ozone Park). Back then, the neighborhood was called West Flushing, but it was renamed Corona in 1872 by music publisher Benjamin W. Hitchcock, who sold hundreds of lots for residential development, including two to the showman P. T. Barnum. After that initial offering, development increased rapidly, especially once the elevated train (which is still in operation) was built in 1917 along Roosevelt Avenue.

Corona was not only attractive as a residential area; it also became home to numerous factories. The stained-glass factory of Louis Comfort Tiffany, which still stands today, was built in 1893 on 97th Place between 43rd and 44th Avenues. Tiffany Studios produced decorative lights, ceramics, jewelry, and metal works, which were then displayed in a Manhattan showroom for some of New York's choosiest customers: the Rockefellers, the Astors, and Mark Twain, among others. Tiffany's fame faded during the Depression, and his business went into bankruptcy. These days, however, he is remembered as a brilliant artisan.

In the early 1970s, Corona had a growing Hispanic population living alongside German, Italian, African American, and Jewish families. Today, more than half of the residents in this north-central Queens neighborhood are Puerto Rican, Dominican, Peruvian, Colombian, or Mexican. While there is also an Asian popula-

The 7 line still runs along elevated tracks over Roosevelt Avenue

tion in the neighborhood, Hispanic influences—including delicious Latin American cuisine—are most apparent. Every summer, these cultures host numerous festivals attended by thousands: Ecuadorian Day Festival, Dominican Day Festival, and Latin Mix Festival are just some of those celebrated at Flushing Meadows–Corona Park, a western portion of which sits in this neighborhood, next to 111th Street (see the Corridor photo spread). Small wonder that Queens native Paul Simon should hail "Rosie, the queen of Corona" in his Latin-flavored "Me and Julio Down by the Schoolyard."

Smaller-scale recreation can be found on a triangle at 108th Street and 51st Avenue, affectionately dubbed "Spaghetti Park" by locals. Here Italian men have been staging bocce ball tournaments for decades, making William F. Moore Park a neighborhood institution for both the elderly participants and the younger spectators who cheer them on.

Also an institution here for almost thirty years was the jazz legend Louis Armstrong, who lived at 34-56 107th Street, off of Northern Boulevard. Armstrong moved to the modest, red-brick, two-story house with his wife, Lucille, in 1943 and the couple, who had no children of their own, became "Aunt Lucille" and "Uncle Louis" to neighborhood kids. Beyond his playful side—the famous musician enjoyed serenading the kids from his front stoop—Louis was a compelling role model for young children. He was an outspoken symbol of the civil rights movement, made a goodwill tour to western Africa, and refused to patronize New York clubs from which he once had been excluded. Armstrong lived in Corona until his death in 1971; Lucille Armstrong stayed on until she passed away in 1983. Today, the house

N E I G H B O R H O O D P R O F I L E

Boundaries: <u>North border:</u> Northern Boulevard; <u>east border:</u> Grand Central Parkway; <u>south border:</u> Long Island Expressway; <u>west border:</u> Junction Boulevard

Subway and Train: <u>7 train:</u> Junction Boulevard, 103rd Street/Corona Plaza, 111th Street, Willets Point/Shea Stadium; <u>LIRR:</u> Shea Stadium

Bus: <u>Q66:</u> Northern Boulevard; <u>Q72:</u> Junction Boulevard; <u>Q48:</u> 108th Street to Roosevelt Avenue; <u>Q23:</u> 108th Street to Horace Harding Expressway; <u>Q58:</u> Corona Avenue to Horace Harding Expressway to College Point Boulevard; <u>Q88:</u> Horace Harding Expressway; <u>x51:</u> Horace Harding Expressway

Libraries: Queens Library, Corona Branch (42-11 104th Street); Langston Hughes Branch (100-01 Northern Boulevard); Lefrak City Branch (98-30 57th Avenue)

Museums: New York Hall of Science (47-01 111th Street); Queens Wildlife Center (53-51 111th Street, Flushing Meadows–Corona Park); Queens Museum of Art (New York City Building, Flushing Meadows–Corona Park); Louis Armstrong House and Archives (34-56 107th Street)

Theaters: Queens Theatre in the Park (Flushing Meadows–Corona Park)

Community Board: Nos. 3 and 4

Police Precinct: 110th Precinct (94-41 43rd Avenue, Elmhurst); 115th Precinct (92-15 Northern Boulevard, Jackson Heights)

Fire Department: Engine 289, Ladder 138, Battalion 46 (97-28 43rd Avenue)

is a national historic landmark and a New York City landmark, as well as a museum, which opened to the public in 2003.

Other museums include the New York Hall of Science, on 111th Street in Flushing Meadows–Corona Park, the only hands-on science and technology center in New York City. Also in the park, straddling the Corona-Flushing border on Grand Central Parkway, is the Queens Museum of Art, which is housed in the New York City Building, the only surviving building erected for the 1939 World's Fair. (From 1946 to 1950 the building was the home of the U.N. General Assembly.) Offering artistic and educational programs and exhibitions that relate to the contemporary life of Queens residents and other New Yorkers, the Queens Museum of Art is best known for its Panorama of New York City, a 9,335-square-foot ar-

"Spaghetti Park"

• The New York World's Fairs

The New York World's Fairs of 1939 and 1964, staged on the present-day site of Flushing Meadows–Corona Park, were two of the largest international expositions of the twentieth century. In total, more than 75 million people attended the events, which showcased the latest innovations of American corporations, as well as the nationalistic pride of dozens of foreign countries.

In the midst of the Great Depression, the 1939 World's Fair, along with the preparations it would entail—including the construction of the Bronx-Whitestone Bridge to access it—was seen by its planners as a means of kick-starting the city's economy. The fair's title, "The World of Tomorrow," embodied that hope, as did the sleek, forward-looking designs of many of the fair's pavilions. Among the more popular exhibits were General Motors's Futurama, a 36,000-square-foot theater featuring a scrupulously detailed diorama, designed by the theatrical and industrial designer Norman Bel Geddes, depicting how American life would look in 1960; the Chrysler exhibit, which introduced the world to "air-conditioning"; and "Voder," a speech synthesizer developed by Bell Labs and operated by keyboard.

After opening on August 20, 1939, to a first-day crowd of 200,000, the 1939 fair attracted more than 25 million visitors before it closed in October 1940. Although revenues topped $48 million, the fair was ultimately a financial flop—organizers spent $67 million on the project, and investments from outside sources exceeded $100 million. In the fair's second season, moreover, the notion of international progress was silenced by the outbreak of World War II—Poland and Czechoslovakia, having fallen to Nazi forces by 1940, failed to return for the final season.

Twenty-five years later, in 1964, Flushing Meadows–Corona Park hosted a second World's Fair, this time under the banner of "Peace Through Understanding." More than 51 million people attended. From the start, however, the fair was marked by controversy. The Bureau of International Expositions (BIE), a multinational oversight committee, refused to sanction the 1964 proposal because it had already approved a similar bid by Seattle for 1962. Against BIE objections, New York City planners pressed on—but not without consequences. Most European countries, as well as the Soviet Union, stayed home. As a result, the 1964 World's Fair was largely a showcase for U.S. corporations, with some foreign representation from Asia, Africa, and South America. General Motors unveiled a new Futurama, this time depicting an unspecified "World of Tomorrow" with design credit going simply to G.M. staff; IBM treated visitors to a hydraulic ride through a computer's inner workings; and Disney showed off the lifelike robots in the exhibit "It's a Small World" that later inhabited its Disneyland themepark.

But like its predecessor the World's Fair of 1964 was a financial disaster, and most of its pavilions were quickly razed. One landmark that did survive was the Unisphere, a hollow, metallic globe inspired by the Perisphere of the 1939 World's Fair. Today, the Unisphere stands in the middle of Flushing Meadows–Corona Park, Queens's most famous landmark and perhaps the most enduring and positive legacy of the site's two international fairs.

Even in winter the "Lemon Ice King of Corona" draws customers

chitectural model that includes every building constructed before 1992 in all five boroughs—895,000 structures. Created for the 1964 World's Fair, the panorama was updated in 1993 with the addition or renovation of more than 60,000 structures. It was renovated again in 2006–7 with new lighting, a multimedia feature, and an audio-visual tour of the buildings. The panorama still depicts the city as it looked in 1992, although once the city has decided on the Ground Zero memorial, the area around the World Trade Center will be updated.

While most of Corona is made up of one- and two-family homes, this neighborhood also houses Lefrak City, a massive rental apartment development covering 40 acres of land. The 5,000-

unit complex—made up of twenty towers, each eighteen stories high—is located in the southwest corner of Corona, bordered by the Long Island Expressway and neighboring Rego Park. Built between 1960 and 1968, the complex is itself a sprawling community. Swimming pools, tennis courts, playgrounds, indoor and outdoor parking, a post office, a public library, office buildings, shopping, and other amenities make Lefrak City a lively, bustling center of exuberant, multicultural Corona.

Aerial view of Lefrak City in 1965 (Queens Library, Long Island Division, Illustrations Collection)

NEIGHBORHOOD FACTS

■ Holding court at 52-02 108th Street is the community icon Peter Benfaremo, better known as the Lemon Ice King of Corona. Benfaremo began selling flavored ices to neighborhood residents in 1944. His tasty treats quickly became legendary, and today the Lemon Ice King of Corona is famous throughout New York.

■ Founded in 1969, the Langston Hughes Community Library and Cultural Center of the Queens Library on Northern Boulevard holds the largest circulating black heritage reference collection in New York City.

■ Queens Theatre in the Park, adjacent to the Queens Museum of Art in Flushing Meadows–Corona Park on the Corona-Flushing border, offers family-friendly and experimental theater, dance, and music on two stages, a 476-seat main stage, and a 99-seat experimental theater.

■ Union Evangelical Church, the oldest building in Corona, is at 41-16 National Street. This nondenominational church was built in 1873.

■ F. Scott Fitzgerald's *The Great Gatsby* (1925), partially set in Corona, memorably refers to the Corona dump heaps as "the valley of ashes." The dumpsite was eliminated in the construction for the 1939 World's Fair.

Winter carnival, Kissena Lake, 1930 (Courtesy of the Queens Library, Long Island Division, Illustrations Collection)

THE CORRIDOR

A detailed map of Queens offers an intriguing revelation: with the exception of Forest Park, in Woodhaven, the other main parks at the center of the borough—Flushing Meadows–Corona Park, Kissena Park, Cunningham Park, and Alley Pond Park—are all connected. The continuous stretch of green, known to many as the Corridor, has historic significance: it follows the route of an old railroad line that was in service around the 1870s.

Perhaps even more surprising, the spectacular Flushing Meadows–Corona Park, the flagship park of the borough, was originally a swamp. In the 1930s, in the largest reclamation project undertaken in the United States during the period, Commissioner of Parks Robert Moses led a team to fill in the area to create a 1,255-acre fairground for the 1939 World's Fair. The popular site was once again home to a World's Fair in 1964, and the structures remaining from the two events (including the Unisphere from the 1964 fair)—as well as the fact that the U.N. General Assembly convened in the park's New York City Building between 1946 and 1950—make Flushing Meadows–Corona one of New York's most historically significant parks. The expansive park truly has something to offer every taste: whether you spend the day relaxing at the humanmade Meadow Lake (at 84 acres, the largest in New York City); cheering on the Mets at Shea Stadium; discovering the world at the New York Hall of Science; enjoying fine arts exhibitions, performances, and films at the Queens Museum of Art or the World's Fair Theaterama; rooting for your favorite tennis stars at the

Alley Pond Park

U.S. Tennis Association's National Tennis Center (which hosts the U.S. Open and other tournaments); perusing exhibits of North American animals in natural settings at the Queens Wildlife Center; helping your little one learn about domestic animals at the Children's Farm; marveling at the tree and flower collections at the 39-acre Queens Botanical Garden; or taking in breathtaking views of the New York skyline from Terrace on the Park, a fourteen-story ballroom and catering hall, you're bound to have an unforgettable experience at Queens's largest park.

Kissena Park takes its name from Kissena Lake, the first piece of this parkland acquired by the city. Later parcels included Samuel Bowne Parsons's nursery (see Flushing), 65 acres of swampland, and a police-horse training farm. The

Queens's most famous landmark, the Flushing Meadows–Corona Park Unisphere, built for the 1964 World's Fair

Junked cars at Alley Pond Park, 1979 (The Queens Library, Long Island Division, Joseph A. Ullman Photographs)

land that linked it to the Corridor was acquired in 1947. In addition to the refurbished Parsons's Nursery and Weeping Beach Park, Kissena Park features the Charlie Emerson Wildlife Garden. It also offers a golf course and tennis and handball courts, and boasts New York City's only public bike track. Built in 1963, the track is the site of an annual junior cycling race and in 1964 hosted the U.S. Olympic Team cycling trials. The park has been renovated many times; in 1942, as part of a Works Progress Administration project, Kissena Lake was drained, surrounded by a stone retaining wall, and refilled.

Cunningham Park was originally probably home to Matinecoc Indians before Dutch and then English settlers began arriving in the seventeenth century. Much of the land was cleared during the Revolution, when British soldiers occupied the area. The city began acquiring the land for the park in 1928; it opened as Hillside Park and was renamed in 1934 for the city comptroller, W. Arthur Cunningham. The needs of the growing borough led to a reduction in the park between 1944 and 1960 to accommodate schools and roads, but today's 358-acre park still offers a variety of recreational facilities, including tennis courts, playgrounds, stables, and bridle paths.

William Buhrman's General Store, Alley Pond Park, after restoration, 1935 (The Queens Library, Long Island Division, Illustrations Collection)

Cunningham Park

Like Cunningham Park, Alley Pond Park was originally home to Matinecoc Indians, who were attracted by the shellfish in Little Neck Bay. English settlers began arriving in 1673, and soon the area featured mills and other light industry. In the eighteenth century it took on the name "The Alley"; it is believed to have been the route George Washington took while touring Long Island in 1790. The area was still largely rural when William Vanderbilt built his private road, Long Island Motor Parkway, in 1908 (see Hollis Hills). The second-largest park in Queens, Alley Pond was acquired by the city in 1929. Today the park includes the Alley Pond Nature Trail (opened in 1935) and the Alley Pond Environmental Center (1976). Bridle paths, tennis courts, picnic areas, a playground, and a soccer field are also part of these rescued park grounds.

Alley Pond Park with William Buhrman's General Store at left, 1932 (Courtesy of the Queens Library, Long Island Division, Gottscho Collection)

NEIGHBORHOOD FACTS

■ Among the historic structures in Douglas Manor are eight houses designed by Josephine Wright Chapman, a renowned architect and one of a handful of women working in the field at the turn of the century.
■ The nonprofit National Art League (originally the Douglaston Art League) at 44-21 Douglaston Parkway was founded in 1930 by the sister and daughter of painter William Merritt Chase and offers art exhibitions, workshops, demonstrations, and instruction. Another longstanding arts organization, Douglaston Community Theater, located at the Zion Episcopal Church at 44th Avenue off Douglaston Parkway, has been bringing theatrical productions to the community for nearly fifty years.
■ John McEnroe, a native of Douglaston Hill, learned to play tennis at the Douglaston Club.

Houses in Douglas Manor boast spectacular views of Little Neck Bay

Douglaston

Million-dollar views of Little Neck Bay. The sure strokes of experienced golfers on Douglaston Park Golf Course. A famous hometown yacht winning the first America's Cup. Residents of Douglaston, a long-established affluent area framed by the lush woodlands of Alley Pond Park to the west and commanding vistas of Little Neck Bay to the north, are rightly proud of the neighborhood's long history, natural and architectural beauty, excellent schools, and relatively easy commute to Manhattan.

Douglaston, one of the oldest neighborhoods in Queens, was settled by Thomas Hicks, who in 1656 led a small army against the Matinecoc Indian fishing village, at today's Marathon Parkway and Northern Boulevard (where the Douglaston–Little Neck Library now stands). There, on a peninsula that was originally called Little Madnan's (or Madman's) Neck, members of the Hicks family established a hamlet known as the Alley (or Alley Pond), stretching from Alley Creek west to modern-day Bell Boulevard in Bayside. In 1683, when Queens County was established and divided into five towns, the hamlet and area that make up today's Douglaston were designated part of the town of Flushing. (In the 1930s the Alley Pond hamlet was sacrificed to make way for the Cross Island Parkway and Long Island Expressway.)

The area remained primarily farmland through the eighteenth century, but during the Revolutionary War, when the British were stationed throughout Queens (many of the settlers were loyal to the crown and tolerated the encampments), most of the forests and farms in today's Douglaston were devastated. Recovery was slow, but new developments in transportation—in particular, the steam railroad, introduced in the early 1800s—set the area on a course to becoming a highly desirable suburb.

Douglaston Hill, which has been on the National Register of Historic Places since 2000 and was designated a New York City landmark in 2004, was one of the earliest such developments. Founded in 1853 as part of the "garden suburb" movement to provide gracious housing for professionals who worked in the city, the area was first briefly called Marathon, a name that lingers in Marathon Parkway, which runs in a north-south direction through nearly half of Douglaston. Today the Hill section offers notable examples of turn-of-the-century architecture with an eclectic mix of Colonial Revival, Queen Anne, and Tudor Revival styles set on ample lots.

But although the neighborhood in general has been an enclave for white, well-to-do families, Douglaston Hill was also home to an early community of African American oystermen, who worked and lived in the Douglaston–Little Neck area. Located mainly along Orient Avenue (243rd Street), the community began to decline after 1909, when the polluted Little Neck oyster beds were condemned. St. Peter's African Methodist Episcopal Church, on Orient Avenue between 42nd and Depew Avenues, was founded in 1872 to serve this community; it continued to offer services until the late 1980s.

An early church that is still in operation is the Zion Episcopal Church at 243-01 Northern Boulevard, which opened in 1830. A fire on Christmas Eve 1924 damaged the church considerably, but it was rebuilt and reopened a year later. The grounds include a historic churchyard containing the remains of about thirty

Matinecoc tribe members who were re-interred here in 1931 after Northern Boulevard was widened over part of their original burial ground. A large rock cut in half with a tree growing through the middle, a symbol of the tribe, marks the new site. Early white Douglaston settlers buried here include Wyant Van Zandt, a wealthy merchant who funded the building of the church in addition to his own home, a large 1819 Greek Revival man-

Northern Boulevard in Douglaston Park, 1925 (Queens Library, Long Island Division, Illustrations Collection)

NEIGHBORHOOD PROFILE

Boundaries: <u>Douglaston</u>: <u>north border:</u> Little Neck Bay; <u>east border:</u> Marinette Street to Douglas Road to Sandhill Road to Little Neck Parkway to 250th Street to Marathon Parkway; <u>south border:</u> Grand Central Parkway; <u>west border:</u> Cross Island Parkway; <u>Douglaston Hill:</u> <u>north border:</u> Long Island Rail Road tracks; <u>east border:</u> Little Neck Parkway to 250th Street; <u>south border:</u> Northern Boulevard; <u>west border:</u> Cross Island Parkway; <u>Douglas Manor:</u> <u>north border:</u> Little Neck Bay; <u>east border:</u> Marinette Street to Douglas Road to Sandhill Road; <u>south border:</u> Long Island Rail Road tracks; <u>west border:</u> Cross Island Parkway; <u>Douglaston Park:</u> <u>north border:</u> Northern Boulevard; <u>east border:</u> Marathon Parkway; <u>south border:</u> Long Island Expressway; <u>west border:</u> Cross Island Parkway
Subway and Train: <u>LIRR:</u> Douglaston
Bus: <u>Q12, N21, N20:</u> Northern Boulevard; <u>Q30:</u> Horace Harding Expressway
Libraries: Queens Library, Douglaston–Little Neck Branch (249-01 Northern Boulevard)
Museums: Alley Pond Environmental Center (228-06 Northern Boulevard); National Art League (44-21 Douglaston Parkway)
Community Board: No. 11
Police Precinct: 111th Precinct (45-06 215th Street, Bayside)
Fire Department: Engine 313, Ladder 164, Battalion 53 (44-01 244th Street)

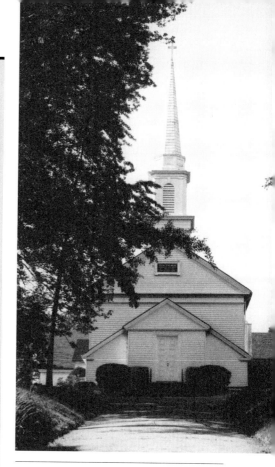

Zion Episcopal Church

sion on West Drive and Manor Road in what is today Douglas Manor.

Van Zandt's land, now the site of the Douglaston Yacht Club, was purchased in 1835 by George Douglas, who bought another 240 acres in the area, including what is now 233 Arleigh Road, the site of the oldest tree on Long Island and in New York City: a six-hundred-year-old white oak. Douglas's son William P. Douglas, famous both for refitting the British yacht *Sappho* (with which he won the 1871 America's Cup) and for introducing polo to America, donated land for an extension of the Long Island Rail Road, as well as a farmhouse to serve as the station, on condition that it be named after him, and in 1866 the station took on the name Douglaston. The peak Hill development took place during the 1920s and 1930s, when it was developed with strict rules regarding fencing and setbacks, but (unlike other communities in Queens) little constraint in terms of architectural style, leading to today's delightfully diverse array of early-twentieth-century home styles: Tudor, Mediterranean, Queen Anne, Arts and Crafts, and Colonial Revival are all represented.

Another enclave established as a planned suburb is **Douglas Manor,** bordering Little Neck Bay, established in 1906. The Douglas Manor Association, formed the same year, is a cooperative ownership of the mile-long waterfront. One of the unique features of this enclave is Shore Road, a lightly traveled waterfront drive that serves as a promenade for neighbors—the original developer, the Rickert-Finlay Realty Company of New York, was considered unusual at the time for favoring public access to the bay. Histor-ically noteworthy houses here include the Cornelius Van Wyck farmhouse at 126 West Drive. This privately owned colonial Dutch residence was built circa 1735 and has been meticulously maintained by its owners. It features original hand-cut moldings, hand-hewn beams and shingles, and wide plank floors. The Allen-Beville farmhouse at 29 Center Drive, built during the late 1840s by the Allen family, is also one of the oldest in the area. Both of the houses are designated New York City landmarks. In fact, all of Douglas Manor is a New York City landmark district—a priceless designation that will forever ensure the character of this exceptional section of Queens.

Farther south Douglaston offers more suburban-style housing in several smaller enclaves, including a section of townhouses located south of the Long Island Expressway near Doug-laston Plaza and Winchester Estates, a tiny, secluded area of private houses in the southwest corner of the neighbor-hood between Douglaston Parkway and the Douglaston Park Golf Course. In the same area is the site of the former Cathedral College of the Immaculate Conception. Founded in 1967 as a four-year college seminary, Cathedral Col-lege closed in 1987 but today houses the Immaculate Conception Center, a religious retreat and conference facility

One of the stately homes in Douglas Manor

visited by 150,000 people each year and still owned by the Roman Catholic Dio-cese of Brooklyn. Douglaston Park Golf Course, covering some 100 acres of roll-ing hills, was established in 1927 as the North Hills Country Club Golf Course and renamed in 1963, when the New York City Department of Parks and Recre-ation purchased most of the land.

The golf course is not to be confused with **Douglaston Park,** a lovely resi-dential community of single-family homes that sits between the Long Island Ex-pressway and Northern Boulevard. Private houses here run the gamut in design, with Colonials, ranches, and Capes. A portion of Alley Pond Park sits in the area, as well as the Alley Pond Environmental Center, located on Northern Boulevard, which was founded in 1972 to promote environmental awareness and responsibil-ity, especially among schoolchildren. Working with the New York City Depart-ment of Parks and Recreation, the center, which was designated a National Envi-ronmental Study Area in 1979, offers courses in ecology and life sciences for pre-kindergarten through high school and beyond.

East

Many people first encounter East Elmhurst as the scenery they see out their airplane or car window on the way to and from La Guardia Airport. But as residents and those who take the time to stop in the neighborhood can tell you, this busy north-central Queens community is worth a much closer look. Now a hub for vacationers and commuters traveling via La Guardia or the parkways and expressways of Queens, East Elmhurst has a history all its own.

In the late 1800s, East Elmhurst was mostly a rural expanse with unobstructed views of the East River, especially Bowery and Flushing Bays. But the beautiful area along the shoreline of Astoria and what is today East Elmhurst also proved to be the perfect spot for the North Beach Bowery Bay Gala Amusement Park. Opened in 1886, the enormous park was conceived and created by William Steinway, of the piano manufacturing company, and George Ehret, a brewmaster. It was a hit. Throngs of

Malcolm X House, at 97th Street (Malcolm X Place) is now a daycare center

Elmhurst

people arrived by steamboat ferry from Manhattan and the Bronx, and by trolley from other parts of Queens and Brooklyn, to amuse themselves at the bathing beaches; ride on the carousels, Ferris wheels, and scenic railways; carouse at the beer garden and restaurants; and party at the dance halls and pavilions. Waterfront hotels sprang up to accommodate them, and the local economy boomed.

Hotel construction increased in the early 1960s to serve the influx of business travelers, the impending ballpark (Shea Stadium) and the 1964 World's Fair in Flushing Meadows–Corona Park (Queens Library, Long Island Division, New York Herald Tribune Photo Morgue)

NEIGHBORHOOD PROFILE

Boundaries: <u>North border:</u> Astoria Boulevard South to 81st Street to 19th Avenue to Hazen Street to Bowery Bay (including La Guardia Airport); <u>east border:</u> Flushing Bay to Grand Central Parkway; <u>south border:</u> Northern Boulevard; <u>west border:</u> Brooklyn-Queens Expressway West

Bus: <u>Q66:</u> Northern Boulevard; <u>Q47:</u> 74th Street to 82nd Street to Marine Air Terminal; <u>Q48:</u> Ditmars Boulevard to 23rd Avenue to La Guardia Airport; <u>M60:</u> Astoria Boulevard to 23rd Avenue to La Guardia Airport; <u>Q33:</u> 82nd Street to La Guardia Airport; <u>Q19:</u> Astoria Boulevard; <u>Q19B:</u> 92nd Street to Astoria Boulevard; <u>Q72:</u> 94th Street; <u>Q23:</u> 103rd Street to Ditmars Boulevard

Libraries: Queens Library, East Elmhurst Branch (95-06 Astoria Boulevard)

Community Board: No. 3

Police Precinct: 115th Precinct (92-15 Northern Boulevard, Jackson Heights)

Fire Department: Engine 316, Battalion 49 (27-12 Kearney Street); Engine 307, Ladder 154 (81-17 Northern Boulevard, Jackson Heights)

The popularity of this family resort began to wane in 1919 with the advent of Prohibition, and North Beach was subsequently torn down. In 1929, a 105-acre portion of the site was used for the privately owned Glenn H. Curtiss Airport. But Mayor Fiorello La Guardia had bigger plans. On December 2, 1939, what is today called La Guardia Airport officially opened to commercial traffic. Masses of people continued venturing to East Elmhurst, this time as spectators, drawn by the novel sight of airplanes landing and taking off.

Today, access to La Guardia is facilitated by the Grand Central Parkway. Run-ning parallel is the largely commercial Ditmars Boulevard, connecting Astoria Boulevard South with busy 82nd, 94th, and 108th Streets. And while there is a constant flow of traffic via land and air, East Elmhurst welcomes those who wish to stay, with the small frame houses that grew up starting in 1905.

45

46   Until recently, these frame houses were inhabited primarily by African Americans. East Elmhurst has been home to a number of renowned jazz talents, including singer Ella Fitzgerald and bassist Ray Brown. Pianists Ray Bryant and Junior Mance, as well as singer and actor Harry Belafonte, all lived here as well. And composer Scott Joplin, the "King of Ragtime," is buried in St. Michael's Cemetery on Astoria Boulevard South.

A darker moment in East Elmhurst's history was the night of February 14, 1965. Longtime neighborhood residents still recall when bottles of gasoline were hurled through the living-room windows of the 97th Street home of former Nation of Islam minister Malcolm X and his family . . . Nobody was hurt that night, but a week later Malcolm X was gunned down and killed in Manhattan.

The ethnic composition of East Elmhurst began changing in the 1990s, as Hispanic and Asian families started moving in. Indeed, the 2000 census showed that East Elmhurst was among the fastest-changing communities in the city. Today the community bulletin board of the East Elmhurst Public Library is dotted with Spanish-language flyers, while beauty salons that once catered to a black clientele now have Spanish-language signs in their windows, and the English Service Ministry of the Korean Church of Queens serves second-generation Korean Americans.

The Vaughn College of Aeronautics and Technology (formerly the College of Aeronautics) draws newcomers to East Elmhurst as well. Founded in 1932 on 23rd Avenue near La Guardia Airport, this four-year private institution offers bachelors and associate degrees in aviation, management, engineering, and technology.

The English Service Ministry of the Korean Church of Queens

Hotels continue to play an important role in shaping the economy and character of the community. But now, instead of housing vacationers seeking out East Elmhurst's waterfront, they shelter the multitudes of out-of-towners traveling through La Guardia, who today arrive to enjoy the vast historical and contemporary treasures of New York. Throughout these changes, some dramatic, in its landscape, this active neighborhood has adapted and thrived, welcoming residents and visitors alike.

NEIGHBORHOOD FACTS

■ Established in 1852, St. Michael's Cemetery is owned and operated by St. Michael's Church, an Episcopalian congregation on the Upper West Side of Manhattan. The cemetery is nonsectarian, however, and throughout its existence has offered affordable burials for people of various religions and ethnicities.

■ In the early 1900s, "Shoot-the-Chutes" was a popular attraction at North Beach and other amusement parks. People would board a toboggan-style contraption that would send them roaring down a steep slope, ending up in a body of water. This was probably the prototype for the modern-day flume ride.

The Vaughn College of Aeronautics

Elmhurst today hosts the sights, sounds, and delicious smells of an international community. For hundreds of years, the neighborhood has been continually revitalized by new immigrants—most recently from countries such as Peru, Chile, Costa Rica, Ecuador, Mexico, the Philippines, India, Korea, China, and Cuba. These pioneers have made Elmhurst what it is today: a celebration of cultural diversity.

Elmhurst's first immigrants were English colonists who settled here in 1652, making Elmhurst one of the oldest areas in Queens. One of the original three towns of Queens, it was first called Middelburgh (or Middleburgh), but in 1683, when the town became the seat of local government, it was renamed Newtown. In 1896, after developer Cord Meyer purchased a number of farms and began building up the area as a residential village, he asked the federal government to change the name—supposedly because people were associating it with the polluted Newtown Creek, which runs along the Queens-Brooklyn border. To make the area marketable, the name became Elmhurst, a tribute to the neighborhood's many majestic elm trees. (The name Newtown survives today on the Grand Avenue Independent subway station, two churches, and a high school.)

Additional development followed quickly after the Queensboro Bridge opened in 1909. A trolley from Manhattan to Queens Boulevard further facilitated access to the area, which was enhanced yet again when the Independent subway opened in 1936. Italian, German, Irish, and Jewish immigrants who had settled in Lower Manhattan relocated to this neighborhood in large numbers. Elmhurst remained a

Elmhurst

predominantly white, middle-class community until the late 1960s, when newly arrived South Americans discovered its many appealing qualities: housing in apartments or private homes, two hospitals (Elmhurst Hospital Center and St. John's), an accessible commute into Manhattan via trains on Roosevelt Avenue and Queens Boulevard, and a wealth of restaurants, services, and shopping along Broadway, Roosevelt Avenue, Junction Boulevard, and, of course, Queens Boulevard.

Queens Boulevard features many varied storefronts of local retailers, and has been home to large retailers such as Macy's. The multilevel Macy's store, which opened in 1965 between 55th and 56th Avenues, was initially designed as a completely circular building, but the plans were thwarted by Mary Sondek, a widow who lived on a corner lot that Macy's needed to complete the sphere. Sondek was offered five times her property's value, but refused to sell. Finally, Macy's built its store around her property, giving the illusion of a full circle by putting up a mammoth store sign that hid her lot. When Sondek passed away a few years later, her house was torn down and a small strip mall was built in its place.

Macy's later became Stern's, which was replaced in 2001 by Queens Place, a shopping center. Elmhurst also claims Queens Center, the borough's only suburban-style shopping mall, which was built in 1974. Today Queens Center, which employs more than 1,700 people, is undergoing a multimillion-dollar redevelopment and expansion, including a new atrium and food court appropriately called "The World's Fare Cafés." Because its customers are of so many different nationalities, the mall employs a foreign-language assistance program that matches shoppers with translators fluent in, among other languages, Arabic, Hungarian, Korean, Chinese, and Spanish.

NEIGHBORHOOD FACTS

■ Visible from Queens Boulevard since 1910, the red-striped Elmhurst Gas Tanks on Grand Avenue, known affectionately as "the tanks," were a radio and television traffic-report reference point until 1993, when they were torn down. The 6.5-acre property on which they stood is now a public park.
■ In the late 1980s, Eddie Murphy and Arsenio Hall shot scenes of their film *Coming to America* at a Wendy's on Queens Boulevard.
■ Two acres on 45th Avenue and Broadway are designated Clement Clarke Moore Homestead Park. Clement Clarke Moore, the great-great-great-grandson of Reverend John Moore, one of the first settlers of Elmhurst, was the author of "A Visit from St. Nicholas," which begins with the famous line, "'Twas the night before Christmas . . .'"

What country would you like to eat in?

Assisting foreign-language speakers is also important at Elmhurst's hospitals. Elmhurst Hospital Center at 79-01 Broadway employs workers who speak more than thirty languages to serve its nearly 1 million constituents. Founded in 1832, Elmhurst Hospital Center was the nation's second public hospital and is noted for its superb maternal and child health care: it was the first hospital to control puerperal fever (an infection that can occur during childbirth) and established the first children's health center (1918) in the country. It was also one of the first hospitals to use hydrotherapy. St. John's Queens Hospital at 90-02

NEIGHBORHOOD PROFILE

Boundaries: <u>North border:</u> Roosevelt Avenue; <u>east border:</u> Junction Boulevard; <u>south border:</u> Long Island Expressway to Woodhaven Boulevard to Eliot Avenue; <u>west border:</u> 74th Street

Subway and Train: <u>R,G,V trains:</u> Woodhaven Boulevard, Grand Avenue/Newtown, Elmhurst Avenue, 74th Street/Broadway/Jackson Heights/Roosevelt; <u>7 train:</u> 74th Street/Broadway/Jackson Heights/Roosevelt, 82nd Street/Jackson Heights, 90th Street/Elmhurst Avenue, Junction Boulevard; <u>E,F trains:</u> 74th Street/Broadway/Jackson Heights/Roosevelt

Bus: <u>Q72:</u> Junction Boulevard; <u>Q53:</u> Broadway; <u>Q45:</u> 81st Street; <u>Q29:</u> Hampton Street; <u>Q58:</u> Corona Avenue; <u>Q59:</u> Queens Boulevard; <u>Q38:</u> Eliot Avenue; Q60: Queens Boulevard

Libraries: Queens Library, Elmhurst Branch (86-01 Broadway)

Community Board: Nos. 3, 4, and 5

Police Precinct: 114th Precinct (34-16 Astoria Boulevard, Astoria)

Fire Department: Engine 287, Ladder 136 (86-53 Grand Avenue), Engine 289, Ladder 138 (97-28 43rd Avenue)

Hospitals and Clinics: Elmhurst Hospital Center (79-01 Broadway); St. John's Queens Hospital (90-02 Queens Boulevard)

ELMHURST, L. I.

Twelve Minutes from 34th St. Ferry
6¼c. commutation, including the Ferry
5c. via Bridge to New York

Handsome Houses Ready
$3,200 TO $6,500
ON EASY TERMS
1,700 RESTRICTED LOTS
CORD MEYER & CO.,
62 WILLIAM STREET, NEW YORK
Office, ELMHURST, L. I.

A real estate ad from 1899 promotes the newly renamed Elmhurst as an ideal commuters' community (Queens Library, Long Island Division, Illustrations Collection)

Queens Boulevard opened in 1891. A community hospital, St. John's until recently was a member of St. Vincent's Catholic Medical Centers of New York. When St. Vincent's filed for Chapter 11 bankruptcy protection in 2005, St. John's became part of a newly created healthcare system anchored by Wyckoff Heights Medical Center on the Ridgewood-Bushwick border in Brooklyn.

Elmhurst is home to settlers from around the world

• Elmhurst's Churches

Elmhurst is home to some of the oldest churches in Queens, with a history of serving diverse communities, a history that continues in what is one of the most ethnically diverse zip codes in Queens. The First Presbyterian Church of Newtown, at 54-05 Seabury Street, may be the oldest congregation in Queens. The original 1652 building, located on present-day Broadway around Dongan Avenue, served as a church, town hall, parsonage, and courthouse, presided over by the Reverend John Moore, its first minister and ancestor of Clement Clarke Moore. An early advocate of religious freedom, the Newtown church in 1657 showed its support for the Quakers of Flushing, who were being persecuted by New Amsterdam governor Peter Stuyvesant, when several Newtown men signed the famous Flushing Remonstrance, one of the first American documents defending religious freedom (see Flushing). The original church building was demolished during the Revolutionary War, but it was rebuilt four years later and dubbed "the Old White Church." The current brownstone sanctuary was dedicated in 1895. In the 1920s the church was seriously damaged by a fire. The sanctuary was also moved back 125 feet for the expansion of Queens Boulevard, but lost its steeple during the move. A more positive change occurred when a church house was built in 1931 behind the sanctuary to hold an auditorium, classrooms, and a full kitchen—all still used today. The church is the spiritual home for people from more than forty countries and the headquarters of South Asian Youth Action, a nonprofit organization providing after-school activities for teens. In 2004, along with the Manhattan-based Green Guerrillas, the Youth Action planted an organic vegetable garden to supply the food pantry at the church.

St. James Episcopal Church, built in 1734 on what is today 51st Avenue and Broadway, is the oldest standing building in Elmhurst. The church was last used for worship in 1848; after that, services were held in a new structure across the street, which subsequently burned down and was replaced by a plain brick building. In 2004, to honor the 300th anniversary of the church, it received an extensive exterior renovation. The building is now used as a community center.

Across Broadway from St. James Episcopal Church is the Reformed Church of Newtown. Founded in 1731 by Dutch farmers and tradesmen, the church today features only the cornerstone of the original 1735 building: a new sanctuary was built in 1832. English eventually replaced Dutch as the language of the church, and in the 1980s services were added in Tamil (an ancient Indian language) and Taiwanese. In the 1990s, the Tamil congregants had moved or been incorporated into the English worship, along with others in the church's multicultural congregation of Greeks, Hispanics, Asians, and Russians, but in 1995 the church began offering Mandarin services in addition to the Taiwanese and English worship, fulfilling its mission of being "a house of prayer for all nations."

Elmhurst's diverse congregations are also served by the Chan Meditation Center of the Dharma Drum Mountain Buddhist Association at 90-56 Corona Avenue, Elmhurst Baptist Church at 87-37 Whitney Avenue, the Korean Evangelical Church of New York at 88-28 Corona Avenue, and St. Matthew's Lutheran Church for the Deaf at 41-01 75th Street, which was established in 1911. One of the more unusual churches of Elmhurst is housed in the Elmwood Theatre, an ornate three-story movie palace on Hoffman Drive that was built in 1928 and closed down in 1999. It was later sold to the Rock Community Churches, an international nondenominational Christian church founded in the 1990s in Jackson Heights. In addition to offering services in several languages, including Spanish and Indonesian, the church has created a performance space, showcasing theater, dance, music, and poetry, and offers art workshops, dance classes, and music, with instructors from the Juilliard School and the Alvin Ailey Dance Company who volunteer their services.

St. James Episcopal Church, 1735, the oldest standing building in Elmhurst (Queens Library, Long Island Division, Illustrations Collection)

St. Bartholomew's Roman Catholic Church, Elmhurst (Courtesy of the Queens Library, Long Island Division, Postcard Collection)

Floral Park

Like their western neighbor Bellerose, Floral Park and New Hyde Park share their names with Nassau County counterparts. They also both border the county line and share post offices with the Long Island communities. (The Queens County line, separating the two Floral Parks and the two New Hyde Parks, was established in 1899.) But residents of these communities do not

Single-family homes on 265th Street in New Hyde Park with North Shore Towers in the distance

NEIGHBORHOOD FACTS

■ Although the luxury cooperative complex North Shore Towers on Marcus Avenue bears a Floral Park address, it is actually situated in Glen Oaks.

■ Because there was also a Hyde Park in upstate New York, the neighborhoods in Queens and Nassau County officially became New Hyde Park in 1871, when a post office opened on the Nassau County side.

have to pay the much higher real estate taxes in nearby Nassau County, even though they have the cachet of living as close to suburbia as one can get. They also benefit from the shopping and entertainment options that Nassau County has to offer.

Much of what are today Floral Park and New Hyde Park was farmland until just before World War II, when the Sperry Gyroscope Company of Brooklyn opened a military plant in nearby Lake Success, drawing a solid labor force of more than 20,000 to the area. (In 1946, the plant housed the U.N. Security Council, while the General Assembly convened in the New York City Building at

& New

Flushing Meadows–Corona Park.) After the war, many white, middle-income families, headed by former GIs, settled in the area looking for steady work and a quiet, safe neighborhood for their children. Remnants of the prewar era are still viewable at the Queens County Farm Museum in Bellerose on the Bellerose–Floral Park border, New York City's largest remaining tract of natural, undisturbed farmland, which boasts a colonial farmhouse circa 1772, orchards, greenhouses, and grazing livestock.

The communities have stayed close to their founding values, even as the neighborhoods welcomed people of various ethnic backgrounds. Today, although a majority of residents are white, an increasing number of Asians, as well as some Hispanics and African Americans, are calling the area home. Many residents live in modest single-family homes typical of those built throughout Queens in the 1940s and 1950s. In 1948, neighbors from both areas formed the Lost Community Civic Association to ensure that their voices would be heard.

And residents have been able to get attention, mobilizing local politicians and city officials in support of basic neighborhood causes such as garbage collection, street repairs, problems connected with flooding, and parking and crowding issues concerning the Long Island Jewish Medical Center, a 48-acre campus that spans both the Queens neighborhood of New Hyde Park and Nassau County's New Hyde Park. One of the top twenty cardiology hospitals in the United States, the medical center also serves as the Long Island campus for the Albert Einstein College of Medicine and has one of the largest medical education programs in the state. More than four hundred physicians and dentists work full-time there as teachers, clinicians, and researchers. The medical center's Schneider Children's Hospital opened its doors in 1983 to provide outpatient medical services for 40,000 children. Today Schneider offers outpatient health care to more than 160,000 children, as well as inpatient pediatric health care, and the facility is undergoing continuous expansion to serve its increasing population. Also part of the medical center is the Zucker Hillside Hospital, a prestigious psychiatric facility that specializes in the diagnosis, treatment, and research of mental illness. Its Clinical Research Center for the Study of Schizophrenia is one of only four such facilities in the country established by the National Institute of Mental Health.

Expansion is under way, due to be completed in 2008, that will consolidate inpatient care in a new 215,000-square-foot-facility including an Ambulatory Care Pavilion, a Child and Adolescent Day Hospital, a Geriatric Day Hospital, an Adult Day Hospital, and an Inpatient Building.

Active residents have also joined

Hyde Park

This new pink McMansion sits among older brick Capes on 262nd Street off 80th Avenue (Sonia S. Estreich)

with teachers and staff at Floral Park's Public School 191, the Mayflower School, on 258th Street—one of the schools that make School District 26 the best-performing in New York City. The *Queens Chronicle* reported in September 2005 that every one of the school's fourth-graders had achieved state standards on the statewide math exam (its reading scores are in the top 5 percent statewide, too). The school features an active arts program, and parents volunteer energetically, organizing after-school classes (taught by school staff) in quilting, soccer, arts and crafts, and drama. The school building is a bit cramped, but teachers don't seem to mind; they report that they enjoy the collegial atmosphere and just make do—in the case of the science and art teachers, by traveling from class to class with a rolling cart.

NEIGHBORHOOD PROFILE

Boundaries: <u>Floral Park:</u> <u>north border:</u> Union Turnpike; <u>east border:</u> 268th Street to Hillside Avenue to Nassau County line; <u>south border:</u> Jamaica Avenue; <u>west border:</u> Little Neck Parkway; <u>New Hyde Park:</u> <u>north border:</u> 74th Avenue to north border of Long Island Jewish Medical Center or North Shore Towers Golf Course; <u>east border:</u> Nassau County line; <u>south border:</u> Hillside Avenue; <u>west border:</u> 268th Street to Union Turnpike to 264th Street to 76th Avenue to 263rd Street

Bus: <u>Q79:</u> Little Neck Parkway; <u>x68,</u> <u>Q43:</u> Hillside Avenue; <u>Q36, Q34:</u> Jamaica Avenue; <u>Q46:</u> Union Turnpike to Lakeville Road

Libraries: Queens Library, Bellerose Branch (250-06 Hillside Avenue, Bellerose)

Community Board: No. 13

Police Precinct: 105th Precinct (92-08 222nd Street, Queens Village)

Fire Department: Engine 251, Battalion 53 (254-20 Union Turnpike, Glen Oaks)

Hospitals and Clinics: Long Island Jewish Medical Center (270-05 76th Avenue); Schneider's Children's Hospital (269-01 76th Avenue)

Long Island Jewish Medical Center (Queens Library, Long Island Division, Illustrations Collection)

Flushing

Although it may be best known today as the Chinatown of Queens, Flushing, one of the original three towns of Queens (along with Jamaica and Newtown) and one of the largest neighborhoods in the borough, encompasses a wealth of cultures. A major center during the development of New York City, Flushing boasts national and city landmarks and memorials in addition to parks, cemeteries, hospitals, and educational institutions. But many residents and visitors alike may not be aware that the physical landmarks are only the outward symbols of Flushing's more vital history: since the seventeenth century the neighborhood has been the site of important struggles in religious freedom, abolition, and civil rights. Even

more surprising, bustling Flushing was for almost two hundred years one of the major horticultural centers in the country.

Flushing was chartered in 1645 as the town of Vlissingen, part of New Netherland. The original settlers were English, and soon after the town was founded it began drawing a large Quaker population, seeking religious freedom they could not find elsewhere in the American colonies. These set-

Northern Boulevard, part of Flushing's Chinatown

NEIGHBORHOOD FACTS

■ It was the glory of Flushing—the 1928 RKO Keith's, a 3,000-seat Spanish Moorish–style landmarked theater on Main Street and Northern Boulevard. When the theater closed in 1986, its fate was unclear, until the community board saved the building by approving a plan for a mixed-use building that would include two hundred condominium apartments, restaurants, retail shops, and a senior center.

■ A number of cultural organizations celebrate Flushing's large Asian community, including the Chinese Cultural Center, at 41-61 Kissena Boulevard, which features a library of Chinese books as well as exhibits of traditional Chinese instruments and masks; the Tung Ching Chinese Center for the Arts, at 136-43 37th Avenue, which offers traditional Chinese theater, opera, and folk dance; the Binari–Korean American Cultural Troupe, at 50-16 Parsons Boulevard, which gives performances of traditional Korean drumming; and the Korean Performing Arts Center, at 142-05 Roosevelt Avenue, which showcases Korean ballet, combining Western and Korean styles of dance.

■ Francis Lewis, a Queens native and signer of the Declaration of Independence, was a vestryman at St. George's Episcopal Church, 135-32 38th Avenue at Main Street, Flushing.

Kissena Park (Sonia S. Estreich)

tlers, who were among Flushing's major landowners and entrepreneurs, helped guide the town for the next two hundred years, spearheading initiatives in religious freedom (the Flushing Remonstrance, a forerunner of the Bill of Rights, was drafted in 1657), abolition (Flushing was an active participant in the Underground Railroad), and civil rights (Flushing Quakers began the first schools for black children and later joined the civil rights struggle, fundraising, holding vigils, and attending the 1965 March on Washington). The influence of Flushing's Quakers can still be seen throughout the neighborhood's several small but distinct communities.

One of the oldest settled areas was in what is now **Downtown Flushing,** the heart of today's Chinatown. It was here in 1661 that Quaker John Bowne bought land and built a house that frequently served as a meetinghouse for local Quakers (and may later have been a stop on the Underground Railroad). Today the oldest structure in Queens, the Anglo-Dutch Bowne House, at 37-01 Bowne Street, is a public museum. (When the English founder of the Quakers, George Fox, paid a visit to Flushing, he gave an address outside the house, on a spot that is now marked by Fox Stone.) Also surviving are the Quaker burying ground, established in 1676 on land donated by Bowne, and the Quaker Meeting House at 137–16 Northern Boulevard, built in 1694. Historians are not really sure how many people are buried in the old Quaker burial ground, because the Quaker

• Flushing, the Garden of Queens

Today one of the largest commercial districts in Queens, Flushing was once the garden of the borough. America's first commercial nursery, a scant, 8-acre plot owned by Robert Prince, was planted in Flushing in 1737. By the 1800s, at least three other local nurseries had formed nearby, turning the quiet Flushing Bay area into the horticultural mecca of an emerging nation.

Prince's Nursery, as the pioneer of these operations, started with trees: importing them from abroad, and reshipping them to American buyers. By the 1770s, the nursery had expanded to 113 acres; its offerings—plum, pear, apple, and nectarine trees, to name a few—were as varied as they were exotic; and its stature in the colonies was quickly rising. In 1789, just months after being elected president, George Washington traveled to the nursery to survey its plots; Thomas Jefferson was also a visitor. Two decades later, when Meriwether Lewis and William Clark returned from charting the Northwest Territory, they asked that a number of their discoveries be sent to the nursery for safekeeping.

Although Bloodgood Nursery, founded in the 1790s, also imported rare plants (the "Bloodgood" Red Japanese Maple was introduced there), Prince's most notable competitor was Parsons's Nursery, which opened in 1838 on the site of present-day Parsons High School. Founded by Quaker Samuel Bowne Parsons, the nursery added dozens of foreign trees to the American market, including the pink-flowered dogwood, the Japanese maple, and the weeping European beech. Frederick Law Olmsted, the co-designer of New York City's Central Park, is said to have enlisted Parsons's services to help landscape the park. Around 1870, Parsons's two sons divided the nursery between them, creating two separate businesses, one of which was Kissena Nursery, part of which still survives in Kissena Park. At Samuel Bowne Parsons's death in 1906, the firm was dissolved, and the city of New York, seeking to create new parkland, purchased Kissena Nursery and converted it to the 14-acre Kissena Grove (the rest of the nursery was sold off for development). But the area became neglected, and in 1981, while clearing an overgrown section of Kissena Park, a group of interns discovered a true treasure—an area of exotic trees that turned out to be the remains of the nursery.

The original Parsons's Nursery also included a 2-acre parcel that is today's Weeping Beech Park, situated at 143–35 37th Avenue and named for the weeping beech imported from Belgium and planted by Samuel Bowne Parsons in 1847. The magnificent tree, designated a "living landmark" in 1966, was rightly honored with a memorial service when it finally died in 1998: during its nearly 151-year life, it grew to a stately 60 feet, with an outer circle of 80 feet, and it was probably the source for all of the weeping beech trees in the United States.

graves did not have headstones until about 1820. John Bowne may be buried there—the Bowne family plot is in there—but if so, his grave is unmarked. But the graves of many important early Quakers are marked, including those of abolitionists William Burling and John Murray, Jr.; Samuel Leggett, founder of the New York Gas Light Company; and members of the prominent Hicks and Lawrence families.

The members of the Bowne family who are buried in the graveyard wouldn't recognize the area today, however, because the land their trees grew on has long been paved over for the densely laid out streets and sidewalks. More than twenty bus lines converge here, and a subway terminal at Main Street and Roosevelt Avenue (the 7 line), as well as a Long Island Rail

Road station, make this neighborhood a commuter hub. But for those who can linger, Main Street is packed with exotic commercial enterprises, a large proportion of them catering to the Asian population (mostly Chinese and Korean) that began settling here starting in the 1970s, when many of the original Jewish, Irish, Italian, and German residents moved toward the suburbs, and increasingly after 1995. Today Flushing has the largest Chinatown in New York (in terms of total population), with a combination of working- and middle-class families. Boasting a profusion of Chinese herbal and medicine shops, Asian groceries, Korean bakeries, music stores with the latest hits from Shanghai, and other businesses—apparel shops, jewelry stores, beauty salons, restaurants—launched by Asian entrepreneurs, Downtown Flushing is the place to go to immerse yourself in Asian culture; even the street vendors sell fried noodles, pan-fried dumplings, and soups. Adding to the exotic atmosphere, many storefront signs are in Chinese or Korean in addition to English.

Downtown Flushing is also home to Flushing Hospital Medical Center, at 4500 Parsons Boulevard, which was founded in 1884 in a rented house by a group of women. Today this 293-bed, not-for-profit teaching hospital is famous for identifying the initial 1999 West Nile encephalitis outbreak. And the headquarters for the Queens Historical Society, at 143-35 37th Avenue, is located in the late-eighteenth-century Kingsland Homestead, a Dutch-English colonial farmhouse that was built by Quaker resident Charles Doughty and originally situated in **Murray Hill.** Doughty's daughter married sea captain Joseph King, and their daughter married into the Murray family, for whom Murray Hill is named, who later owned tree nurseries in the area.

A residential area, today's Murray Hill largely owes its growth to the opening of a Long Island Rail Road station. Houses and buildings are somewhat close together, though a few older, stately structures can still be found among the one-, two-, and three-family homes that serve a largely Korean population. For instance, at 149-19 38th Avenue sits the pink Victorian Voelker Orth Museum, Bird Sanctuary, and Victorian Garden. The grand house dates back to the 1890s and was bequeathed by its owner for historic purposes.

North of Murray Hill are two neighborhoods that developed in the late nineteenth and early twentieth centuries, **Broadway-Flushing** and **Linden Hill.** Broadway-Flushing, a lovely residential area replete with beech, maple, and oak trees, was developed around 1909, and each house deed included covenants and restrictions still applicable today. In fact, in 1988 the Broadway-

Flushing Homeowners Association went all the way to the State Supreme Court to ensure that the covenants would stand against developers' plans to build multifamily dwellings in areas that had been restricted to single-family homes. Home styles range from English Tudors to Victorians, Colonials, ranches, and Capes.

Adding to the bucolic, tranquil setting is Bowne Park, just south of 29th Avenue between 155th and 159th Streets. Named after Walter Bowne, a descendant of John Bowne's who served as a state senator and New York City mayor and once had a summer mansion on these grounds, the more than 11-acre park is overseen by the New York City Department of Parks

Shoppers on Northern Boulevard and Main Street

NEIGHBORHOOD
PROFILE

Boundaries: <u>Flushing</u>: <u>north border</u>: 25th Avenue to Willets Point Boulevard to 25th Avenue; <u>east border</u>: Utopia Parkway to Francis Lewis Boulevard to 47th Avenue to 46th Avenue to 47th Avenue to Fresh Meadow Lane; <u>south border</u>: Union Turnpike to Parsons Boulevard to Kissena Boulevard to Melbourne Avenue (southern border of Queens College campus) to 149th Street to Gravett Road to Main Street to Mount Hebron Cemetery to Flushing Meadows–Corona Park; <u>west border</u>: Grand Central Parkway to Flushing Bay to Whitestone Expressway; <u>Downtown</u> <u>Flushing</u>: <u>north border</u>: Northern Boulevard; <u>east border</u>: Parsons Boulevard; <u>south border</u>: 45th Avenue to Colden Street to Elder Avenue to Main Street to Dahlia Avenue to Crommeling Street to Blossom Avenue to College Point Boulevard to Fowler Avenue; <u>west border</u>: Van Wyck Expressway to Long Island Rail Road tracks to Grand Central Parkway; <u>Murray Hill</u>: <u>north border</u>: Northern Boulevard; <u>east border</u>: 162nd Street; <u>south border</u>: 46th Avenue; <u>west border</u>: Parsons Boulevard; <u>Broadway-Flushing</u>: <u>north border</u>: 25th Avenue; <u>east border</u>: Utopia Parkway; <u>south border</u>: Crocheron Avenue to 162nd Street to Northern Boulevard; <u>west border</u>: 154th Street; <u>Linden Hill</u>: <u>north border</u>: 25th Avenue to Willets Point Boulevard to 25th Avenue; <u>east border</u>: 154th Street; <u>south border</u>: Northern Boulevard; <u>west border</u>: Whitestone Expressway; <u>Auburndale</u>: <u>north border</u>: Crocheron Avenue to Utopia Parkway; <u>east border</u>: Francis Lewis Boulevard; <u>south border</u>: 47th Avenue to 46th Avenue to 47th Avenue to Fresh Meadow Lane to Pidgeon Meadow Road; <u>west border</u>: 46th Avenue to 162nd Street; <u>Kissena Park</u>: <u>north border</u>: Parsons Boulevard to 46th Avenue; <u>east border</u>: Pidgeon Meadow Road to Fresh Meadow Lane; <u>south border</u>: Booth Memorial Avenue; <u>west border</u>: Kissena Boulevard to Poplar Avenue to Colden Street to 45th Avenue; <u>Queensboro Hill</u>: <u>north border</u>: Blossom Avenue to Crommeling Street to Dahlia Avenue to Main Street to Elder Avenue to Colden Street to Poplar Avenue; <u>east border</u>: Kissena Boulevard to Booth Memorial Avenue to 164th Street; to the Long Island Expressway to Kissena Boulevard; <u>south border</u>: Melbourne Avenue (southern border of Queens College campus) to 149th Street to Gravett Road to Main Street to Mount Hebron Cemetery; <u>west border</u>: Van Wyck Expressway to College Point Boulevard; <u>Pomonok</u>: <u>north border</u>: Long Island Expressway; <u>east border</u>: 164th Street; <u>south border</u>: 73rd Avenue; <u>west border</u>: Kissena Boulevard; <u>Flushing Heights</u>: <u>north border</u>: Booth Memorial Avenue; <u>east border</u>: Fresh Meadow Lane; <u>south border</u>: 73rd Avenue; <u>west border</u>: 164th Street; <u>Hillcrest</u>: <u>north border</u>: 73rd Avenue; <u>east border</u>: Fresh Meadow Lane; <u>south border</u>: Union Turnpike; <u>west border</u>: Parsons Boulevard
Subway and Train: <u>7 train</u>: Flushing/Main Street, Willets Point/Shea Stadium; <u>LIRR</u>: Shea Stadium, Flushing/Main Street, Murray Hill, Broadway, Auburndale

Relaxing in Linden Hill

and Recreation and by the Bowne Park Civic Association. The park includes a pond and the city's first modular playground, a novelty when it was installed in 1969.

Linden Hill, situated between Willets Point Boulevard to the north and Northern Boulevard, is characterized mainly by six-story cooperative apartment buildings in neatly aligned blocks. But there are a few surprises: for instance, 146th Street between 29th Road and Bayside Avenue offers a charming display of brick single-family houses shadowed by large, lush trees. Also here is the historic Flushing High School, at 31-01 Union Street. The original high school building was located on Sanford Avenue,

Bus: Q48: Roosevelt Avenue; Q58: Horace Harding Expressway to College Point Boulevard; Q16: Bayside Avenue to 29th Avenue; Q76: Francis Lewis Boulevard; x32: Parsons Boulevard to Roosevelt Avenue to 29th Avenue; Q15: Sanford Avenue to 150th Street; Q28: Northern Boulevard to Crocheron Avenue; QBx1: Linden Place to Main Street; Q25, Q34: Linden Place to Kissena Boulevard; Q17: Kissena Boulevard to Horace Harding Expressway; Q27: Kissena Boulevard to 46th Avenue; Q26: 46th Avenue; Q66: Northern Boulevard; x51: Kissena Boulevard to Sanford Avenue to Northern Boulevard; Q65: Main Street to Kissena Boulevard to Sanford Avenue to 164th Street; N21, N20, Q12, Q3: Northern Boulevard; Q44, Q20B, Q20A: Main Street; Q74: Main Street to Melbourne Avenue; Q65A: Jewel Avenue, Q46: Union Turnpike; Q14: Union Street

Libraries: Queens Library, Auburndale Branch (25-55 Francis Lewis Boulevard); East Flushing Branch (196-36 Northern Boulevard); Main Library (41-17 Main Street); McGoldrick Branch (155-06 Roosevelt Avenue); Mitchell-Linden Branch (29-42 Union Street); Pomonok Branch (158-21 Jewel Avenue); Queensboro Hill Branch (60-05 Main Street); Hillcrest Branch (187-05 Union Turnpike)

Museums: Bowne House (37-01 Bowne Street); Queens Botanical Garden (43-50 Main Street); Queens Historical Society (143-35 37th Avenue); Godwin-Ternbach Museum (405 Klapper Hall, Queens College, 65-30 Kissena Boulevard); Voelker Orth Museum, Bird Sanctuary and Victorian Garden (149-19 38th Avenue); Flushing Council on Culture and the Arts (137-35 Northern Boulevard); New York Hall of Science (47-01 111th Street)

Theaters: Brooklyn Conservatory of Music at Queens (42-76 Main Street); Selma and Max Kupferberg Center for the Visual and Performing Arts at Queens College (65-30 Kissena Boulevard); Tung Ching Chinese Center for the Arts (136-43 37th Avenue); Binari–Korean American Cultural Troupe (50-16 Parsons Boulevard); Korean Performing Arts Center (142-05 Roosevelt Avenue)

Community Board: Nos. 7, 8, and 11

Police Precinct: 107th Precinct (71-01 Parsons Boulevard); 109th Precinct (37-05 Union Street)

Fire Department: Engine 273, Ladder 129 (40-18 Union Street); Engine 274, Battalion 52 (41-20 Murray Street); Engine 299, Ladder 152 (61-20 Utopia Parkway); Engine 320, Ladder 167, Battalion 53 (36-18 Francis Lewis Boulevard)

Hospitals and Clinics: Flushing Hospital Medical Center (4500 Parsons Boulevard); Long Island Care Center (144-61 38th Avenue); New York Hospital Medical Center of Queens (56-45 Main Street); St. Vincent Catholic Medical Center–St. Joseph's Hospital (158-40 79th Avenue); Cliffside Nursing Home (119-19 Graham Court); Woodcrest Nursing Home (119-09 26th Avenue)

but between 1912 and 1915 the present building was erected. The oldest public school in the city, Flushing High was chartered in 1875 and designated a New York City landmark in 1991.

Just south of the high school is arguably one of the most important structures of this neighborhood: Town Hall, on Northern Boulevard. Erected in 1862, the early–Romanesque Revival building was the center of political, cultural, and social events during its day, functioning at various times as a jail, a bank, a theatrical space, and a public assembly hall—the abolitionist Frederick Douglass spoke there in 1865. From 1902 until the early 1960s it was used as a courthouse. Today it is home base for the Flushing Council on

Looking south on Main Street from Northern Boulevard (Sonia S. Estreich)

Culture and the Arts. It is also a New York City landmark (1967) and on the National Register of Historic Places (1972).

A historic structure of another sort is Latimer House (34-41 137th Street), a New York City landmark saved in 1988 from demolition and moved to its present location in Leavitt Field thanks to a thirteen-year effort by local activists and politicians. It was the home of African American inventor Lewis H. Latimer (1848–1928), who greatly improved upon Thomas Edison's lightbulbs, prepared Alexander Graham Bell's telephone patent, and invented a forerunner of the modern air conditioner.

The remains of a large African American population can be found beneath a small playground in **Auburndale** along 46th Avenue between 164th and 165th Streets at Martins Field. This playground was paved over by the city in 1935, but it was originally a burial ground for more than a thousand African Americans and Native Americans, for whom a memorial park is under way. Auburndale, which is south of Crocheron Avenue, was once farmland owned by Thomas Willett, who became the first mayor of New York City back in the 1660s. This village was developed in 1901, around the time that the Long Island Rail Road put in a station at 192nd Street and 39th Avenue. Another station erected around this time is the Broadway station on what is today known as Northern Boulevard. Brick one-family houses, tree-lined

streets, and lovely front lawns here create an oasis from the hustle and bustle of the rest of the borough. Adding to the tranquil air is Flushing Cemetery on 46th Avenue. Established in 1853, this 75-acre cemetery holds the remains of many persons important to Flushing's history, including members of the Parsons and Bowne families; it is also the burial site of more contemporary luminaries such as Louis Armstrong.

The southernmost tip of the cemetery nearly touches the northernmost point of the public Kissena Park Golf Course, adjacent to the expansive Kissena Park (see the Corridor photo spread), with its lake, biking trail, and the 14-acre Kissena Grove, a beautiful forested area that was part of the original Parsons's Nursery (the rest of the nursery was sold to become a real estate development). While these pastoral grounds take up a large portion of the park's 235 acres, there are still residential parts to **Kissena Park.** Roomy single- and two-family houses on ample lots characterize much of this area. Attentive residents have been working to maintain the ambience here—Kissena Park's civic association was established in 1937—a job made more difficult because of the many illegal multifamily con-

The oldest structure in Queens, the 1661 Bowne House, where Quaker meetings were held, may have been a stop on the Underground Railroad (Queens Library, Long Island Division, Illustrations Collection)

versions that have been occurring throughout the borough. Flushing also shares a portion of the Flushing Meadows–Corona Park, site of two World's Fairs, the original home of the U.N. General Assembly, and Shea Stadium (see Corona, the Corridor photo spread, and Shea Stadium photo spread).

South Flushing, better known as **Queensboro Hill,** boasts another testament to Flushing's past—the Queens Botanical Garden, at 43-50 Main Street, created as an exhibit for the 1939 World's Fair, which continues the horticultural tradition begun in 1737 with Prince's Nursery. The Botanical Garden celebrates Flushing's natural beauty with rose, bee, herb, and perennial gardens, changing displays, and numerous public programs. Serenity and solitude can also be found south of the small residential part of this neighborhood, just beyond the Long Island Expressway, at Mount Hebron Cemetery and Cedar Grove Cemetery. And east of those is the campus of Queens College, at 65-30 Kissena Boulevard, founded in 1937 and incorporated into the City University of New York (CUNY) system when it was created in 1961. With some 13,000 undergraduates and 4,500 graduate students as well as adult and continuing education programs, Queens College is one of the largest senior colleges in CUNY and one of the most prestigious: in 2004, it had the highest graduation rate of all CUNY colleges (comedian Jerry Seinfeld is one famous graduate), and in 2006 Princeton Review's Best Value Colleges ranked it eighth in the nation. Among the college's offerings are the renowned Selma and Max Kupferberg Center for the Visual and Performing Arts (formerly the Colden Center), which has featured such talented—and diverse—performers as Luciano Pavarotti and Janis Joplin, and Godwin-Ternbach Museum, a teaching museum with a collection of

Pomonok Houses, 1951 (Queens Library, Long Island Division, Illustrations Collection)

2,500 works of art from antiquity to the present.

Near the campus, at 65-21 Main Street, is the CUNY School of Law. Founded in 1983, the school has been honored as the most diverse in the country. It is especially noted as a welcoming school for women: female students make up more than half the student body, and Princeton Review has ranked CUNY School of Law first in the country for women faculty.

To the east of Queensboro Hill is **Pomonok,** a complex of apartment houses built on grounds that originally contained a country club and golf course. Pomonok Houses is a federally subsidized thirty-five-building development run by the New York City Housing Authority. Dating from the same era is Electchester, a union-

Auburndale's lush trees and gardens offer a quiet oasis amid Flushing's bustle

In 1968 the late-eighteenth-century Kingsland Homestead was moved from Murray Hill to Downtown Flushing, where it serves as headquarters of the Queens Historical Society (Queens Library, Long Island Division, Illustrations Collection)

hensive Energy Management Program to offer residents energy-efficient housing. Customers were compensated for using less electricity during peak or difficult times; computers were used to initiate duty cycling; and amenities like cinemas, libraries, hospitals, and shopping malls were created to draw customers to air-conditioned places during times of peak use. The complex still has strong ties to the union: some 50 percent of its residents are electricians, and about 10 percent more are relatives of union members. The union leader, Harry Van Arsdale, lived in one of the units until his death in 1986.

East and south of Pomonok are two middle-class areas

sponsored cooperative complex of thirty-eight buildings erected in the 1950s and 1960s to provide affordable housing for members of Local 3 of the International Brotherhood of Electrical Workers. In addition to being intended as a home for electricians, the complex was designed as part of the Compre-

known as **Flushing Heights** and **Hillcrest,** which were named for hills between Flushing and Jamaica—in fact, Hillcrest was known simply as "The Hills" before residential development in 1907. Both communities are ethnically diverse and benefit from the commercial bustle of Union Turnpike, in addition to the convenient transportation connections in Downtown Flushing. And while each of these neighborhoods carries its own distinctive moniker, if you ask residents where they live, their most likely response—"Flushing"—speaks to the communities' shared history.

• The Society of Friends and Flushing Meeting

For close to two hundred years, the history of Flushing could be said to be the history of Flushing's Quakers, members of the Society of Friends who started settling in the town, fleeing religious persecution, soon after it was chartered. When New Netherland governor Peter Stuyvesant issued an edict against them, Flushing's Quakers (supported by other Queens residents) drafted what is considered the first American document on the issue of religious freedom, the Flushing Remonstrance (1657), which demanded that Quakers be given the same rights granted all settlers under the Flushing charter. More Quakers settled in the region, including John Bowne, who allowed meetings in his home. Angered by Bowne's activities, Stuyvesant banished him from the colony, but Bowne went to Holland and petitioned the Dutch West India Company (owner of New Netherland) for redress; their response—that "the consciences of men at least ought ever to remain free and unshackled"—established religious freedom in the colony.

Flushing's Quaker population helped make the area a leader in the struggles for abolition as well. A 1718 anti-slavery address by William Burling, a member of the Flushing Meeting, is one of the earliest published in America. Flushing Meeting formally condemned slavery in 1767 and, as the site of the New York Yearly Meeting in 1774, banned members from owning slaves. Flushing's Quaker women also joined the struggle: in 1814 the Flushing Female Association established a school for poor children, black and white, which continued until 1862. (Patrick Healey, the first African American to receive a Ph.D. and later president of Georgetown University, may have been a graduate of the school.) The association survived until 1989. Horticulturalist Samuel Bowne Parsons was a leader in the town's active Underground Railroad, one of the first in the country, as was merchant John Murray, Jr., who along with John Jay, Alexander Hamilton, Egbert Benson of Queens, and others, helped found the New York Society for the Manumission of Slaves and the New York African Free School, which provided the first public school instruction for African Americans in New York City.

Flushing's Quakers were active in more than social causes; in addition to Parsons's Nursery, Quaker-established businesses included the New York Gas Light Company, founded by Samuel Leggett, the first company to lay underground gas pipes in New York City (Leggett's home was the first in New York to be lit by gas lights). John Murray, Jr., was director of the Bank of New York; his brother Lindley Murray ran a successful publishing business; and Samuel Parsons, Jr., became New York Parks Commissioner.

The 1828 schism that divided Quakers throughout the country affected the Flushing Quakers as well, who split into a Hicksite faction (which retained the Meeting House) and an Orthodox faction, which built a new meetinghouse (now demolished). The numbers of Flushing's Quakers declined, and in the late nineteenth century few were left. But beginning in 1939, Flushing Meeting once more became active, first in protests against conscription during World War II, then as a meeting place for members of the United Nations when it was headquartered in Flushing Meadows–Corona Park (1946–50). Flushing's Quakers could be said to have returned to their roots during the 1950s and 1960s when they became involved in the civil rights movement and, later, protests against the Vietnam War. Today, as the Meeting celebrates more than 350 years of Flushing history, Flushing's Quaker community continues to play a vibrant role in the neighborhood.

S H E A   S T A D I U M

Rock and roll legends Jimi Hendrix, the Beatles, Simon and Garfunkel, the Rolling Stones, the Who, Elton John, Janis Joplin, the Police, Bruce Springsteen . . . they've all played here. So have Billy Graham, the Ice Capades, wrestlers, boxers, soccer teams, and even cricket stars. Local pro football teams the Jets and the Giants have also played here. But for Mets fans, the only playing that truly matters in Shea Stadium is baseball.

Shea Stadium, at 123-01 Roosevelt Avenue in Flushing, is part of New York City's Flushing Meadows–Corona Park, and has been a Queens fixture since it opened on April 17, 1964, with the New York Mets playing the Pittsburgh Pirates. The stadium was named after William A. Shea, an attorney at the forefront of the drive to return National League baseball to New York with a home for the Mets, following the departure of the Brooklyn Dodgers and New York Giants.

Since then, more than 70 million fans have poured through the stadium gates, arriving by car, bus, train, and even ferry from the boroughs of New York as well as from Long Island, Connecticut, and New Jersey. And Shea has been the site of

Opening Day 2005 (Marc S. Levine/NY Mets)

Carlos Beltran congratulates Carlos Delgado after Delgado homers against the St. Louis Cardinals in the 2006 National League Championship Series at Shea Stadium (Marc S. Levine/NY Mets)

A view of Shea Stadium from La Guardia Airport

several historic events—for instance, when some 60,000 crazed Beatles fans awaited the arrival of the Fab Four for their outdoor concert on August 15, 1965. Footage of young girls screaming so loudly that the band members could barely hear themselves sing was broadcast worldwide, making Shea Stadium a household name overnight.

Other memorable moments at the stadium include October 14, 1969, when "the Amazing Mets," who had spent their first seven years as one of the worst teams in the National League, became the first expansion team to win a World Series; the 1974–75 baseball season, when both the Mets and the Yankees played ball at Shea while Yankee Stadium was undergoing renovations; the Mets' second World Series title on October 27, 1986; the 2000 Subway Series, in which the Yankees defeated the Mets 4–1; and the return of the team to postseason play in 2006 as National League East Champions with a league-best 97 wins.

But soon Shea will rock no more—nor will it thrill to the crack of a bat or the cheers of baseball fans. The ballpark will be torn down to make way for a new, larger-capacity stadium. The Mets have begun construction of their new ballpark just beyond the outfield fence in the parking lot due east of Shea. The 45,000-capacity ballpark will open in 2009.

Jose Reyes, Carlos Delgado, and Jose Valentin celebrate the Mets clinching the National League Eastern Division on September 18, 2006, at Shea Stadium (Marc S. Levine/NY Mets)

Bruce Springsteen and the E Street Band play to a sold-out Shea Stadium in October 2003 (Marc S. Levine/NY Mets)

68

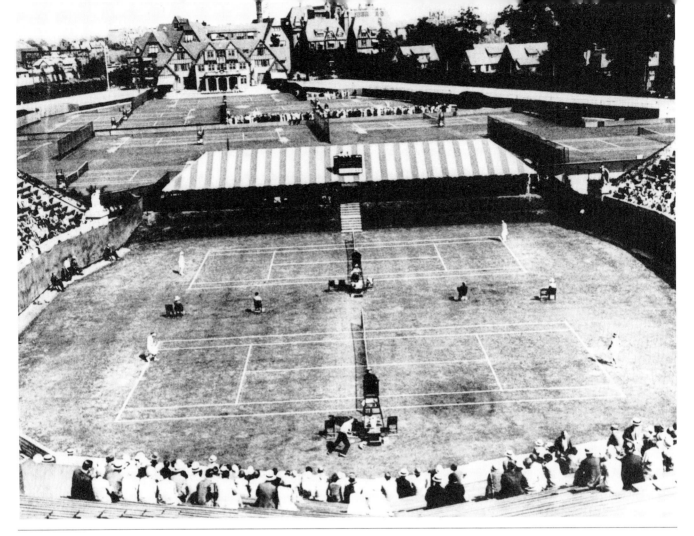

West Side Tennis Club (Queens Library, Long Island Division, Illustrations Collection)

Forest Hills, named for its proximity to Forest Park, has two distinct but related personalities. To the east and north of Queens Boulevard, the neighborhood has a cosmopolitan flair, with luxury cooperative apartment buildings towering over the many stores that line this active thoroughfare. From Jewel Avenue along 108th Street and up to the Long Island Expressway are dozens of blocks of additional, well-maintained residential buildings. And aligned in a grid pattern typical for Queens, pristine one-family houses of various architectural types can also be found throughout the northern area.

Forest Hills

This section of the neighborhood was farmland until the early 1900s, when it was developed by Cord Meyer Development Company. Single-family houses were initially built from 108th to 112th Streets and between Queens Boulevard and 67th Road, and streets were named alphabetically, from Atom (75th Avenue) to Zuni (63rd Drive). Schools and churches were built, and the community flourished, particularly after the Long Island Rail Road opened a station there in 1911, offering a mere half-hour commute into Manhattan. By the end of the 1920s, construction had begun on apartment buildings along Queens Boulevard.

The population continued to grow, especially after 1936, when the Independent subway opened a station on Union Turnpike. New apartment buildings were constructed to meet the influx of residents. By the end of World War II, Forest Hills was populated primarily by middle-class Jewish and Italian residents. Today, the residents are mainly immigrants who discovered the neighborhood in the 1980s and thereafter: Asians, Russian Jews, and Hispanics, who mingle with people of Polish, Iranian, Italian, and German descent.

Southwest of Queens Boulevard, beyond the thriving chain-store, boutique- and restaurant-lined Austin Street, a different persona emerges: **Forest Hills Gardens.** To venture into the narrow, lushly landscaped streets that encircle ele-

Residential apartment buildings lining Queens Boulevard

• West Side Tennis Club

The historic West Side Tennis Club, formerly the Forest Hills Tennis Stadium, became in 1915 the new location of the U.S. Lawn Tennis Association National Championship (a forerunner to the U.S. Open), and remained a center of activity for the tennis world until 1978, when the event was moved to the larger stadium at Flushing Meadows. During its time in the spotlight, the club hosted such tennis legends as Jimmy Connors, John McEnroe, Billie Jean King, Althea Gibson, Tracy Austin, and Martina Navratilova—and was legendary for being the place where the color line was broken in tennis (by Althea Gibson, who became the first black champion in 1950); a metal racquet was first used to win a Grand Slam title (Billie Jean King in 1967); and the tie-breaker was introduced (in 1970). But the site was also famous for its concerts. Frank Sinatra, Jimi Hendrix, the Rolling Stones, Bob Dylan, the Who, and the Beatles were just some of the many musicians who played there. Today's West Side Tennis Club still hosts tennis matches and special events; it also boasts a Junior Olympic–size swim complex, thirty-eight tennis courts on various surfaces, and an elegant Tudor clubhouse built in 1913.

gant brick and stucco Georgian- and Tudor-style row houses and detached homes is to step into a storybook setting in the heart of Queens.

Forest Hills Gardens, the nation's first planned community, was fashioned after an English village by renowned landscape architect Frederick Law Olmsted, Jr. (whose father co-designed Central Park), and architect Grosvenor Atterbury. In 1906 businessman and real estate developer Cord Meyer sold a section of land south of Queens Boulevard to Margaret Slocum Sage, the wife of Russell Sage and benefactor of the Russell Sage Foundation. The initial intention behind the 1912 creation of Forest Hills Gardens by the foundation was to create a development for working-class residents. But this turned out to be a short-lived plan because of the rising costs of land and construction details, which included expensive design elements on the houses such as terra-cotta-tiled sloping roofs.

The Russell Sage Foundation also added picturesque visuals to the neighborhood setting—period lampposts, winding cobble-stone streets and lanes, a town square, and village greens—all of which remain today. Station Square, dating back to 1912, is the gateway to Forest Hills Gardens from the Long Island Rail Road, where a quaint railroad station adds to the feeling of stepping back in time. (In 1917, Theodore Roosevelt gave a speech in support of America's involvement in World War I from the station.) This is

NEIGHBORHOOD PROFILE

Boundaries: <u>Forest Hills</u>: <u>north border:</u> Long Island Expressway; <u>east border:</u> Grand Central Parkway; <u>south border:</u> 78th Crescent to Union Turnpike; <u>west border:</u> Woodhaven Boulevard to Metropolitan Avenue to Selfridge Street to Fleet Street to Thornton Place to 67th Avenue to Queens Boulevard to 102nd Street; <u>Forest Hills Gardens</u>: <u>north border:</u> Burns Street; <u>east border:</u> Union Turnpike; <u>south border:</u> Kessel Street to 77th Avenue to Whitson Street to Ascan Avenue to Greenway South to Groton Street; <u>west border:</u> 70th Avenue (Herrick Avenue) to Dartmouth Street to 69th Avenue (Stafford Avenue)

Subway and Train: <u>LIRR</u>: Forest Hills; <u>E, F, R, V, G trains:</u> Forest Hills and 71st Avenue; <u>E, F trains:</u> 75th Avenue

Bus: <u>Q23:</u> 108th Street to Union Turnpike; <u>Q54:</u> Metropolitan Avenue; <u>Q65A:</u> Jewel Avenue; <u>Q88:</u> Horace Harding Expressway; <u>Q58:</u> Horace Harding Expressway; <u>x51:</u> Horace Harding Expressway; <u>Q60:</u> Queens Boulevard

Libraries: Queens Library, Forest Hills Branch (108-19 71st Avenue); North Forest Park Branch (98-27 Metropolitan Avenue)

Community Board: No. 6

Police Precinct: 112th Precinct (68-40 Austin Street)

Fire Department: Engine 305, Ladder 151 (111-02 Queens Boulevard)

Hospitals and Clinics: North Shore University Hospital at Forest Hills (102-01 66th Road); Forest View Nursing Home (71-20 110th Street); Jamaica Hospital Medical Center Advanced Center for Psychotherapy (103-26 68th Road); Parkway Hospital (70-35 113th Street); Forest Hills Hospital (102-01 66th Road)

also the site of the former Forest Hills Inn, a charming multistory structure that today houses cooperative apartments. A few blocks from the railroad station is 1 Tennis Place, a graceful Tudor building that houses the West Side Tennis Club. Forest Hills Gardens is privately owned, maintained, and regulated by property residents, who formed the Forest Hills Gardens Corporation in the 1920s.

Heading farther south the English village motif finds expression in the surprisingly rural barns and horse stables of Lynn's Riding School, located at 88-03 70th Road, and DD Stables at 88-11 70th Road. Both facilities offer riding lessons and the chance for city slickers to saddle up and ride the heavily wooded trails bordering Forest Park, just past Union Turnpike.

But this is Queens, not rural England, and these pastoral, equine locales can be reached via modern-day mass transit with a pleasant walk from the E or F trains at Continental (71st) Avenue. The subways (the R, G, and V lines are also here) and express buses along Queens Boulevard (as well as along a variety of major highways, among them Grand Central Parkway, Jackie Robinson Parkway, and the Long Island Expressway) offer easy access to Manhattan, an attractive quality for Forest Hills residents who commute there.

Greenway Terrace, Forest Hills Gardens
(Sonia S. Estreich)

72

NEIGHBORHOOD FACTS

■ Bramson ORT College, whose main campus is located at 69-30 Austin Street, is a private two-year college operated by ORT Operations USA, the American branch of the Jewish charity ORT (Organization for Educational Resource and Technological Training). Established in 1942 to serve World War II refugees, Bramson offers technical, business, and health services education.

■ Everybody loved comedian Ray Romano when he was growing up in Forest Hills. Other famous residents have included Helen Keller, former Democratic vice-presidential candidate and congresswoman Geraldine Ferraro, newspaper columnist Jimmy Breslin, and Dale Carnegie. The punk group the Ramones formed in Forest Hills in 1974.

■ Peter Parker, the alter-ego of Marvel Comics superhero Spider-Man, grew up in Forest Hills with his Uncle Ben and Aunt May Parker.

■ The mast of the yacht *Columbia*, the America's Cup winner in 1899 and 1901, stands as a monument in Forest Hills Gardens.

■ The paperback publishing house Dover Publications was founded in 1941 by the late Hayward Cirker and his wife, Blanche, who named the Mineola-based company after the Forest Hills apartment building in which they were living at the time.

Playing chess in a community park

A strong Jewish presence can still be found on 108th Street (note the kosher Chinese restaurant on the left)

Fresh

Single-family homes in Utopia Estates
(Sonia S. Estreich)

Despite its name, the ambience of much of Fresh Meadows is distinctly urban. Originally a farming village called Black Stump (so-called because during colonial times farmers marked their land boundaries with rows of black stumps), the northern side of 73rd Avenue (formerly Black Stump Road) around 188th Street and the Long Island Expressway is where the

NEIGHBORHOOD PROFILE

Boundaries: <u>Fresh Meadows:</u> <u>north border:</u> 47th Avenue to Hollis Court Boulevard to 47th Avenue to Francis Lewis Boulevard to Long Island Expressway; <u>east border:</u> Clearview Expressway; <u>south border:</u> Grand Central Parkway to 188th Street to Union Turnpike; <u>west border:</u> Utopia Parkway to Fresh Meadow Lane; <u>West Cunningham Park:</u> <u>north border:</u> 73rd Ave to 197th Street to 67th Ave; <u>east border:</u> Francis Lewis Boulevard; <u>south border:</u> Grand Central Parkway; <u>west border:</u> 188th Street; <u>Utopia:</u> <u>north border:</u> 73rd Avenue; <u>east border:</u> 188th Street; <u>south border:</u> Union Turnpike; <u>west border:</u> Utopia Parkway

Bus: <u>Q31:</u> Utopia Parkway; <u>Q30:</u> Utopia Parkway to Horace Harding Expressway; <u>Q46:</u> Union Turnpike; <u>Q17, x32:</u> Horace Harding Expressway to 188th Street; <u>Q88:</u> Horace Harding Expressway to 188th Street to 73rd Avenue; <u>Q76:</u> Francis Lewis Boulevard; <u>Q75:</u> 188th Street

Libraries: Queens Library, Fresh Meadows Branch (193-20 Horace Harding Expressway)

Community Board: No. 8

Police Precinct: 107th Precinct (71-01 Parsons Boulevard, Flushing); 111th Precinct (45-06 215th Street, Bayside)

Fire Department: Engine 274, Ladder 129 (40-18 Union Street, Flushing)

Hospitals and Clinics: St. Joseph's Hospital Division of Catholic Medical Center of Brooklyn and Queens (158-40 79th Avenue, Flushing)

Meadows

landscaped rental apartment complex that is also called Fresh Meadows was built after World War II as a "model urban community." Lauded at the time by community planner Lewis Mumford, it is one of the largest in Queens, spread out over almost 150 acres that once housed the Fresh Meadows Country Club, a well-known golf course that opened in 1923 and once hosted the U.S. Open.

Developed by the New York Life Insurance Company in 1949, the massive residential cluster, designed for middle-income households, was long home to white families but now includes Hispanics, African Americans, and residents of Chinese, Japanese, Korean, and Indian descent. The Fresh Meadows apartment compound consists of 140 buildings, among them two- and three-story garden apartments, a twenty-story high rise, and two thirteen-story structures. It also contains the Fresh Meadows Shopping Center, which hosts more than forty retailers, and a seven-screen Loews Cineplex, whose original single screen was built in 1949.

But just outside the complex residents have long relished the tranquil environment of other parts of Fresh Meadows, exemplified for years by the Klein farm, built in 1895 at 194-15 73rd Avenue. The Kleins sold freshly harvested produce from their stand and lived in a 1930s red-brick house on 2 acres. Originally the property spanned some 200 acres, but over the years it was sold out in parcels to developers. The farm was finally sold in 2003, though development plans remain at a standstill because of neighborhood opposition. Nevertheless, that part of Fresh Meadows, which some residents refer to as **West Cunningham Park,** retains characteristics of a well-heeled suburb in the city. Cunningham Park, part of the borough's connected park system (see the Corridor photo

NEIGHBORHOOD FACTS

■ St. Francis Preparatory School, at 6100 Francis Lewis Boulevard, is the largest private Catholic secondary school in the United States and was the first private Catholic school on Long Island. Founded in 1858 as the all-male St. Francis Academy in Brooklyn, St. Francis Prep, as it is familiarly known, took its present name in 1935 and moved to Queens in 1974, at which time women were admitted. The school was a recipient of the U.S. Department of Education's Excellence in Private Education Award and takes pride in the fact that 98 percent of its graduates go on to college. The school's varsity football team, considered one of the best among American Catholic schools, has won more championships in New York than any other. Among the school's famous alumni are former Green Bay Packers coach Vince Lombardi and N.Y. Yankees manager Joe Torre.

■ Fresh Meadows residents might be surprised to learn that an overgrown lot at 73rd Avenue and 182nd Street is a burial site for seventy-seven members of the Brinkerhoff family. Brinkerhoff descendants, who included some of the first farmers in Queens, came here from New Amsterdam as early as 1642. The burial ground in Fresh Meadows also contains members of the Snedeker, Hoogland, and Bennet families, with some of the earliest markers dating to the 1700s.

■ Fresh Meadows octogenarian Leonard LeShay, a member of the Metropolitan Association of Sea Kayaking (MASK), has no qualms about paddling around Manhattan: he's made the thirty-three-mile trip, which takes ten hours, about four times now.

■ An annual Sunday softball game has been taking place at Utopia Playground from March through November since 1948. Open to all, the weekly pickup game starts at 6 A.M.

spread), largely sits in the West Cunningham Park area.

Also within Fresh Meadows, between 73rd Avenue and Union Turnpike, and from 188th Street to Utopia Parkway, is an area called **Utopia,** developed in the mid-1900s. Rather than apartment buildings, its residential development, called Utopia Estates, is made up of attractive single-family homes. The houses are similar to one another in general plot size (40 feet by 100 feet) and style—many are Capes and Colonials. Utopia was initially acquired in 1905 by the Utopia Land Company, which planned to create a cooperative community for Jewish families then living on the Lower East Side of Manhattan. It was to cover a tract of 50 acres, and street names would emulate those on the Lower East Side: Ludlow, Hester, Essex, and so on. The plan for this "utopian" society was abandoned when the development company couldn't secure enough funding. The optimistic moniker stuck, however, and was also used for a thoroughfare, Utopia Parkway, and a 3-acre park, Utopia Playground, on 73rd Avenue, where a historic plaque outlines in detail the plan for the Jewish community that never was.

Fresh Meadows garden apartments
(Sonia S. Estreich)

Glendale

Glendale may be the quietest neighborhood in Queens—but then again, no other communities in the borough have about half of their land devoted to cemeteries. Historically also something of a party town, today Glendale is home to a diverse population of residents who take great pride in their community.

Glendale, once primarily farmland, was developed in the mid-1800s when real estate agent John C. Schooley laid out streets and sold off 25-foot by 100-foot lots for housing. In 1868 Schooley reportedly called the settlement Glendale after his hometown of Glendale, Ohio. A large German community thrived in the neighborhood back then, and taverns were an important feature of the area, along with "picnic parks," where sports, dancing, singing, and imbibing were common activities—that is, until Prohibition curtailed public revels. (One of the largest of the old picnic parks was Schuetzen Park, which also boasted a hotel, on the north side of Myrtle Avenue at 88th Street.) The manufacture of products such as textiles, matchsticks, silk ribbons, and airplanes provided labor for the increasing number of people moving into the area's affordable attached and semi-attached row houses. But by the

1930s, the last of the picnic parks was redeveloped as part of today's Jackie Robinson Parkway, which runs through the southern part of the neighborhood.

This southern section is informally known as Cemetery Belt for its vast number of burial grounds, the result of a mid-nineteenth-century prohibition on further burials in Manhattan. Glendale and neighboring Middle Village became home to a number of new cemeteries, which in Glendale now include Mount Lebanon Cemetery (7800 Myrtle Avenue), Hungarian Union Field Cemetery (8299 Cypress Avenue), Mount Neboh Cemetery (8207 Cypress Hills Street), Mount Carmel Cemetery (8345 Cypress Hills Street), Machpelah Cemetery (8230 Cypress Hills Street), and Beth El Cemetery (8012 Cypress Hills Street). Cypress Hills Cemetery and Cemetery of the Evergreens cover so much property that they both extend into Brooklyn, which borders Glendale to the west and south.

Cypress Hills Cemetery, the only national cemetery in New York City, is the final resting place of the celebrated and the infamous: not only baseball players Jackie Robinson and Lou Gehrig, writers Emma Lazarus and Sholem Aleichem, and actors Mae West and Edward G. Robinson are interred there but six notorious Mafia figures as well, including Charles (Lucky) Luciano, Vito (Don George) Genovese, and Carlo Gambino.

NEIGHBORHOOD FACTS

■ The Queens Symphony Orchestra, based on Cooper Avenue, has been making beautiful music for more than fifty years. It is the only professional orchestra in Queens and the oldest and largest professional arts organization in the borough.

■ A silent film studio was based on the north side of Myrtle Avenue in the 1920s.

■ The house featured in the opening credits of the classic CBS sitcom *All in the Family* is at 89-70 Cooper Avenue.

Only about eight miles from Manhattan, Glendale features public transportation (an express bus) on Myrtle Avenue, the neighborhood's commercial strip, serving the Chinese, Dominican, Polish, Romanian, and other residents who live in Glendale today. Myrtle Avenue is also home base for the Glendale Civilian Observation Patrol (G-COP), which over the past twenty-five years has worked hand in hand with the 104th Precinct to keep the neighborhood safe. A volunteer ambulance corps, the Glendale Property Owners Association, and other groups are also active.

Row houses on Cooper Avenue, similar to those that appear in the opening credits of *All in the Family*

Atlas Terminal in 1905 (Queens Library, Long Island Division, Illustrations Collection)

The partial transformation of Atlas Terminal—a 25-acre longtime industrial park that once housed General Electric and Kraft Foods—into the up-scale Shops at Atlas Park shows how Glendale has changed from a strictly blue-collar neighborhood to an increasingly upwardly mobile one. The shopping complex, located on Cooper Avenue, opened in 2006 and when completed will offer some sixty retail stores and restaurants, office space, a daycare facility, and ample parking. The area also features a 2.5-acre public park, with fountains, a food market, and—in a nod perhaps to the "picnic park" days of long ago—picnic tables for all to enjoy.

Cypress Hills Cemetery, one of the many burial grounds making up the Cemetery Belt, lies in both Queens and Brooklyn

NEIGHBORHOOD PROFILE

Boundaries: <u>North border:</u> 67th Avenue to Long Island Rail Road Tracks to Cooper Avenue to Metropolitan Avenue; <u>east border:</u> Woodhaven Boulevard to Union Turnpike to Pedestrian Way to western border of Forest Park (east section); <u>south border:</u> Myrtle Avenue to Woodhaven Boulevard to Forest Park to 83rd Drive to northeastern border of Forest Park Golf Course to Jackie Robinson Parkway to eastern border of Forest Park to Kings County border (from Cypress Hills Cemetery through the Ridgewood Reservoir); <u>west border:</u> Kings County line to Robert Place to Robert Street to Heath Place to Jackie Robinson Parkway, around the Cemetery of the Evergreens to Long Island Rail Road tracks to Fresh Pond Road

Subway and Train: <u>M train:</u> Fresh Pond Road, Fresh Pond Road and 67th Avenue

Bus: <u>Q55:</u> Myrtle Avenue; <u>B13:</u> Cypress Hills Street to Fresh Pond Road; <u>Q54:</u> Metropolitan Avenue; <u>Q29:</u> 80th Street; <u>Q23:</u> Woodhaven Boulevard; <u>Q11:</u> Woodhaven Boulevard; <u>Q53:</u> Woodhaven Boulevard; <u>B20:</u> Fresh Pond Road and 67th Avenue; <u>Q58:</u> Fresh Pond Road; <u>Q39:</u> Forest Avenue to 61st Street

Libraries: Queens Library, Glendale Branch (78-60 73rd Place)

Community Board: No. 5

Police Precinct: 104th Precinct (64-2 Catalpa Avenue, Ridgewood)

Fire Department: Engine 286, Ladder 135, Battalion 51 (66-44 Myrtle Avenue)

Hospitals and Clinics: Catholic Medical Center of Brooklyn (8000 Cooper Avenue)

Glen Oaks

Like many neighborhoods in Queens, Glen Oaks offers residents great schools (School District 26 is rated the best in New York City), affordable, safe homes within reasonable commuting distance of Manhattan, and shopping and entertainment right at their doorsteps. But the small neighborhood typifies another aspect of postwar urban development: although it does have a section of single-family homes, the area is dominated by an enormous cooperative garden-apartment complex called Glen Oaks Village. The complex surrounds the lovely 3-acre Tenney Park at 74th Avenue and 260th Street, and it is so expansive that twenty-four of its buildings are actually in Bellerose, to the west. The Glen Oaks section consists of 110 two-story buildings and 2,328 apartments of various sizes.

Glen Oaks was originally the site of the William K. Vanderbilt country estate. In 1923 the property was converted into the Glen Oaks Golf Club. But soon thereafter, a large segment of the golf course was slated for development. In 1944 the Gross-Morton Company bought 175 acres of land and built Glen Oaks Village as

NEIGHBORHOOD FACTS

■ Glen Oaks Village developer Jerry Tenney was a loyal New Yorker. Born in the Bronx, he made a career out of financing and developing real estate in the city. He was especially devoted to making Glen Oaks a good place to live: during its development, he spent seven days a week on-site supervising every aspect of the construction, and during his later years he continued to improve the garden community. In recognition of his service to the entire neighborhood, the New York City Department of Parks and Recreation renamed the Glen Oaks Park after him in 1977.
■ The highest point in Queens is in Glen Oaks: 258.2 feet above sea level, near the 17th tee of the North Shore Towers Country Club golf course.

The Glen Oaks Little League enjoys summer at Jerry M. Tenney Park

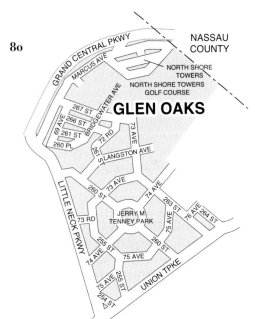

GLEN OAKS

The cooperative garden apartments of Glen Oaks Village

a residential rental-only development with two-story buildings in the Colonial style. The apartments were promptly snapped up by thousands of returning World War II veterans.

In 1972 the rest of the golf course was developed as the North Shore Towers and Country Club complex, three thirty-three-story buildings of luxury apartments set on 100 acres off Marcus Avenue. Originally a rental complex, North Shore Towers began conversion to co-ops in 1985. The complex offers residents on-site shopping, a deluxe health club, a private eighteen-hole golf course, tennis, swimming, twenty-four-hour security, and concierge services.

Like North Shore Towers, today's Glen Oaks Village, which is home to white, Asian, Hispanic, and African American occupants, is patrolled by private security guards, and has convenient amenities just steps away: park-

NEIGHBORHOOD PROFILE

Boundaries: <u>North border:</u> Grand Central Parkway; <u>east border:</u> Nassau County line to North Shore Towers golf course to 74th Avenue to 263rd Street to 76th Avenue to 264th Street; <u>south border:</u> Union Turnpike; <u>west border:</u> Little Neck Parkway
Bus: Q79: Little Neck Parkway; Q46: Union Turnpike
Libraries: Queens Library, Glen Oaks Branch (256-04 Union Turnpike)
Museums: Queens County Farm Museum (73-50 Little Neck Parkway, Bellerose)
Community Board: No. 13
Police Precinct: 105th Precinct (92-08 222nd Street, Queens Village)
Fire Department: Engine 251, Battalion 53 (254-20 Union Turnpike)
Hospitals and Clinics: Hillside Hospital (75-59 263rd Street)

ing garages, playgrounds, tennis courts, laundry facilities, a library, post office, and supermarket, banks, shopping, and transportation. This self-reliance and built-in organization are a bonus for residents, but they have left the relatively few private homeowners who live in Capes and ranches along the outskirts of the co-ops feeling somewhat isolated. These resourceful residents have shown their community spirit—and sense of humor. Forming the aptly named Lost Community Civic Association, the homeowners of Glen Oaks have united to mobilize local politicians and officials in support of their neighborhood.

Hollis

Hollis is where gritty hip-hop bangs up against the middle-class dream—where friends Daymond John, J. Alexander Martin, Keith Perrin, and Carl Brown teamed up in 1992 to create the urban sportswear clothing line Fubu ("For us, by us") and middle-class African American families have long settled, attracted by the quiet residential streets of single-family homes. A magnet for families looking for good schools, Hollis now draws people from a variety of ethnic backgrounds—and has been home to a number of very well-known residents.

Founded by Dutch settlers in the seventeenth century, Hollis was primarily a farming community for its first 150 years. The area's earliest brush with fame occurred during the American Revolution's Battle of Long Island, when Brigadier General Nathaniel Woodhull was captured by the British in a tavern owned by Increase Carpenter at today's Jamaica Avenue and 197th Street. Although it is unclear whether Woodhull actually refused to declare "God save the Queen" and instead shouted "God save us all" before being stabbed by a sword, the legendary story still inspires.

In the 1880s a railroad station was built in Hollis, at around the same time that Frederick W. Dunton was wondering what to call his new development. He thought of naming it after Woodhull, but finally chose Hollis, a reminder of his own hometown in New Hampshire. Woodhull was commemorated instead by elementary school P.S. 35, located two blocks from the site of Carpenter's Tavern. Also named after Woodhull is an

> **NEIGHBORHOOD FACTS**
>
> ■ The Art Deco Hollis Cinema at 191-12 Jamaica Avenue used to show adult films. In 1978 it closed and has since been converted into the Greater Forbes Temple, a Pentecostal church.
>
> ■ When Hollis Park Gardens was developed in the early 1900s, decorative pillars bearing the enclave's monogram were erected during construction. Some of these pillars still stand today.

Jamaica Avenue

82 avenue where lovely Victorian houses were erected in the early 1900s. A few of those structures still stand, although many were demolished as the demand for housing increased and blocks of apartment buildings and row houses were constructed in their place.

The mid-1950s was the start of a transition for Hollis, as it was for much of Queens. During this time and continuing into the 1960s and 1970s, white families began moving out of the area once known as East Jamaica, and blacks discovered the tranquil streets and stately Victorians, Colonials, and orderly row houses of Hollis. The three-bedroom, ivy-covered bungalow in Hollis where former Secretary of State Colin Powell spent his late teen years, for example, was surrounded by a lawn and fruit trees. Powell's home, at 183-68 Elmira Avenue, was a definite step up from the tenements of the South Bronx where he had grown up. As Powell recalled in his autobiography, "The neighborhood looked beautiful to us, and the Hollis address carried a certain cachet, a

Graduating class of P.S. 35 (near what is now 89th Avenue), ca. 1910 (The Queens Library, Long Island Division, Frederick J. Weber Photographs)

cut above Jamaica, Queens, and just below St. Albans, then another gold coast for middle-class blacks." Today Powell's old address is even trendier: Hollis's border has shifted north, and Elmira Avenue is now part of St. Albans.

Other famous Hollis residents also prized the neighborhood, including the Reverend Al Sharpton, who for a time lived at 100-50 199th Street, and former U.N. ambassador Andrew Young, who made his home at 111-35 200th Street. Pulitzer Prize–winning author and humor columnist Art Buchwald grew up in Hollis as well. But perhaps most notably, Hollis has been home to well-known musicians over the years, including pioneer jazz artist Clarence Williams, pianist and composer Jaki Byard, and trumpeter Roy Eldridge. More recently, Hollis has

"The Castle" apartments on Woodhull Avenue, 1975 (Queens Library, Long Island Division, Illustrations Collection)

NEIGHBORHOOD PROFILE

Boundaries: <u>North border:</u> Hillside Avenue; <u>east border:</u> Francis Lewis Boulevard; <u>south border:</u> 104th Avenue to Liberty Avenue; <u>west border:</u> 183rd Street to 93rd Avenue to 180th Place to 180th Street
Subway and Train: <u>LIRR:</u> Hollis
Bus: <u>Q1, Q43, x68, N22A, N22, N26, Q36:</u> Hillside Avenue; <u>Q110:</u> Jamaica Avenue; <u>Q2:</u> Hollis Avenue; <u>Q77:</u> Francis Lewis Boulevard; <u>Q3:</u> 190th Street; <u>N1, N2, N3, N6, N24:</u> Hillside Avenue to Francis Lewis Boulevard
Libraries: Queens Library, Hollis Branch (202-05 Hillside Avenue); South Hollis Branch (204-01 Hollis Avenue)
Community Board: No. 12
Police Precinct: 103rd Precinct (168-02 P.O. Edward Byrne Avenue, Jamaica); 113th Precinct (167-02 Baisley Boulevard, Jamaica)
Fire Department: Engine 301, Ladder 150, Battalion 54 (91-04 197th Street)
Hospitals and Clinics: Medisys Family Center (188-03 Jamaica Avenue and 200-16 Hollis Avenue)

Hession farm potato field, with Joe Hession, Edward Donohum, and Hugh Hession, Jr., on wagon (The Queens Library, Long Island Division, George Winans Collection)

• Hollis Hip-Hop

"The time is now, the place is here, and the whole wide world is filled with cheer." So sentimentalized neighborhood natives Joseph Simmons, Darryl McDaniels, and Jason Mizell, better known as rappers Run-DMC, in their popular song "Christmas in Hollis." A virtual breeding ground for musical talent, Hollis has been home to rappers Ja Rule (Jeff Atkins), Jimi Kendrix (Kendred T. Smith), and producer Om'Mas Keith. LL Cool J (James Todd Smith), who grew up in neighboring St. Albans, was also part of Hollis's early hip-hop scene.

Run-DMC, perhaps the best-known hip-hop group to come out of Hollis, was formed in the 1980s by friends and neighbors Simmons ("Run"), McDaniels ("DMC"), and Mizell ("Jam Master Jay"). The group was originally managed by Simmons's older brother Russell, today a multimillionaire who made a fortune not only in the hip-hop world, as cofounder of Def Jam Records, but also in fashion—in 1992, he launched the clothing line Phat Farm, which just over ten years later he sold for nearly $140 million. (In 2004, Simmons told the CBS news program *60 Minutes* that his mentor is Donald Trump, another Queens native who made it big.)

More than simply music, hip-hop reflects a way of life, one that is sometimes violent, and many hip-hop stars have met tragic ends, including Jam Master Jay, who was killed in 2002. But the dream of success, given voice in LL Cool J's "Hollis to Hollywood," continues to fuel this urban sound.

produced a remarkable number of rap music moguls, including Russell Simmons (founder of the hip-hop label Def Jam Records), Ja Rule (Jeff Atkins), and Run-DMC (Joseph Simmons, Darryl McDaniels, and the late Jason Mizell).

Hollis continues to appeal to middle-class families. Within close range of the Jamaica transit hub and with its own Long Island Rail Road Station on 193rd Street and Woodhull Avenue, the neighborhood is ideal for commuters. It is also conveniently close to shopping along Jamaica and Hillside Avenues. But while the majority of Hollis's population is African American, Latin Americans, Filipinos, Indians, and Guyanese have also made their home here—creating what residents call a "global community in Queens." Potluck parties and community flower-planting gatherings promote a sense of goodwill and spirit of solidarity in this diverse, centrally located neighborhood.

This house on Elmira Avenue where Colin Powell's family lived in the 1950s is now part of St. Albans (Sonia S. Estreich)

Hollis Hills

Hollis Hills

Hollis Hills is a little hideaway in northeastern Queens, a verdant neighborhood flanked by the woodsy barriers of the Grand Central Parkway to the south, Cunningham Park to the west, and Alley Pond Park to the east. Its northern border follows a portion of what used to be the Long Island Motor Parkway but is now a landscaped biking and jogging path for residents—a feature that further cloisters Hollis Hills and adds to its allure as a well-kept secret in the borough.

"We don't want people to know about us," maintains a long-time neighborhood resident with a wink. That's because life is good here—it is quiet and peaceful, and there is a strong spirit of community, with annual block parties and planting get-togethers at various triangles. The public schools, part of District 26, are consistently top-notch, and well-maintained homes (Colonials, ranches, split levels, and Tudors situated on ample lots) were built here fairly recently, after World War II. The oldest portion of this area, Surrey Estates, was built in 1939 and runs from Hartland Avenue to 223rd Street, by Springfield Boulevard.

Hollis Hills, long a mostly white

Elegant homes line 85th Avenue
(Sonia S. Estreich)

community with many Jewish residents, is attracting a growing Asian population. Many of these residents are professionals—public officials, politicians, doctors. In fact, Hollis Hills boasts the world's youngest doctor. According to the *Guinness Book of World Records*, Balamurali Ambati was just seventeen when he graduated from Mount Sinai School of Medicine in 1995.

Because there is no subway or Long Island Rail Road station here, the only means of commuting into Manhattan, which is about fourteen miles away, is bus service from Union Turnpike. But that's just fine with Hollis Hills residents, because mass transit would surely attract many to this quiet corner of Queens.

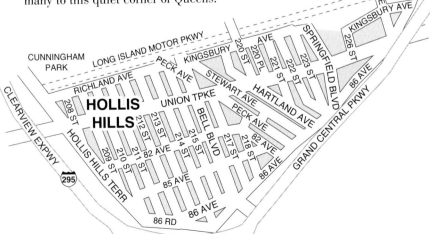

• Long Island Motor Parkway

Built by William K. Vanderbilt, great-grandson of shipping and railroad magnate Cornelius Vanderbilt, the Long Island Motor Parkway was one of the earliest concrete roads in the country. Stretching some forty-eight miles from Queens to Lake Ronkonkoma in Suffolk County, the parkway included twelve tolls and overpasses.

Vanderbilt was a racing enthusiast, and in 1908 he organized the annual Vanderbilt Cup Race along the first ten miles of the parkway that were completed by that time. But two years later a car crash during the race killed many spectators, and the races were stopped. The parkway continued to be used as a scenic road by motorists until master builder Robert Moses's intricate network of roadways was created. Although the parkway was still privately owned by Vanderbilt, in 1938 Moses tore down the famous thoroughfare, whose narrow roads and tolls just couldn't compete with the more modern highways.

Today, the New York City Greenway program, a collaboration of the Department of Transportation, the City Planning Office, and the City of New York Parks and Recreation Department, maintains the remaining sections of the Motor Parkway for pedestrian use.

NEIGHBORHOOD FACTS

■ Donny Deutsch, advertising guru and host of CNBC's *The Big Idea with Donny Deutsch*, grew up in Hollis Hills.

■ The Alley Pond Striders, a Hollis Hills running and walking group, makes full use of the beautiful biking, jogging, and walking trail linking Cunningham and Alley Pond Parks (see the Corridor photo spread). The more than three hundred members of the group, which has been going strong for twenty-five years, organize the annual five-mile Alley Pond Challenge, one of the largest in the New York City area, as well as casual weekend runs and walks for members of all abilities.

Long Island Motor Parkway is now a runners' and bikers' haven (Sonia S. Estreich)

85th Avenue at 218th Street

NEIGHBORHOOD PROFILE

Boundaries: <u>North border:</u> Long Island Motor Parkway along Richland Avenue to Peck Avenue to Bell Boulevard to Kingsbury Avenue; <u>east border:</u> Grand Central Parkway; <u>south border:</u> 86th Road; <u>west border:</u> Clearview Expressway
Bus: <u>Q46:</u> Union Turnpike; <u>Q27, Q88, Q32:</u> Springfield Boulevard
Libraries: Queens Library, Windsor Park Branch (79-50 Bell Boulevard)
Community Board: No. 11 and 13
Police Precinct: 111th Precinct (45-06 215th Street, Bayside)

Holliswood

In Holliswood, winding streets lead to unexpected charms: well-kept homes on sprawling lots, towering trees and beautiful gardens, and the blissful feel of a country retreat. Although it is just north of Hollis, separated by Hillside Avenue and developed around the same time as that neighborhood, Holliswood has an expansive, rural quality all its own.

The rolling hills and abundant trees that grace this area were what drew Frederick W. Dunton to develop the neighborhood in the late 1800s. Dunton, whose uncle was Austin Corbin, then president of the Long Island Rail Road, gave Holliswood's curving streets romantic, exotic names like Palermo, Sancho, and Marengo. He fashioned the now-defunct trotting racecourse Epsom Course just south of where the Grand Central Parkway and Francis Lewis Boulevard cross today. And on Dunton Avenue, along the southern part of the neighborhood, he constructed his mansion, Hollis Hall, which in subsequent years became the restaurant Brown's Chop House. Today, a lovely garden apartment complex is at this site. Built in 1949, Holliswood Gardens includes 262 two-story apartments. More important, it maintains the integrity of Holliswood with carefully landscaped courtyards, grassy lawns, and wide, tree-lined streets. Hollis Park Gardens, covering five blocks along Foothill Avenue, was another early development. Built in the 1910s and 1920s, the magnificent homes on large lots have always attracted affluent homebuyers to the neighborhood.

Holliswood is not exclusively residential: Holliswood Hospital, at 87-37 Palermo Street, is a private psychiatric facility. Holliswood Jewish Center/Young Israel of Holliswood, an orthodox organization at 86-25 Francis Lewis Boulevard, is part of the Northeast Queens Jewish Community Council, an association of thirty synagogues and other religious, education, fraternal, and community organizations.

Residents representing many diverse nationalities and cultures, with a relatively even number of whites and African Americans and smaller populations of Asians and Hispanics, have actively worked with the Department of City Planning to maintain the character of their neighborhood. When Holliswood was threatened by zoning that permitted

NEIGHBORHOOD FACTS

■ Holliswood resident Sue Levi-Pearl made history in 2001 when she was admitted as the first woman of the previously all-male Cunningham Park Bocce Club.

■ In 2005, after a request from Congressman Gary Ackerman, the U.S. Postal Service officially renamed the Holliswood post office, which had previously been called Station D, Holliswood Station. The move reflects a borough-wide change that took place in 1998, also at Ackerman's urging, to name post offices after their neighborhoods, instead of assigning each Queens zip code to Flushing, Jamaica, or Long Island City.

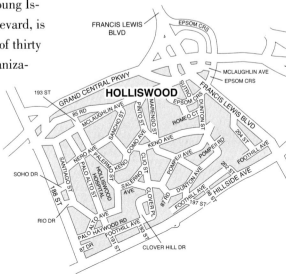

more single-family homes to be replaced with multiple dwellings on the same lots, neighborhood residents took stock of the alarming effects—Santiago Street, a woodsy cul-de-sac that originally served two homes, was leveled and rebuilt to accommodate seven houses—and lobbied officials until the designation was changed.

It is that persistence, as well as the essence of Holliswood—the quiet, winding streets with almost no sidewalks, the upscale houses, the beautiful landscaping and towering trees—that for years has attracted families like the Cuomos, who settled here in the 1930s. A three-term governor of New York, Mario Cuomo wrote in his 1984 memoir *Diaries of Mario Cuomo,* "We had just moved from South Ja-

Sancho Street is one of the many winding roads of Holliswood (Sonia S. Estreich)

NEIGHBORHOOD PROFILE

Boundaries: <u>North border:</u> Grand Central Parkway; <u>east border:</u> Epsom Course to Francis Lewis Boulevard; <u>south border:</u> Hillside Avenue; <u>west border:</u> 188th Street
Bus: <u>Q76:</u> Francis Lewis Boulevard; <u>Q75, Q17, x32:</u> 188th Street; <u>Q1, Q43, x68, N22A, N22, N26, Q36, N1, N2, N3, N6, N24:</u> Hillside Avenue
Community Board: Nos. 8, 13
Police Precinct: 107th Precinct (71-01 Parsons Boulevard, Flushing)
Fire Department: Engine 301, Ladder 150, Battalion 54 (91-04 197th Street, Hollis)
Hospitals and Clinics: Holliswood Hospital, psychiatric care (87-37 Palermo Street)

maica into Holliswood. We had left the place behind the store and for the first time had our own house. It even had some land around it, even some trees—one in particular, was a great blue spruce that must have been forty feet high. It was beautiful." The spruce became uprooted during a heavy storm after the family moved into the neighborhood. But the senior Cuomo would not allow it to die. Instead, he recruited his children, Mario, Frank, and Marie, to help him set the roots back in place. The tree thrived, and Cuomo incorporated this lesson in perseverance into the children's book *The Blue Spruce* (1999). Like the spruce, Holliswood endures, thanks to the community spirit of its residents.

Howard

When William Howard advertised his hotel as the "Coolest Place in Greater New York," he didn't mean it was hip. He was touting the nautical breezes and other benefits of the summertime waterfront hotel he built in 1899 to lure well-to-do city folks to his resort, which was based along Grassy Bay and Jamaica Bay in this southern section of Queens. Because of the bays and canals surrounding the resort and adjacent bungalows, the area came to be dubbed "Little Venice."

The grand Victorian Howard Hotel originally stood on a 2,000-foot-long pier at the end of what is now 98th Street. In 1907 a boardwalk and eighteen of the original rental cottages burned to the ground, but Howard rebuilt the area to become

Ramblersville, or Old Hamilton Beach, a tiny, quaint community at sea level, most of whose homes are set on stilts to avoid flooding. Another feature of Howard's resort—a casino—is now the site of Frank M. Charles Memorial

Can this be New York City? A canal in Hamilton Beach

Beach

Park, at 165th Avenue between Shellbank Basin and Hawtree Creek, which offers a sandy, peaceful retreat for locals.

The neighborhood generally known today as Howard Beach, which is divided by a canal, is inhabited predominantly by white residents, although there are some Hispanic, Asian, and African American residents as well, and it includes several other smaller communities. These smaller communities are surprisingly sheltered considering they are surrounded by—and accessible via—one of the busiest roads in Queens: the Belt Parkway, which runs across it in an east-west direction and is the main thoroughfare for John F. Kennedy International Airport.

In the southeast corner is the secluded fishing village of **Hamilton**

Beach (also called West Hamilton Beach), which sits on a narrow peninsula bordered by the airport to the east, 160th Avenue to the north, and Shellbank Basin to the west. High tides frequently cause flooding in this picturesque, rural community, which is accessible only via a narrow vehicle bridge and a pedestrian bridge. The small cottages here are set on narrow streets, with virtually no sidewalks; in fact, boardwalks link some homes to others because

LINDENWOOD

HOWARD BEACH

HAMILTON BEACH

SOUTH CONDUIT AVE
NORTH CONDUIT AVE
27
LINDEN BLVD
BLAKE AVE
DUMONT AVE
75 ST
76 ST
77 ST
80 ST
78 ST
149 AVE
151 AVE
151 AVE
83 ST
84 ST
85 ST
86 AVE
86 ST
88 ST
88 AVE
89 ST
90 ST
151 AVE
153 AVE
SOUTH CONDUIT AVE
NORTH CONDUIT AVE
BELT PKWY
155 AVE
151 AVE
153 AVE
155 AVE
155 AVE
156 AVE
SHORE PKWY
SHORE PKWY
156 AVE
157 AVE
KILLARNEY ST
LAHN ST
HURON ST
BRIDGETON ST
COHANCY ST
94 ST
95 ST
98 ST
84 ST
157 AVE
157 AVE
158 AVE
158 AVE
100 ST
101 ST
102 ST
103 RD
159 AVE
159 RD
COLEMAN SQ
ARSON BRIDGE ST
RUSSELL ST
CHURCH ST
158 AVE
159 AVE
160 AVE
160 AVE
161 AVE
95 ST
96 ST
97 ST
98 ST
99 ST
102 ST
BAYVIEW AVE
RUSSELL ST
103 RD
104 ST
JOHN F KENNEDY INTERNATIONAL AIRPORT
CROSS BAY BLVD
SHELLBANK BASIN
162 AVE
161 AVE
162 AVE
163 AVE
1ST ST
RAU CT
DAVENPORT CT
163 DR
164 AVE
164 RD
164 DR
165 AVE
HAWTREE CR
PARK
SPRING CREEK PARK
78 ST
79 ST
80 ST
81 ST
82 ST
83 ST
84 ST
86 ST
87 ST
88 ST
89 ST
90 ST
91 ST
92 ST
160 AVE
162 AVE
163 AVE
164 AVE
165 AVE
164 AVE
165 AVE
FRANK M CHARLES MEM PARK
GRASSY BAY
77 ST
78 ST
80 ST
156 AVE
157 AVE
SPRING CR
RALPH CR
OLD MILL CR
KINGS COUNTY
JAMAICA BAY
PUMPKIN PATCH CHANNEL
CONGRESSMAN JOSEPH P ADDABBO BRIDGE

• **Spring Creek Park**

The development of the busy Shore Parkway section of the Belt Parkway also led to the creation of another rural refuge tucked into the busy city: Spring Creek Park, a 62.2-acre salt marsh designed to combat pollution and provide a safe respite for wildfowl. The original land for the park was acquired as part of the parkway's initial development in 1938. Land has since been added to make it an expansive part of the Jamaica Bay ecosystem (which also includes Sparrow Marsh and Fresh Creek Park): in 1992, the New York Department of Real Property more than doubled the size of the park, with the southern portion (below 157th Avenue) contained in Queens, and in 1994 and 1995 two more parcels in Queens, on Fairfield Avenue, were included. Along with the larger Spring Creek Park Preserve, the park is part of the city's "Forever Wild" program, created to protect the city's most ecologically valuable land. In keeping with the wilderness of the surrounding area, the park has been left as mostly undeveloped marshland—an inviting habitat for the many great blue herons, egrets, red-winged blackbirds, pheasants, and mallards, as well as deer, raccoons, and muskrats, who make the area their home.

canals meander through the area. But the twenty-first century is slowly creeping in: this tight-knit village was delighted recently to get its first-ever city sewer system. Gravel roads have been paved as well. And after some forty years, new houses are going up, with developers eyeing the ample spaces between houses.

To the west is the area that people generally think of when they say "Howard Beach": a section of the neighborhood dominated by one- and two-family homes inhabited by mostly Italian and Jewish families. Just to the north of Shore Parkway is Rockwood Park, with expensive contemporary houses, and **Lindenwood,** which includes a cooperative complex built in 1952. A couple of years later, a subway line—the A train—was extended to the neighborhood, furthering development. Cross Bay Boulevard, which meets North Conduit Avenue, serves the entire area with a variety of shopping, services, and entertainment.

Residents of Howard Beach still grapple with the aftereffects of a 1986 tragedy in which twelve white teenagers armed with baseball bats attacked three African American youths whose car had broken down in this predominantly white neighborhood. One of the black youths was killed when he ran into oncoming traffic on the Belt Parkway. The racial incident outraged the city, and to many, Howard

NEIGHBORHOOD PROFILE

Boundaries: Howard Beach: north border: North Conduit Avenue; east border: John F. Kennedy International Airport; south border: Grassy Bay and Jamaica Bay; west border: Kings County line; Hamilton Beach: north border: 160th Avenue; east border: John F. Kennedy International Airport; south border: Grassy Bay; west border: Shellbank Basin; Lindenwood: north border: North Conduit Avenue; east border: Cross Bay Boulevard; south border: Belt Parkway; west border: Kings County line

Subway and Train: A train: Howard Beach; AirTrain: John F. Kennedy International Airport

Bus: B15: South Conduit Avenue; Q21: 157th Avenue to Cross Bay Boulevard; Q41: 157th Avenue to Cross Bay Boulevard to 84th Street; Q53: Cross Bay Boulevard; Q11: 102nd Street to 160th Avenue to 104th Street to 165th Avenue

Libraries: Queens Library, Howard Beach Branch (92-06 156th Avenue)

Community Board: No. 10

Police Precinct: 106th Precinct (103-51 101st Street, Ozone Park)

Fire Department: Engine 331, Ladder 173, Battalion 51 (158-57 Cross Bay Boulevard)

Hospitals and Clinics: Medisys Family Center (157-02 Cross Bay Boulevard)

NEIGHBORHOOD
F A C T S

■ Founded in 1928, the West Hamilton Beach Fire Department is an
all-volunteer fire company, one of
the few remaining in New York
City.

■ Developer William Howard's line
of work was leather manufacturing. When he purchased the original 37 acres of land on Hawtree
Creek, he also imported Angora
goats from Mexico, hoping to breed
them for his business. But it seems
that in 1903 a massive rainstorm
flooded Ramblersville, drowning
the poor goats (which in any event
had been having a hard time ad-
justing to the cold weather of
Queens).

■ The highest numbered avenue in
Queens, 165th Avenue, is located at
the southern end of Hamilton
Beach. Many streets in Howard
Beach—such as Rau Court, Davenport Court, 1st Street, and Bayview
Avenue—have not generally appeared on maps of the area. In
2004 the New Hamilton Beach
Civic Association initiated efforts
to get their streets onto the city
maps.

■ Folk legend Woody Guthrie once
lived in Howard Beach, and his
son, singer Arlo Guthrie, often
copyrights his songs with Howard
Beach Music.

Lindenwood Gardens, a cooperative complex built in the 1950s

Beach remains synonymous with racism, especially following another attack on black youths in 2005. Some Howard Beach residents consider this charge un-just—those familiar with the area claim that Hispanics, Asians, and African Americans reside here peacefully alongside their white neighbors—but the inci-dents have led the community to focus on education, especially of the young, and awareness. In 1988 a multiracial group, Concerned Citizens for South Queens, was formed, and local Howard Beach leaders held discussion groups and undertook other initiatives, such as holding seminars for the Howard Beach Little League on racial and reli-gious sensitivity, to ensure that such events became part of Howard Beach's past, not its future.

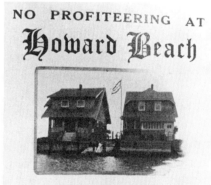

NO PROFITEERING AT

Howard Beach

Same prices are quoted to-day as in 1914
for choice Building Lots.

Buy a Home Site Now and Build
Next Spring.

LOTS $600, ON EASY TERMS.   16% DOWN, 1% MONTHLY
BUILDERS ON PREMISES
Howard Estates Development Company
Property Office: 51 CHAMBERS STREET
Phone 368 Richmond Hill   NEW YORK CITY

Although 1921 prices may have been "as low as in 1914," today choice lots at Howard Beach retail for $650,000 to $900,000 (Queens Library, Long Island Division, Illustra-tions Collection)

Jackson

Rows of two-family semi-attached homes, such as these on 89th Street, are flanked by apartment buildings on the avenues

Cravings for foods as different as Colombian plantains, Argentinean churros, and Indian kulfi can all be satisfied in Jackson Heights. This multiethnic community in northwestern Queens has long welcomed immigrants from such countries as Argentina, Mexico, Ecuador, Bangladesh, China, Pakistan, Colombia, and India—and embraced their contributions to the neighborhood's cuisine, music, and lively, eclectic spirit.

In the 1800s Jackson Heights was mostly farmland, part of Trains Meadow, a section of the town of Newtown, one of the original three Queens settlements. The area's transformation began in 1908, when a group of bankers and real estate developers known as the Queensboro Realty Company (or the Queensboro Corporation) purchased the land. A year later the Queensboro Bridge opened. By 1910 the syndicate, led by visionary Edward A. MacDougal, owned 350 acres of land, which it promptly began developing. But unlike other area neighborhoods, Jackson Heights was modeled after the Garden City movement of nineteenth-century England, according to which urban towns were planned around open, airy spaces, and were limited in size and density.

Jackson Heights became the nation's first "garden apartment" community. While semi-detached single- and two-family houses flanked the neighborhood's east-west borders, the buildings in the heart of the residential area, from 37th Avenue to Jackson Avenue (now Northern Boulevard), were constructed around the concept of com-

JACKSON HEIGHTS GREENMARKET

JACKSON HEIGHTS ART CLUB

NORTHERN BLVD

34 AVE

34 RD

JUNCTION BLVD

34 AVE

69 ST
70 ST
71 ST
72 ST
73 ST
74 ST
75 ST
76 ST
77 ST
78 ST
79 ST
80 ST
81 ST
82 ST
83 ST
84 ST
85 ST
86 ST
87 ST
88 ST
89 ST
90 ST
91 ST
92 ST
93 ST
94 ST
95 ST

35 AVE

35 AVE

37 AVE

JACKSON HEIGHTS

37 AVE

ELMHURST AVE

WARREN ST

LEVERICH ST

35 RD

71 ST
72 ST
74 ST
75 ST

37 AVE

37 RD

BROADWAY

ROOSEVELT AVE

Heights

munal gardens. Complete blocks were developed at once, with buildings set back from the street to allow for landscaping. Each structure offered ample sunlight and ventilation through numerous windows, and apartments faced interior court-yards complete with flowering gardens, sitting areas, and walkways. The build-ings, many designed with ornate architectural details, were given elegant names such as the Chateau, Cambridge Court, and the Towers.

The Queensboro Realty Company went even further to lure urban profes-sionals into the neighborhood: in addi-tion to churches and playgrounds, a golf course, tennis courts, and commu-nity clubhouse were created. Mean-while, Roosevelt Avenue was built to accommodate an extension of the In-terborough Rapid Transit (IRT) line, with four train stations (at 74th Street, 82nd Street, Elmhurst Avenue, and Junction Boulevard) facilitating a mere twenty-minute commute to Manhattan.

In the 1920s, Queensboro Realty in-troduced another innovative housing concept—the cooperative apartment, for which, at least in those years, "so-cial and business references" were re-quired for purchase. Jackson Heights boomed, especially when the Indepen-dent subway opened in 1933, opening the door for further transport to Man-hattan and other boroughs. During the Depression, only a few of the estab-

Day or night, Roosevelt Avenue is hopping

Queens Pride

Once a year, in June, Jackson Heights lets loose with a celebration of sexual diversity and community openness: the Queens Pride Parade. The event, which draws forty thousand participants and spectators, is an exuberant expression of personal freedom that steps off from the corner of 37th Avenue and 89th Street and is organized by the Queens Lesbian and Gay Pride Committee (which also coordinates a daylong multicultural festival following the parade).

Although the parade and festival are its main events, the group has many other outreach activities based in Jackson Heights and throughout the borough, as it seeks to "educate the public about the history of LGBT [lesbian, gay, bisexual, and transgendered] rights and create and support activities commemorating events of importance within the LGBT movement."

Like many communities in the United States, Jackson Heights has a painful history when it comes to gay rights. On July 2, 1990, Julio Rivera, a gay model, was murdered in the schoolyard of P.S. 69 in a vicious hate crime. The community rallied in support, and on April 17, 2000, New York City Mayor Rudy Giuliani officially named the southwest corner of 78th Street and 37th Avenue "Julio Rivera Corner" in memory of the tragic event. Today, Jackson Heights takes pride in its thriving homosexual, bisexual, and transgendered community.

lished co-ops failed, and developers who saw room for growth tore down the golf course and other open areas to make way for more buildings.

Even with the loss of some open space, MacDougal's vision of a green, urban community has proven resilient. Residents living in the original garden apartments of his era have maintained the grounds so that trees, shrubbery, flowerbeds, rose gardens, and fountains still flourish within the residential areas of Jackson Heights.

In the 1970s and 1980s, after many of the neighborhood's earliest citizens (who were generally of Eastern European descent) flocked to nearby suburbs, Jackson Heights became a haven for immigrants from other areas. Jackson Heights's diversity is apparent not only in the neighborhood's exotic culinary fare but also in its shopping and entertainment options. For instance, fans of Asian-Indian films can view the latest Bollywood hits at the Eagle Theater on 73rd Street. A visit to one of the area's retail hubs, 74th Street and 37th Avenue, may inspire the purchase of anything from ornate Indian jewelry to colorful silk saris. A stroll along the shops of Roosevelt Avenue and 82nd Street will delight the Latin music lover. And Junction Boulevard and

Looking down 82nd Street and 37th Avenue ca. 1942 (Queens Library, Long Island Division, Illustrations Collection)

96

English garden houses on 30th Street (now 87th Street), 1929
(Queens Library, Long Island Division, Illustrations Collection)

Landscaped garden of the Chateau Garden Apartments, 1928
(Queens Library, Long Island Division, Illustrations Collection)

37th Avenue, another commercial center, offers a wide array of clothing and home goods at bargain prices.

For a period during the 1970s and 1980s, Jackson Heights shared the problems of increased drug trafficking and other crimes that afflicted a number of Queens neighborhoods. This prompted concerned citizens to band together to reclaim their community. Among those neighborhood activists was Ralph Moreno, a Colombian immigrant who founded the Jackson Heights Action Group from an office in his home. Working closely with nearby police precincts and the Queens District Attorney's office, the group founded sports programs, graffiti-removal campaigns, and a civilian observation patrol. Such efforts have kept Jackson Heights a friendly, exciting place to live and visit.

Various forms of culture enliven the neighborhood as well. For more than fifty years, the Jackson Heights Art Club, located at 33-50 82nd Street, has been a center for the creative and visual arts, offering classes in a variety of media—in-

98 cluding oil, pastel, acrylic, watercolor, and pencil—for adults and children of all artistic levels. Every year, the club sponsors demonstrations by visiting artists, art workshops for public schools, a juried art show, outdoor shows, and exhibits at local banks and restaurants. In addition, folk musicians, blues and classical performers, poets, photographers, painters, and writers have the opportunity to be part

NEIGHBORHOOD FACTS

■ Jackson Heights was named after John C. Jackson, who built Jackson Avenue, now Northern Boulevard. The road opened in 1860 and was the only road in Queens to have milestone markers.

■ The Jackson Heights Greenmarket, which offers farm-fresh produce, is located at Travers Park, on 34th Avenue between 77th and 78th Streets. The market operates from July to October on Sundays between 10 A.M. and 3 P.M.

■ In 1931 Jackson Heights resident Alfred Mosher Butts created a word board game he called Lexico. In 1938 he applied for a patent for his game, renaming it Criss-Cross Words. In 1948 the game was trademarked as Scrabble. The neighborhood celebrates its famous homegrown game with a street sign featuring Scrabble "scoring": at the corner of 35th Avenue and 81st Street, the site of the Community Methodist Church where Butts perfected his idea, the letters of the sign are followed by small numbers, in a creative nod to America's second-favorite board game.

■ Radio personality and "shock jock" Howard Stern was born in Jackson Heights. So were actresses Mercedes Ruehl and Lucy Liu. Comedian and actor John Leguizamo grew up in Jackson Heights, as did actress Susan Sarandon. Jazz and Big Band greats Benny Goodman, Woody Herman, Mezz Mezzrow, Glenn Miller, and Charlie Spivak all once called Jackson Heights home. Betty Suarez, the fictional heroine of the popular television comedy *Ugly Betty* (premiered 2006), about the clash of cultures between Queens and Manhattan, also lives in Jackson Heights.

■ One of the pioneers of modern American cryptology, Herbert O. Yardley, once lived in the Chateau in Jackson Heights. Yardley became famous in 1931 after his memoir, *The American Black Chamber*, was published. In his bestselling book, which nearly caused him to be charged with treason, Yardley revealed his work with MI-8, the first U.S. peacetime cryptanalytic organization, funded by the U.S. Army and the Department of State.

The latest Bollywood film releases are featured at the Eagle Theater

These tennis courts, photographed in 1928, gave way to more development after the Depression (Queens Library, Long Island Division, Illustrations Collection)

of LACE—Local Art Collaborative Exchange, located at 33-47 91st Street. A project of the Jackson Heights Community Development Corporation, LACE serves as a network of visual and performing artists, arts groups, and cultural institutions devoted to expanding the role of the arts in Jackson Heights, Corona, and East Elmhurst.

But Jackson Heights is much more than a potpourri of cultural offerings—as of 1994, its thirty-six-block residential center is also a New York City landmark historic district, one of the city's largest. Credit for achieving the designation is given to the Jackson Heights Beautification Group, founded by residents in 1988 to combat graffiti and crime and to preserve the neighborhood's residential character, which is rich in history and innovative architecture.

NEIGHBORHOOD PROFILE

Boundaries: <u>North border:</u> Northern Boulevard; <u>east border:</u> Junction Boulevard; <u>south border:</u> Roosevelt Avenue; <u>west border:</u> Amtrak tracks to 69th Street

Subway and Train: <u>7 train:</u> 69th Street, 74th Street/Broadway, 82nd Street, 90th Street/Elmhurst Avenue; <u>R, G, V trains:</u> 74th Street/Broadway; <u>E, F trains:</u> 74th Street/Broadway

Bus: <u>Q66:</u> Northern Boulevard; <u>Q53:</u> Roosevelt Avenue; <u>Q32:</u> Roosevelt Avenue; <u>Q47:</u> 74th Street; <u>Q33:</u> 83rd Street to Roosevelt Avenue; <u>Q19B:</u> 35th Avenue; <u>Q72:</u> Junction Boulevard

Libraries: Queens Library, Jackson Heights Branch (35-51 81st Street)

Museums: Queens Museum of Art at the Bulova Corporate Center (75-20 Astoria Boulevard)

Theaters: The Yueh Lung Shadow Theatre (33-47 91st Street); The Jackson Heights Art Club and AARK Theatre at St. Mark's (33-50 82nd Street)

Community Board: No. 3

Police Precinct: 114th Precinct (34-16 Astoria Boulevard, Astoria); 115th Precinct (92-15 Northern Boulevard)

Fire Department: Engine 316, Battalion 49 (27-12 Kearny Street); Engine 307, Ladder 154 (81-17 Northern Boulevard)

Hospitals and Clinics: Regal Heights Rehabilitation and Health Care Center (70-05 35th Avenue); Jackson Heights Hospital, Division of Wyckoff Heights (34-01 73rd Street)

Jamaica

There is an air of promise and possibility in Jamaica today. Its revitalizing downtown, as well as the launch of a new electric-train service linking commuters to John F. Kennedy International Airport, has given a new lift to this neighborhood—one of the oldest in Queens, with a rich, diverse, and sometimes troubled history.

Jamaica was founded on grand expectations of prosperity. Back in 1655, English settlers from Hempstead, Long Island, established a town, which they called Rusdorf, in the area called Rustdorp, under a grant from Peter Stuyvesant. Eventually, the town came to be known as Jamaica, a name that may have derived from the Jameco, or Yamecah, Indians who first inhabited the area (*jameco* is the Algonquian word for "beaver"). Jamaica became the county seat when Queens County was formed in 1683; the county clerk's office is still here, as is the family court, surrogate court, and civil court,

and the New York State Supreme Court House. Back then the town served as a colonial trading post, and for decades thereafter its geographic centrality made it an ideal place for commerce, education, finance, government, entertainment, and transportation.

Indeed, transportation fueled much of this neighborhood's growth. In its earli-

The Spanish Baroque–style Loews Valencia (1929), once the largest movie theater in Queens, now houses the Tabernacle of Prayer

est days, Jamaica Avenue (first called Jamaica Plank Road) was a significant Indian trail and colonial road that stretched from Brooklyn to Long Island. Later, the opening of the Long Island Rail Road in 1836; the elevated line, which ran along Jamaica Avenue starting in 1918 (until it was removed in 1980); and the Independent subway, which opened in 1937, offered mass transit for residents throughout Queens and the outer boroughs hoping to conduct business and shop in Jamaica. Those who lived in **South Jamaica,** the residential area of mostly one- and two-family houses below the railroad tracks, also benefited from the substantial shopping available on Jamaica Avenue.

The commercial district didn't just thrive: it boomed. Among the banks and trust companies, rows and rows of retailers—including the Macy's and Gertz department stores, the Wallach's and Burden's clothing stores, and the "five-and-dime" store, Woolworth's—lined Jamaica Avenue and its side streets. And it was here that Michael J. Cullen leased a vacant garage and in 1930 turned it into America's first supermarket, King Kullen Grocery Company.

With commerce came more development, including the area called **Baisley Park** (also known as Southside), which was developed as a residential community in the 1920s and named

NEIGHBORHOOD PROFILE

Boundaries: Jamaica: north border: Hillside Avenue; east border: 180th Street to 180 Place to 93rd Avenue to 183rd Street to Dunkirk Street to 110th Avenue to 178th Street to 109th Avenue to Merrick Boulevard to Baisley Boulevard to Irwin Place to Roe Road to 120th Avenue to Long Island Rail Road tracks to 121st Avenue to Farmers Boulevard; south border: North Conduit Avenue to 150th Street to Rockaway Boulevard; west border: Van Wyck Expressway; South Jamaica: north border: Long Island Rail Road tracks; east border: 183rd Street to Dunkirk Avenue to 110th Avenue to 178th Street to 109th Avenue to Merrick Boulevard; south border: Baisley Boulevard to Guy R. Brewer Boulevard to Linden Boulevard to Sutphin Boulevard to Rockaway Boulevard; west border: Van Wyck Expressway; Baisley Park: north border: Linden Boulevard; east border: Guy R. Brewer Boulevard; south border: Baisley Boulevard; west border: Rockaway Boulevard to Sutphin Boulevard; Rochdale Village: north border: Baisley Boulevard; east border: Bedell Street to 134th Road to 173rd Street; south border: 137th Avenue; west border: Guy R. Brewer Boulevard; Locust Manor: north border: Baisley Boulevard to Irwin Place to Roe Road to 120th Avenue; east border: Long Island Rail Road tracks to 121st Avenue to Farmers Boulevard; south border: North Conduit Avenue; west border: Guy R. Brewer Boulevard to 137th Avenue to 173rd Street to 134th Road to Bedell Street

Subway and Train: F train: Sutphin Boulevard, Parsons Boulevard, 169th Street, 179th Street; E train: Jamaica/Van Wyck Expressway; E, J, Z trains: Sutphin Boulevard/Archer Avenue; LIRR: Jamaica; AirTrain: John F. Kennedy International Airport

Bus: 165th Street Terminal: Q1, Q2, Q75, Q76, Q17, Q3, Q36, Q77, Q6, Q8, Q9, Q9A, x32, Q41, N1, N2, N3, N6, N22, N22A, N24, N26; Q111: Guy R. Brewer Boulevard; Q112: Guy R. Brewer Boulevard/South Road; Q113: Guy R. Brewer Boulevard; Q85: Liberty Avenue/Archer Avenue/Bedell Street; Q3: Farmers Boulevard; Q6: Merrick Boulevard/Jamaica Avenue/Archer Avenue/Sutphin Boulevard/Rockaway Boulevard; Q8: Merrick Boulevard/Jamaica Avenue/Archer Avenue; Q9: Merrick Boulevard/Jamaica Avenue/Archer Avenue; Q41: Merrick Boulevard/Jamaica Avenue/Archer Avenue; N4: Archer Avenue/Merrick Boulevard; Q4: Liberty Avenue/Archer Avenue/Merrick Boulevard/Linden Boulevard; Q5: Liberty Avenue/Archer Avenue/Merrick Boulevard; x63: Merrick Boulevard; Q84: Archer Avenue/Linden Boulevard/Merrick Boulevard; Q9A: 168th Street/Linden Boulevard/Merrick Boulevard; Q75: 188th Street; Q17: 188th Street/Hillside Avenue; x32: 188th Street; Q110: Jamaica Avenue; Q83: 150th Street/Liberty Avenue; x64: Farmers Boulevard/Liberty Avenue; Q43: Hillside Avenue; Q1: Hillside Avenue; x68: Hillside Avenue; N22A: Hillside Avenue; N26: Hillside Avenue; Q22: Hillside Avenue; Q40: 142nd Street; Q30: 169th Street/Archer Avenue; Q31: 169th Street/Archer Avenue; Q25: Parsons Boulevard; Q34: Parsons Boulevard

Libraries: Queens Library, Central Library (89-11 Merrick Boulevard); Baisley Park Branch (117-11 Sutphin Boulevard); Rochdale Branch (169-09 137th Avenue); South Jamaica Branch (108-41 Guy R. Brewer Boulevard)

Museums: King Manor Museum (151-01 Jamaica Avenue); Queens Library Gallery (89-11 Merrick Boulevard); Jamaica Center for Arts and Learning (161-04 Jamaica Avenue); Independent Arts Gallery (140-40 Jamaica Avenue); York College Jazz Museum and Archive (94-20 Guy R. Brewer Boulevard); Dinizulu Center for Culture and Research (115-62 Sutphin Boulevard)

Theaters: The Afrikan Poetry Theatre (176-03 Jamaica Avenue)

Community Board: No. 12

Police Precinct: 103rd Precinct (168-02 P.O. Edward Byrne [91st] Avenue); 113th Precinct (167-02 Baisley Boulevard)

Fire Department: Engine 275, Battalion 50 (111-36 Merrick Boulevard); Engine 298, Ladder 127, Battalion 50 (153-11 Hillside Avenue); Engine 315, Battalion 50 (159-06 Union Turnpike)

Hospitals and Clinics: St. Vincent's Catholic Medical Center's Mary Immaculate Hospital (152-11 89th Avenue); Jamaica Hospital Medical Center (8900 Van Wyck Expressway); Charles R. Drew Center (166-10 Archer Avenue); Queens Health Network Medical Center (90-73 Parsons Boulevard); Catholic Medical Center of Queens (88-25 153rd Street); Monsignor Fitzpatrick Skilled Nursing Pavilion (152-11 89th Avenue); Medisys Family Center (90-16 Sutphin Boulevard)

Soldiers and Sailors Monument (1896) by Frederick Wellington Ruckstuhl at Major Mark Park, Hillside Avenue (Sonia S. Estreich)

after David Baisley, a farmer who owned and operated a local grain mill powered by the pond he and other farmers created. Single-family homes are in easy walking distance of shops, services, and Baisley Pond Park, which offers a quiet refuge in this busy neighborhood and an important natural habitat for turtles, bullfrogs, waterfowl, and eight varieties of dragonfly.

As Jamaica grew, a number of important institutions were established in the area. Union Hall Academy, founded in 1792, was the third academic building on Long Island and for many years one of the leading schools in the area; it opened a female seminary in 1834. Although the school no longer exists, the 1820 building on Union Hall Street still stands. The *Long Island Farmer*, the first newspaper in Queens, published its first issue on January 4, 1821, from Jamaica. The weekly newspaper eventually became a daily, and in 1920 it became the *Long Island Daily Press* (shortened to the *Long Island Press* in the 1960s). The paper ended its 156-year run when it closed in 1977. Jamaica Hospital Medical Center, on the Jamaica–Richmond Hill border at 8900 Van Wyck Expressway, was

George Washington slept here: Pettit's Hotel in 1905 (Queens Library, Long Island Division, Illustrations Collection)

Jamaica Avenue near 163rd Street

founded in 1891 and continues to serve the surrounding neighborhoods. The Central Library of the Queens Library system opened in 1930 at 89-11 Merrick Boulevard. The building has been renovated and enlarged several times, most recently in 1989. Now the largest unit of the Queens Library, the Central Library offers the most public services on a single floor of any library in the three New York City library systems.

Among its recent additions is the Cyber Center, opened in 1999, which has forty-eight workstations for library patrons. The library's Long Island Room has an extensive collection of archival photographs, several of which were used for this book.

For sport, the Jamaica Race Track, which had opened in 1903, provided thoroughbred racing until it was torn down in 1960 (see Ozone Park). Three years later **Rochdale Village** was constructed in its place. A massive, middle-class cooperative apartment complex with twenty fourteen-story buildings, Rochdale Village is neighbored to the south and east by a quiet residential area called **Locust Manor.** A Long Island Rail Road station here takes commuters into Manhattan in about twenty-five minutes.

Entertainment was also provided by an abundance of movie houses, among them the Spanish-palatial-style Loews Valencia Theatre (165-11 Jamaica Avenue), built in 1929. The largest theater in the borough, with seating for more than 3,500 film lovers, the Valencia still stands but since 1977 has been home to

NEIGHBORHOOD FACTS

■ In the mid-nineteenth century when Brooklyn city workers began dredging Baisley Pond, which the Brooklyn Water Works had recently acquired for the city water supply, they made an unusual discovery: the remains of a ten-thousand-year-old American mastodon (*Mammut americanum*), a large, elephant-like herbivore. After Brooklyn became part of the consolidated New York City, the pond and surrounding Baisley Pond Park, where a sculpture of a mastodon commemorates the find, were given to the city.

■ Pettit's Hotel, formerly known as Queen's Head, had an important overnight visitor—George Washington—in 1790. It also was a vital gathering place for those deciding in 1872 where to put the new Queens Courthouse, a critical seat of power for the borough (Long Island City won the 4–2 vote). The hotel was demolished in 1906.

■ Prospect Cemetery, on 158th Street between Liberty and Archer Avenues, is the oldest in Queens, founded in 1668. Fifty-three veterans of the Revolution and forty-three Civil War veterans are buried there, as well as members of prominent early Queens families like the Lefferts, Sutphins, and Baisleys. Designated a New York City landmark in 1977, the privately owned cemetery is maintained by the Prospect Cemetery Association, which is currently renovating the cemetery's Chapel of the Three Sisters (1853), the gift of Nicholas Ludlum, who named it for his three daughters who had died in childhood. Egbert Benson, an early American patriot, abolitionist, and New York State attorney general, is also buried there. (Another early patriot, Melancton Smith, a Jamaica resident and delegate to the Continental Congress of 1785–87, is buried in Jamaica Cemetery.)

■ Former New York governor Mario Cuomo's parents, Italian immigrants, lived in South Jamaica for a time. Curtis Jackson—better known as rapper megastar 50 Cent—also hails from that area.

the Tabernacle of Prayer for All People, one of the variety of churches that have been serving Jamaica's spiritual life since its founding. The First Presbyterian Church, on 164th Street, was organized in 1662; it may be the oldest continuous Presbyterian congregation in the United States (the current building is around the corner from the original structure). The oldest Episcopal congregation can be found at Grace Church, founded in 1702. The Gothic Revival–style structure on Jamaica Avenue, the third building since the church's founding, was built in 1862. And the 1858 Romanesque Revival–style First Reformed Church of Jamaica, also on Jamaica Avenue, is a New York City landmark. Vacant since the

1980s, this structure will soon be home to the Jamaica Arts and Business Center, part of Cultural Collaborative Jamaica, a not-for-profit partnership of leading arts, cultural, educational, and business organizations in the neighborhood.

The first black church in Jamaica, the Greater Allen African Methodist Episcopal Cathedral of New York, was established in 1834. It is located at 110-31 Merrick Boulevard, and former U.S. Congressman the Reverend Dr. Floyd H. Flake leads its more than 18,400 members in devotional services. That this venerable African American congregation was able to flourish in Jamaica is due in part to the area's distinguished history of civil rights leadership. Rufus King, one of the signers of the Constitution, was an ardent opponent of slavery who served as a U.S. senator for nineteen years and as ambassador to England for ten. King lived in Jamaica from 1805 until his death in 1827. (He is buried at Grace Church Cemetery.) King's son John continued King's abolition work in the New York State Assembly and Senate, in the U.S. Congress, and as governor of New York. Their home, King Manor, at 151-01 Jamaica Avenue, has been a museum since 1900. Built around 1733, with additions in 1806 and thereafter, the 11-acre King Manor Museum, a New York City landmark, reopened to the public in 1992 after major restoration work.

Long before the official civil rights movement, Elizabeth Cisco, an African

American woman living in Jamaica, led an important and successful effort to give young black people a fairer education. Thanks to the work of Cisco and like-minded thinkers, in 1900 a New York State law was passed outlawing separate public schools for blacks; as a result, "colored" public schools in Flushing and Jamaica were abolished.

The work begun by King and continued by Cisco and others finds expression today in organizations like the Center for Culture's Afrikan Poetry Theatre, located at 176-03 Jamaica Avenue, which provides a wide range of cultural, educational, recreational, and social programs for anyone interested in African culture; and the Dinizulu Center for Culture and Research, at 115-62 Sutphin Boulevard, which sponsors the Dinizulu Dancers, Drummers, and Singers and the African Diaspora Children's Museum, an interactive museum designed to increase African American children's awareness of their African roots and global African family.

The AirTrain at Jamaica station

By the 1960s, Jamaica had become home to the largest concentration of African Americans in Queens, due in part to a major population shift that began after World War II, when a large proportion of the German, Italian, Irish, and Jewish residents moved out to the newly developed suburbs. Later, immigrants from Guyana, India, the Caribbean, and Latin America settled in the neighborhood.

Retailers also changed in the postwar years. As suburban shopping malls became increasingly popular with consumers, long-established businesses like Macy's ceased operations, leading to unemployment and economic depression. And as Jamaica's appeal as a business and merchant hub dissipated, the neighborhood became associated with crime. In response, neighborhood coalitions developed, such as the Dunton Block and Civic Association, to keep the areas safe for residents, with tenant patrols and other initiatives that are closely coordinated with the local police precinct.

Downtown Jamaica today is experiencing a dramatic revitalization, one that will benefit the entire area. True, the AirTrain was built under certain controversy, with neighborhood residents fearing noise pollution, property damage during construction, and a loss in property values. But grand plans for Jamaica are under way, and for many Jamaica residents, such plans are welcome.

The Greater Jamaica Development Corporation (GJDC), founded in 1967, is one of the major organizations encouraging thoughtful development. One of GJDC's first projects was bringing York College to Jamaica in 1971, scattered first among a number of neighborhood properties and then, in 1986, established at its current site on the south side of the Long Island Rail Road tracks on Guy R. Brewer Boulevard. Although York maintains a liberal arts emphasis, it is unique in the City University of New York system in its partnership with the U.S. Food and Drug Administration, which opened its Northeast Regional Laboratory there and offers internships to students.

Another early GJDC project was the 1974 opening of the Jamaica Center for Arts and Learning, set in the old Registry building at 161-04 Jamaica Avenue, a New York City landmark. The nonprofit center promotes ethnic and cultural education in the arts and humanities through workshops, performances, and exhibits. The GJDC was

The Supreme Court House in 1940, a year after it was dedicated by Mayor Fiorello La Guardia (Queens Library, Long Island Division, Illustrations Collection)

also instrumental in the creation of Jamaica Market, which opened in 1992, and in the construction of the fifteen-screen Multiplex Cinema (159-02 Jamaica Avenue), which has been entertaining movie buffs since 2002. In addition, the organization has successfully lobbied for the establishment of BIDs (Business Improvement Districts), in which commercial property owners pay into a common fund for improvements such as graffiti removal, sanitation, storefront upgrades, holiday lights, flower plantings, and store promotions. There are four in Jamaica today, the latest on Sutphin Boulevard, where the neo-Classic Supreme Court House stands and where the AirTrain is situated.

The award-winning Jamaica Market, located at Parsons Boulevard and 160th Street, has been honored twice by the American Institute of Architects for its building design. The colorful and innovative shopping center has launched many thriving small businesses. Several of the current vendors within the market actually began by selling their wares from carts, eventually expanding to storefront operations with the help of the GJDC. Vendors, all of them Queens-based, range from independently owned delis and restaurants to flower shops, gift stands, and ethnic arts and crafts. The market is an attraction and convenient shopping center for the downtown Jamaica community during weekdays. And on many warm weekends, visitors and locals are treated to an outdoor Farmer's Market, with fresh produce from Long Island, upstate New York, and New Jersey. A Harvest Festival takes place every October.

Today more positive changes are on the way in Jamaica, including a proposed "airport village"—complete with hotels, office complexes, housing, restaurants, and retailers. After a long and sometimes difficult history, residents of Jamaica can point with pride to the imminent return of their neighborhood's former luster.

King Manor was the home of two of Jamaica's great statesmen and abolitionists, founding father Rufus King and his son John King, a governor of New York

Jamaica

Residents of Jamaica Estates have always been protective of their community, and for good reason: all want to preserve the gorgeous homes that preside over its rolling, landscaped lawns and the stately oak and maple trees that grace its picturesque residential streets. This refined neighborhood, developed to resemble the hilly, wooded villages of England, stands today as a wonderful example of how neighbors who stay involved can keep the best features of their communities thriving while welcoming newcomers.

Jamaica Estates was developed around 1908 as an affluent retreat, complete with a stone gatehouse (which still stands) greeting visitors and residents on Midland Parkway and Hillside Avenue; and almost from the neighborhood's establishment highly active community groups—in particular, the Jamaica Estates Association, created in 1929, and the Committee for the Preservation of Jamaica Estates, founded in 2004—have worked diligently to maintain its pristine character, which features single-family homes with a few apartment buildings, located mainly along the outskirts, on Hillside Avenue. Even the Grand Central Parkway, which runs through the neighborhood, is heavily landscaped so that it blends with the lush greenery of the community. This east-central Queens neighborhood, which is home to mostly white, Asian, African American, and Hispanic residents, is considered prestigious not only because of its fine houses. Many of the people who live here are high-level white-collar professionals such as real estate mogul Fred Trump, whose son "the Donald" grew up here.

Jamaica Estates is also a college

NEIGHBORHOOD PROFILE

Boundaries: North border: Union Turnpike; east border: 188th Street; south border: Hillside Avenue; west border: Home Lawn Street to Utopia Parkway to 82nd Avenue across St. John's University to 170th Street
Subway and Train: F train: Jamaica and 179th Street and Hillside Avenue
Bus: Q46: Union Turnpike; Q30, Q31: Home Lawn Street; Q75, Q17, x32: 188th Street; Q43, Q44, x68: Hillside Avenue
Theaters: Bukharian Jewish Theatre (Vozrozhdenie) (179-30 80th Road)
Community Board: No. 8
Police Precinct: 107th Precinct (71-01 Parsons Boulevard, Flushing)
Fire Department: Engine 315, Battalion 50 (159-06 Union Turnpike, Jamaica Hills)
Hospitals and Clinics: Jamaica Hospital Medical Center Advanced Center for Psychotherapy (178-10 Wexford Terrace)

Estates

town. The Queens campus of the Roman Catholic St. John's University was built in 1956 on the former site of the Hillcrest Golf Club at 8000 Utopia Parkway, in the northwestern corner of the neighborhood. When applications to St. John's University surged from 7,500 in 1998 to 20,500 in 2005, the university added six residence halls to accommodate its growing student body. Another academic institution here is the private United Nations International School on

Beautiful homes grace Utopia Parkway near St. John's University

St. John's University

NEIGHBORHOOD
FACTS

■ The Chung Cheng Art Gallery, at the Center for Asian Studies in St. John's University, features a thousand-piece collection of Chinese artifacts, including paintings, porcelains, and photos. The gallery was named in 1977 after Chiang Kai-shek (Chiang Chung-cheng), president of the Chinese Nationalist government.

■ One of the early developers of Jamaica Estates was Michael J. Degnon, a contractor who helped build municipal subways and tunnels. His own mansion was set on a 12-acre tract between Edgerton Boulevard and Midland Parkway. In 1925, the property was purchased by Roman Catholic Passionist monks, who expanded the house so that it could become the Roman Catholic Bishop Molloy Retreat House. The Passionists also staff the Immaculate Conception Church and School on Dalny Road.

Croydon Road, serving students from kindergarten through eighth grade. In addition, the neighborhood offers several religious schools, including the all-girl Catholic high school Mary Louise Academy on Wexford Terrace and the Immaculate Conception School on Dalny Road.

Shopping in Jamaica Estates is convenient and plentiful thanks to a commercial center built in 2003 just a block from St. John's University, at the southeast corner of Union Turnpike and Utopia Parkway. A pleasant hang-out for students and neighborhood residents alike, the complex features national chains as well as local retailers.

A thriving Jewish population lives in Jamaica Estates, although owing to declining membership at the Conservative Synagogue of Jamaica Estates the congregation combined with other nearby synagogues in 2004 to form the Israel Center of Conservative Judaism,

One of the few apartment buildings in Jamaica Estates, on Utopia Parkway

Wexford Terrace off Midland Parkway today (Sonia S. Estreich)

whose temple is based in Flushing. But Young Israel of Jamaica Estates, an Orthodox youth group, is still located at 83-10 188th Street. And the neighborhood is unique in being the headquarters for Congregation Bene Naharayim, at 85-34 Midland Parkway, which serves Iraqi Jews, originally of Babylonian descent. There are an estimated six thousand Iraqi Jews in the tri-state area today, compared to the fewer than one hundred estimated to be still living in Iraq. Thousands of Iraqi Jews fled to Israel and the United States because of the oppressive regime, and more than four hundred of them now belong to Bene Naharayim, which in 1983 found a home in Jamaica Estates.

Wexford Terrace off Midland Parkway, 1910–30 (Queens Library, Long Island Division, Illustrations Collection)

Jamaica

Along the hilly side of a terminal moraine that extends the length of Long Island and divides northern from southern Queens lies Jamaica Hills (or Hill; both names are common), a community prized for its top schools, ethnic diversity, and beautiful Tilly Park. This neighborhood of mainly one- and two-family houses is proudly called home by residents of many backgrounds, including Bangladeshis, Guyanese, Haitians, South Americans, African Americans, and Chinese.

Now a haven for the middle class, the neighborhood was at first a retreat for well-to-do residents who delighted in the expansive views. Mansions sprang up in the early 1900s, and the neighborhood was somewhat secluded until the arrival in 1913 of the Long Island Rail Road. With the advent of mass transit came the development in the 1920s and 1930s of today's middle-class homes. The 1970s brought an influx of residents from many nations and faiths, including a growing number of Islamic families, who celebrate their faith at the Jamaica Muslim Center, founded in 1976, one of the oldest mosques in New York City. Headquartered at 85-37 168th Street since 1985, the center has further expanded

NEIGHBORHOOD PROFILE

Boundaries: <u>North border:</u> Union Turnpike; <u>east border:</u> 170th Street along St. John's University to 82nd Avenue to Home Lawn Street; <u>south border:</u> Hillside Avenue; <u>west border:</u> Parsons Boulevard
Subway and Train: <u>F train:</u> Parsons Boulevard, 169th Street
Bus: <u>Q25:</u> Parsons Boulevard; <u>Q34:</u> Parsons Boulevard; <u>Q46:</u> Union Turnpike; <u>Q30, Q31:</u> Home Lawn Street; <u>Q65:</u> 164th Street; <u>Q43, Q44, x68:</u> Hillside Avenue
Community Board: No. 8
Police Precinct: 107th Precinct (71-01 Parsons Boulevard, Flushing)
Fire Department: Engine 315, Battalion 50 (159-06 Union Turnpike)
Hospitals and Clinics: Queens Hospital Center (82-70 164th Street)

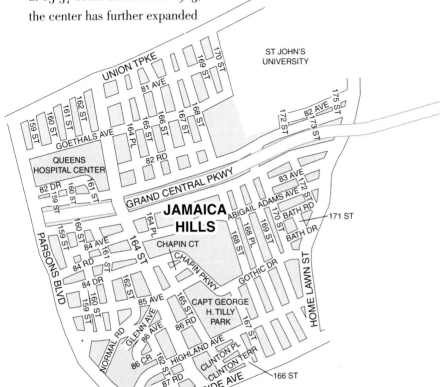

Hills

to include neighboring structures, and now accommodates some 2,000 worshipers.

Most of the early mansions are gone, but residents are dedicated to retaining the ambience of today's Jamaica Hills. Like other Queens neighborhoods, this area could easily fall prey to developers who demolish single-family houses and replace them with multiple dwellings. Activists fearful of losing their neighborhood's character to overcrowded schools and thinly stretched public services have worked to rezone most of Jamaica Hills from five zones to two, to ensure the stability of the one- and two-family detached houses that currently exist, as well as to limit future development.

Residents are equally protective about Captain George H. Tilly Park, one of Jamaica Hills's most valuable assets, and its centerpiece, Goose Pond. The 9-acre park on 165th Street between Highland Avenue and 85th Avenue was built on property long ago owned by the prominent Tilly family. By the early 1900s, the park belonged to the Highland Park Society, made up of several Jamaica landowners who raised geese and ducks there. The so-

Small stores along 164th Street

ciety deeded the site to New York City in 1908 for a dollar, under an agreement that it would thereafter remain a park. Today children romp on the playground facilities while nearby Jamaica High School students hang out after school. And older residents frequent the park to socialize with neighbors and attend concerts and other events.

Goose Pond, always a point of interest in the park, was once a haven for recreational fishing, toy boating, and ice skating. It lost its appeal around 1995 when the springs that fed the pond dried up and the water became clouded with algae. But in 1998, a large-scale renovation was undertaken: the pond was excavated and deepened, a clay liner and filtration system were installed, a well was dug, an island was placed in the middle of the pond as a refuge for wildlife, and the playground was expanded. New plantings and sod were also installed in the park, giving new life to a treasured recreational area.

NEIGHBORHOOD FACTS

■ Joseph Austin Playground, adjoining Thomas A. Edison Vocational and Technical High School, is a 4-acre park named after a longtime youth sports coach who was active in the community. Austin's most famous baseball apprentice was perhaps the young Mario Cuomo, who played from age eight until he was a teenager and then went on to the Pittsburgh Pirates as a minor leaguer. Cuomo dropped out of the team after one year to marry and pursue a political career.

■ Public School 131 on 84th Avenue (Abigail Adams Avenue) between 170th and 172nd Streets boasts some 800 students of 100 nationalities who collectively speak 40 languages.

Jamaica Hills residents also take pride in their three public high schools: Hillcrest High School, at 160-05 Highland Avenue, is the recipient of a Blue Ribbon School of Excellence Award from the State Department of Education; Thomas A. Edison Vocational and Technical High School, at 165-65 84th Avenue, is unusual for offering both high-level vocational training (teams from Edison consistently perform well in New York City's annual auto repair competitions) and college preparatory education; and the imposing Jamaica High School at 167-01 Gothic Drive, founded in 1892 (the current building was built in 1927), boasts a roster of famous alumni, including directors Josef von Sternberg and Francis Ford Coppola, composers Gunther Schuller and Paul Bowles, humorist Art Buchwald, science writer Stephen Jay Gould, and Olympic

Queens Hospital Center

Neat rows of attached brick homes on 84th Road

champion Bob Beamon, the first man to surpass 29 feet in the long jump.

Kew

Kew Gardens is a place where the old blends gracefully with the new. In this beautiful neighborhood, grand historical buildings fit well next to newer architectural achievements and families descended from early immigrants mingle easily with more recent arrivals.

The development of Kew Gardens was spurred by the 1875 establishment of the not-for-profit, nonsectarian Maple Grove Cemetery, which covers 65 pastoral acres on the northeast section of the neighborhood. With its lush, well-maintained grounds, the cemetery—entered at 83-15 Kew Gardens Road—is a peaceful place of remembrance for visitors coming to tend the 80,000 gravesites. In order to provide easier access to the cemetery, the Hopedale Long Island Rail Road station, situated along Union Turnpike and what is today Queens Boulevard, was opened around 1880.

Eventually the railroad added a ground-level station on Lefferts Boulevard. The tracks leading to and from the station cut through the Richmond Hill Golf Club, which had been built by the heirs of Albon P. Man (who developed neighboring Richmond Hill). But Man's heirs approved of the rail-

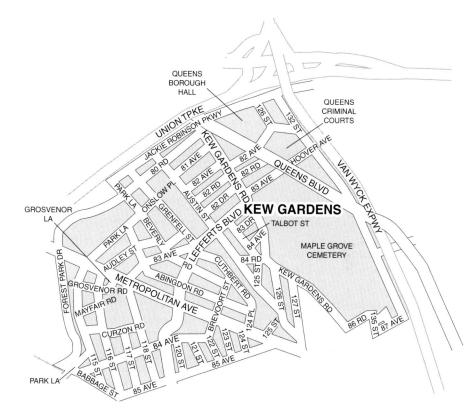

road station, believing that it would spur growth. Sure enough, with it a new community was born—Kew Gardens, named for the Royal Botanical Gardens in Kew, England.

In addition to impressive houses, numerous apartment buildings sprang up. The first was the Kew Bolmer on Kew Gardens Road, erected in 1915. Colonial Hall was built in 1921, followed by Kew Hall a year later. By 1936 there were more than twenty such apartment buildings. Newly developed parkways such as the Grand Central,

Gardens

NEIGHBORHOOD FACTS

■ As Jacob Cohen, Rodney Dangerfield grew up over a bar on Austin Street near Lefferts Boulevard. The Cohen family, living beyond their means in this affluent neighborhood, took in boarders, even though they lived in only a three-room apartment. But Dangerfield had the last laugh, earning as a stand-up comic the financial success that eluded his family—although he continued to complain that he "got no respect."

■ *Civic Virtue*, a statue at Queens Borough Hall sculpted by Frederick MacMonnies in 1922, stands at 17 feet and weighs 10 tons. The statue was originally placed in front of City Hall in Manhattan, but because Mayor Fiorello La Guardia didn't like the image of the unclothed mythological warrior with two nude female figures at his feet—and it caused controversy—he gave it to Queens County in 1941, in honor of the grand opening of the new Borough Hall.

■ Kew Gardens has been called home by Will Rogers, George Gershwin, Dorothy Parker, and Burt Bacharach.

■ Vintage photographs comparing changes in neighborhood houses and streets can be viewed on the Internet at www.oldkewgardens .com. The Web site, originally created by attorney Joseph De May, contains a vast array of photos and old postcards donated by Kew Gardens residents, past and present.

and the opening of the Independent subway line on Queens Boulevard, prompted a steady interest in Kew Gardens as a superb residential neighborhood, stimulating a great deal of construction in this area, which became heavily populated by Jewish German immigrants during World War II.

Kew Gardens is today the site of Queens Borough Hall and the Queens Criminal Courts, both on Queens Boulevard (neighboring Jamaica is the Queens County seat). But these official structures are not the only attractions for those who admire grand historical buildings: many stately English- and Neo-Tudor homes still grace the neighborhood. As a testament to their significance, architectural historian Barry Lewis, a Kew Gardens native famous for his televised walking tours of New York City, wrote *Kew Gardens: Urban Village in the Big City* (1999). The book is an illustrated historic overview of the neighborhood's fine residences, which are protected in part by efforts of the Kew Gardens Improvement Association, a state-chartered, tax-exempt organization founded in 1970. Excellent examples of fine architecture can be found along the eastern portion of Forest Park Road and on Park Lane at Curzon Road, Mayfair Road, and Grosvenor Road, where about a dozen charming houses on each block sit on uphill slopes. The Arts and Crafts–style house that formerly belonged to Charlie Chaplin is located on Mowbray Drive (82nd Drive). Another famous former resident is Ralph Bunche, win-

Civic Virtue was donated to Queens after causing a controversy in Manhattan

ner of the 1950 Nobel Peace Prize, who lived here until his death in 1971 at the national historical landmarked house at 115-25 Grosvenor Road.

The apartment building at 82-70 Austin Street became the focus of far different attention on March 13, 1964, when twenty-eight-year-old Catherine (Kitty) Genovese was stabbed to death there, and it was widely reported that although she cried for help none of the thirty-eight residents purportedly within earshot came to her aid or even called the police. The event sparked not only citywide but national and international outrage, stemming from deep concern over growing urban apathy. Although questions have been raised about how much the residents

Shops along Lefferts Boulevard at Austin Street

Airport and John F. Kennedy International Airport. Neighborhood residents have plenty of restaurants, services, and entertainment options here, as well as ample shopping on Queens Boulevard and in clusters of neighborhood stores on Lefferts Boulevard, Metropolitan Avenue, Union Turnpike, and Austin Street.

actually saw or heard, the case did lead psychologists to investigate what became known as bystander effect. In addition, the tragedy spurred the New York Police Department to overhaul its inefficient telephone reporting system, and residents began to organize Neighborhood Watch programs as a way of protecting their neighbors.

Kew Gardens still has a high concentration of Jewish families, and today more often than not they are Orthodox Jews. In the late 1970s, Iranian Jews also settled here, and since then a mix of other ethnic groups and nationalities have joined the Kew Gardens community, among them Israelis, Chinese, Indians, and Koreans. This neighborhood has also been dubbed "Crew Gardens" because it has attracted a vast number of airline personnel employed at nearby La Guardia

NEIGHBORHOOD PROFILE

Boundaries: <u>North border</u>: Union Turnpike; <u>east border</u>: Van Wyck Expressway; <u>south border</u>: 87th Avenue to 135th Street to 86th Road to Kew Gardens Road to 127th Street to Metropolitan Avenue to 85th Avenue; <u>west border</u>: Babbage Street along Long Island Rail Road to Forest Park Drive to Park Lane

Subway and Train: <u>E, F trains</u>: Union Turnpike and Queens Boulevard; <u>LIRR</u>: Kew Gardens

Bus: <u>Q10A, x63, x64</u>: Queens Boulevard to Van Wyck Expressway; <u>Q54</u>: Metropolitan Avenue; <u>Q10</u>: Lefferts Boulevard; <u>Q37</u>: Park Lane South

Community Board: No. 9

Police Precinct: 102nd Precinct (87-34 118th Street, Richmond Hill)

Fire Department: Engine 305, Ladder 151 (111-02 Queens Boulevard, Forest Hills)

These Kew Gardens houses date from the mid-1900s

Kew Gardens

Saturdays are tranquil in Kew Gardens Hills. Because its population is predominantly Orthodox Jewish, this community, with its grand views of Flushing Meadows–Corona Park and easy access to cultural offerings at Queens College, pauses to observe the weekly Sabbath.

Kew Gardens Hills was mostly rural, and until the 1920s, when it was called Queens Valley, it was the site of a number of beautiful golf courses, including the Queens Valley, Arrowbrook, and Pomonok clubs. That changed in the 1930s when the Independent subway line came to town, the Grand Central Parkway first connected the Kew Gardens interchange to the Triborough Bridge, and the World's Fair drew attention to the area. A flurry of residential development ensued, led by the Wolosoff brothers, developers in Kew Gardens and Forest Hills. German, Irish, and Italian families flocked to Kew Gardens Hills, which the Wolosoffs named in part after their other successful housing ventures.

In the 1960s Orthodox Jewish families began moving into the area. Orthodox families tend to be large, so single-family homes with many bedrooms had great appeal. (In recent years some tension has developed among those wishing to expand their homes to accommodate more children and neighbors hoping to preserve the look and feel of the community.) But garden apartments such as Hyde Park Gardens, an apartment complex with one-, two-, and three-bedroom apartments off Jewel Avenue at Park Drive East, and co-ops are the most prevalent housing option.

Locals, who also include residents of Asian and Hispanic descent, have ample shopping along Main Street; and nestled among the cleaners, hardware stores, clothing shops, and pizza parlors is a

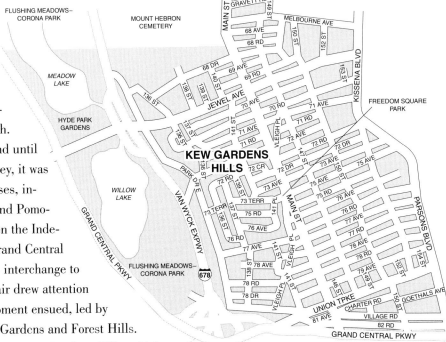

Hills

N E I G H B O R H O O D
F   A   C   T   S

■ Queens County Savings Bank at 75-44 Main Street was built in 1953 as a replica of Independence Hall in Philadelphia. In the lobby is a life-sized model of the Liberty Bell.

■ Mayor Fiorello La Guardia had a summer residence in Kew Gardens Hills.

■ Scenes from the 2000 movie *Boiler Room* were shot in Kew Gardens Hills.

plethora of Israeli and Jewish businesses and kosher grocery stores. There's even a kosher ice cream parlor, Max & Mina's at 71-26 Main Street.

Famous for its unusual concoctions, such as horseradish, garlic, lox, and jalapeño ice cream, in 2002 the shop was thrown into the national limelight when its owners, brothers Mark and Bruce Becker, were listed among *People* magazine's Fifty Top Bachelors.

In response to the increasingly Orthodox Jewish population in Kew Gardens Hills, more than thirty synagogues of various affiliations have sprung up for worshipers. One housing developer, too, the Dermot Company, is building an Orthodox-friendly apartment complex on 153rd Street. The apartments at Estates at Kew Gardens Hills, situated on 5 acres, include kitchens containing double sinks for

• Simon and Garfunkel

Public School 164 on 77th Avenue may look like an ordinary Queens elementary school, but in 1952, for two sixth-grade boys, it was a serendipitous meeting ground that would spark a legendary musical partnership. When the eleven-year-old Paul Simon and Art Garfunkel met there, they found out that they were neighbors, on 72nd Avenue and 136th Street. They went on to attend Parsons Junior High School, then Forest Hills High School together—after which they launched a musical career that was to span decades and win them international acclaim. At age sixteen, they released their first hit, "Hey, Schoolgirl," followed in later years by a number of songs that included references to the borough they grew up in, among them, "The 59th Street Bridge Song (Feelin' Groovy)." The bridge of the song, also known as the Queensboro Bridge, connects Queens to Manhattan. "Me and Julio Down by the Schoolyard," too, refers to nearby Corona. But for those seeking a picture of the neighborhood, some of the songs can be misleading. To those who aren't familiar with Kew Gardens Hills, for example, Simon's "My Little Town" might be interpreted as autobiographical, and lyrics like "coming home after school, flying my bike past the gates of the factories" as a childhood reminiscence. But there were never any factories in Paul Simon's neighborhood. By the time Simon and Garfunkel were born, in 1941, Kew Gardens Hills was a middle-class community of private one- and two-family houses. In fact, the duo recorded some of their earliest songs in the basement of the Garfunkels' single-family home.

Arabic and Hebrew signs share space on Main Street

Elegant houses give the neighborhood a suburban feel

NEIGHBORHOOD PROFILE

Boundaries: <u>North border:</u> Flushing Meadows–Corona Park to Mount Hebron Cemetery to Main Street to Gravett Road to 149th Street to Melbourne Avenue (southern border of Queens College campus); <u>east border:</u> Kissena Boulevard to Parsons Boulevard; <u>south and west borders:</u> Grand Central Parkway
Bus: <u>Q65A:</u> Jewel Avenue; <u>Q74:</u> Main Street; <u>Q44:</u> Main Street; <u>Q20A, Q20B:</u> Main Street; <u>Q46:</u> Union Turnpike
Libraries: Queens Library, Kew Gardens Hills Branch (72-33 Vleigh Place)
Community Board: No. 8
Police Precinct: 107th Precinct (71-01 Parsons Boulevard, Flushing)
Fire Department: Engine 315, Battalion 50 (159-06 Union Turnpike, Jamaica Hills)

separate meat and dairy preparation; elevators that stop on each floor during the Sabbath, when touching electrical devices is forbidden; and rooftops large enough to accommodate the temporary shelters that pop up during the harvest festival of Sukkoth.

Freedom Square Park at Main Street, Vleigh Place, and 75th Avenue also has ties to Jewish culture. In 1960 a flagpole there was dedicated to Theodor Herzl, a Hungarian Jew who founded the Zionist movement. And the Rabbi I. Usher Kirshblum traffic triangle, at 73rd Avenue and Main Street, honors the late rabbi of the Jewish Center of Kew Gardens Hills, who settled in 1946 and helped found the center's congregation.

More expansive park grounds are at the southernmost portion of Flushing Meadows–Corona Park, along East Park Drive on the western side of the neighborhood. A highlight of the Kew Gardens Hills section of that park is Willow Lake, which, unlike its nearby counterpart Meadow Lake, has been kept in a natural state since development began encroaching on the area in the 1930s. Protected by law since 1976, the lake is one of a very few freshwater wetland refuges in New York City. A half-mile nature trail leads visitors through 55 acres of plant life, migratory bird habitats, and wildlife native to New York.

Jewish center and synagogue on Main Street

Laurelton

Every year, war breaks out in Laurelton—a war of the roses, that is, as well as of violets, lilies, and azaleas. Laurelton's Garden Club, founded in 1986, is famous throughout Queens for its annual block competitions. Aspiring gardeners vie for a prize for the best blooms, which are planted on about half of this neighborhood's seventy-six garden "malls," or street medians.

The garden malls are a unique feature of Laurelton, an affluent southeastern neighborhood bordering Nassau County, and its mostly African American residents are understandably passionate about keeping them beautiful: these gorgeous spots of color fit well with the attractive neighborhood of mostly single-family Cape Cods, Spanish-style, and English Tudor–style houses; clean streets; and an abundance of enormous, stately maple trees.

The neighborhood was developed in the 1910s by former New York State senator William H. Reynolds, founder of the Laurelton Land Company (Reynolds also later founded Long Beach, Long Island), and was supposedly named for the many laurel trees in the area. Reynolds built single-family houses in the area over several years, but by the 1920s demand for housing had increased: as Jewish, Irish, Italian, and German families began moving in, a local golf course was quickly turned into a large development of many homes. Predominantly Jewish in the 1940s and 1950s, Laurelton began attracting middle-class blacks from nearby Springfield Gardens and elsewhere in the next decades. In the 1980s immigrants from Jamaica and, later, Haiti, Guyana, and Trinidad and Tobago began moving in as well.

Laurelton's commercial strip, the "Laurelton Mile," runs down Merrick Boulevard from Springfield Boulevard to Laurelton Parkway. Once the heart of the neighborhood, the strip consisted largely of small shops, including the famous Zickerman's, a hardware store at 227-15 Merrick Boulevard. "Zickie's," founded in 1928, was so prosperous in its time that it took up

NEIGHBORHOOD FACTS

■ Since 1997, several Laurelton residents have been trained by Trees New York, a Manhattan-based nonprofit organization, to become licensed caretakers of area trees. This effort has special meaning to those living in Laurelton, because in 1997 four children were crushed to death when a large tree that hadn't been pruned in many years fell on their van.

■ In 2004 the *New York Post* named Laurelton artist Spencer Lawrence one of eight African American unsung heroes who donate their time to make New York City a better place. Lawrence's paintings, many of which portray elements of black history, have been exhibited at the Duke Ellington School of the Arts and at Howard University, both in Washington, D.C.

Long Island Rail Road station, 225th Street and 141st Road, ca. 1941 (Queens Library, Long Island Division, Illustrations Collection)

four adjacent buildings and the surrounding yard. "If you can't find it at Zickerman's, you can't find it anywhere," was the store's motto. Zickerman's closed in 2001, after seventy-three years as a family-owned-and-operated business, and the area began experiencing some growing pains as residents turned to more upscale options, such as the Green Acres Mall in nearby Valley Stream.

But in 2002, concerned residents formed the Laurelton Local Development Corporation, which is organizing a Business Improvement District (BID) for the roughly nineteen-block area. (In a BID, commercial property owners pay into a common fund for improvements such as graffiti removal, sanitation, storefront upgrades, holiday lights, flower plantings, and store promotions.) Laurelton merchants are also participating in "Safe Haven," a public safety initiative that gives residents who feel threatened a safe place to wait for law enforcement officers.

Other measures to enhance the quality of life for Laurelton residents are in full swing. The Laurelton Medical Center on Merrick Boulevard, founded in 2000 by internist Dr. Samuel Akuoku, a native of Ghana, offers comprehensive health care services for area residents. And the Laurelton branch of the Queens Library has led the way in responding to the community's need for youth programs. With the help of community organizations, including local law enforcement, it obtained a federal grant to turn part of the library into a teen-friendly center. An on-site youth counselor creates programs for—and mentors—young adults, and a social worker is on-site part-time to handle any needed referrals.

Laurelton's appearance is also being attended to. Much to the delight of the

Landscaped street medians along 139th Avenue

NEIGHBORHOOD PROFILE

Boundaries: <u>North border:</u> Montefiore Cemetery to 121st Avenue; <u>east border:</u> Laurelton Parkway; <u>south border:</u> North Conduit Avenue; <u>west border:</u> Long Island Rail Road to Springfield Boulevard
Subway and Train: <u>LIRR:</u> Laurelton
Bus: <u>Q84:</u> 238th Street; <u>Q4:</u> Merrick Boulevard to Hook Creek Boulevard; <u>x63:</u> Merrick Boulevard to Hook Creek Boulevard to Francis Lewis Boulevard; <u>Q85:</u> North Conduit Avenue
Libraries: Queens Library, Laurelton Branch (134-26 225th Street)
Community Board: No. 13
Police Precinct: 105th Precinct (9208 222nd Street, Queens Village)
Fire Department: Engine 314, Battalion 54 (142-04 Brookville Boulevard, Rosedale)

Concerned Citizens of Laurelton, the largest civic association in the neighbor-hood, the Metropolitan Transit Authority recently refurbished the 1917 Laurelton Long Island Rail Road station, on 224th Street and 141st Road. Another favorite landmark that has recently received a facelift is the Laurelton Playground, built in 1935 and sandwiched between Laurelton and neighboring Springfield Gardens. In 1999 new drinking fountains, swings, a water sprinkler, and play equipment were installed. The New York City Parks Department also planted a slew of crimson pygmy shrubs, cherry laurel, ivy, and three different types of perennials—in keep-ing with the garden club's zeal for beautifying the neighborhood with flowers.

Laurelton homeowners take pride in their gardens

From its creation Laurelton was touted as a garden suburb, as in this 1910 advertise-ment (Queens Library, Long Island Divi-sion, Illustrations Collection)

Little Neck

Ask residents of Little Neck why they love their neighborhood, and they'll probably mention their top school district, the suburban feel of the tree-lined streets, and the cama-raderie among neighbors. Tucked away at the northwest edge of an urbanized borough, with a peninsular toe dipped in Little Neck Bay, the community is both lively and a comfortable place to raise a family.

The Little Neck peninsula, once abundant in clams and oysters, was originally inhabited by the Matinecoc Indians, who were forced out in the 1600s by English settlers. By the 1800s, oystermen, many of them African Americans, were working the oyster beds at the foot of Old House Landing Road (which is today Little Neck Parkway), supplying clams and oysters to the surrounding areas. A railroad was extended there

Korean businesses are adding to Northern Boulevard's commercial offerings

in 1866 (the station is at Little Neck Parkway and 39th Road), and by 1873 Little Neck was a hamlet of twenty-three houses, a hotel, and a church. The oysterbeds were condemned in 1909 as polluted, destroying the industry.

But as the oyster industry died out the neighborhood began to be developed as part of the garden suburb movement. Between 1905 and 1930, the Rickert-Finlay Company began laying out a development south of the railroad station.

**NEIGHBORHOOD
PROFILE**

Boundaries: <u>North border:</u> Udalls Cove Park at Little Neck Bay; <u>east border:</u> Nassau County line; <u>south border:</u> Grand Central Parkway; <u>west border:</u> Marathon Parkway to 250th Street to Little Neck Parkway to Sandhill Road to Douglas Road to Marinette Street
Subway and Train: <u>LIRR:</u> Little Neck
Bus: <u>Q79:</u> Little Neck Parkway; <u>Q12, N21, N20:</u> Northern Boulevard; <u>Q30:</u> Horace Harding Expressway
Libraries: Queens Library, Douglaston–Little Neck Branch (249-01 Northern Boulevard); North Hills Branch (57-04 Marathon Parkway)
Community Board: No. 11
Police Precinct: 111th Precinct (45-06 215th Street, Bayside)
Fire Department: Engine 313, Ladder 164, Battalion 53 (44-01 244th Street, Douglaston)
Hospitals and Clinics: Little Neck Community Hospital (5515 Little Neck Parkway)

Thirteen protective covenants (including "No house or business building shall be erected costing less than $3,000.00") were written to cover some three hundred houses in what was known as the Westmoreland development, situated in the northern part of Little Neck. (Little Neck Hills, an area just south of Northern Boulevard, was also developed around this time.) The Westmoreland covenants are still included with every property title and deed, although some of them are outdated. And the Westmoreland Association, which was incorporated in 1924,

Annandale Lane gives Little Neck the feel of suburbia

continues to strictly enforce the covenants.

The association is protective for good reason: situated along the Nassau County border, Little Neck has retained its character as a suburban town within a generally urbanized borough. Along tree-lined streets are an assortment of attached and semi-attached Colonials and high ranches blending seamlessly with Tudors, Capes, and Arts and Crafts–style homes. And while more contemporary garden apartment co-ops can be found, primarily south of the Long Island Expressway in the Deepdale Gardens area, no high-rise buildings exist in the neighborhood. Ample shopping for all can be found along Northern Boulevard.

A demographic change has brought new awareness of what makes good communities thrive. In addition to the African Americans, Little Neck, like other

Eunhae Presbyterian Church serves the growing Korean communities of Little Neck and Douglaston

NEIGHBORHOOD FACTS

■ One of Little Neck's most unusual residents was Bloodgood H. Cutter (1817–1906), known variously as "the laureate of Little Neck" and "Long Island's Farmer Poet" (a 500-page book of poems he published with a vanity press was entitled *A Long Island Farmer's Poems*). A prosperous gentleman farmer, Cutter was known for wandering the streets, Bible in hand, and accosting passersby with readings. After making a trip to the Holy Land in 1867 as part of a group that included Mark Twain, Cutter found himself immortalized as "the Poet Lariat" in Twain's account of the trip, *The Innocents Abroad.*

■ Every spring peaceful Little Neck comes alive to the sound of the biggest Memorial Day parade in the nation: with bands playing and banners flying, the town pays homage to U.S. veterans and celebrates its community spirit. The combined Little Neck–Douglaston parade is attended by the mayor of New York and draws enormous crowds with performing groups as varied as the USO Torch Singers and the Federation of Black Cowboys.

■ The natural, undeveloped tidal salt marsh known as Udalls Cove, along the northernmost part of Little Neck, was the site of the thriving oystering industry. Even after the area was condemned in the early twentieth century interest in its natural assets remained strong: after developers began scouting the area in the 1960s, the Udalls Cove Preservation Committee was formed in 1969, led by the late Aurora Gareiss. The committee not only cleared the cove of several tons of refuse but was also instrumental in mobilizing the New York City Parks and Recreation Department to designate it a preserve in 1972. In 2004, the 1-acre Aurora Pond (named after Gareiss) on Sandhill Road received a healthy grant for restoration, and residents hope that the Udalls Cove Park Preserve can remain clean and vital for generations to come.

Queens neighborhoods, was first settled by Italian, German, Irish, and Jewish families; Little Neck Jewish Center, a conservative synagogue at 49-10 Little Neck Parkway, has served the Little Neck, Douglaston, and Great Neck, Long Island, communities since the mid-twentieth century. Increasingly in Little Neck, however, Asians— mostly Korean and Chinese families— have been purchasing homes, churches, and businesses.

The change has led to some challenges, such as the protest in 2001 when construction of the Korean Eunhae Presbyterian Church began on 249th Street, just across the border in neighboring Douglaston. Homeowners worried that the three-story, 20,000-square-foot structure would not include enough parking spaces for parishioners, who would then park on nearby residential blocks. But civic leaders, church members, and political representatives worked through the issue, and in May 2004 the church opened its doors to a peaceful reception from neighbors.

Another recent source of concern has involved Korean-only store signs that have popped up along Northern Boulevard. Longtime Little Neck residents have complained that they pose a safety problem if English-speaking emergency personnel are unable to identify the business from which a call was made. But minor differences like these are sure to be resolved in this co-operative community, in which obvious signs of mutual respect abound, such as at Emperor's Garden, on Northern Boulevard, a vegetarian Kosher Chinese restaurant that caters to the large Jewish population in the neighborhood.

Mayor Abe Beame (left) announcing a $95,000 commitment to clean up Udalls Cove, 1977, with Aurora Gareiss at right (Courtesy of Queens Library, Long Island Division, Aurora Gareiss Papers)

Long Island

The Pepsi-Cola sign welcomes visitors from Manhattan

Part residential area, part business, arts, and industrial center, high-energy Long Island City, geographically the largest neighborhood in Queens and the most heavily industrialized, is being rediscovered by visionaries who are drawn to its museums, easy commute, and array of work, shopping, and entertainment options. But the neighborhood's prime location—right across the East River from Manhattan—has attracted interest since some of the earliest European settlers built homes there in the seventeenth century.

Owing to frequent flooding the area remained mostly farmland until the mid-nineteenth century, when Neziah Bliss and Eliphalet Nott began developing it. The arrival of the railroad in the 1850s and 1860s, as well as a ferry to Manhattan in 1859, brought industry to the region, and in 1870, recognizing that the area was becoming too popular and urbanized to remain part of rural Newtown, the New York State legislature formed Long Island City as a distinct township.

Then in 1898 western Queens became part of New York City. All the local township governments were disbanded, and for a time the first borough government, led by Borough President Frederick Bowley of Long Island City, was housed in Bowley's home neighborhood. The first Borough Hall was, briefly, the Long Island City Courthouse, built between 1872 and 1876. Designated a New York City landmark in 1976 and also listed on the New York State and National Registers of Historic Places, the courthouse was rebuilt in 1904 in the neoclassical style after a fire gutted the original struc-

City

ture. (The building was used as a setting for Cecil B. De Mille's 1922 *Manslaughter* and Alfred Hitchcock's 1956 *The Wrong Man.*)

The courthouse is located on the border of **Hunters Point,** one of the many distinctive smaller areas within Long Island City. Hunters Point is perhaps best known as the home of a 120-foot-long red neon Pepsi sign—an artifact from a now-closed bottling plant and an icon familiar to all those who cross the Queensboro Bridge ("the 59th Street Bridge" of the Simon and Garfunkel song). The area is now an industrial neighborhood in transition—though in other eras it had a very different look. It is named for George Hunter, who acquired a large parcel here in 1817 that was purchased by Brooklyn real estate agent Jeremiah Johnson after Hunter's death. In its early days, after swamps and sand hills were filled and leveled, Hunters Point

NEIGHBORHOOD FACTS

■ Long Island City is a place where people have historically come forward to help one another and be heard. The tradition was perhaps launched in 1861, when a group of Catholic nuns opened Queens's first hospital in the neighborhood. But Margaret Sanger brought an element of outspoken activism to the mix as well, when in the early 1900s she began educating the public about family planning. Sanger was arrested in 1917 for distributing information about contraceptives and sentenced to thirty days in the Queens County jail in Long Island City. Today neighborhood activists like the nonprofit organization Materials for the Arts, which solicits donations and offers free art supplies to city agencies, public schools, and other community-service organizations, and Queensbridge Community in Action, a group dedicated to improving community involvement in public education, continue the tradition of fostering earnest reformers.
■ One famous temporary resident of Ravenswood was James Fenimore Cooper: he spent the summer of 1825 at his friend Colonel George Gibbs's house in what was then called Sunswick, later renamed Ravenswood. At the time, Cooper was working on his novel *The Last of the Mohicans.*
■ *Gangs of New York, Mr. Deeds,* and *When Harry Met Sally* are among dozens of movies shot at Silvercup Studios. Opened in 1983 at the site of the former Silvercup Bakery, the studio is the largest independent, full-service film and television production facility in the northeastern United States. The main lot is at 42-22 22nd Street.

was a well-to-do residential area. In addition to waterside manors like Bodine Castle, a Gothic Revival house built in 1853 by a wealthy wholesale grocer and exporter (torn down in 1966), the area boasted elegantly constructed brownstones built in the late 1800s; in fact, near-perfect examples of exquisite Italianate row houses can still be

An 1895 photograph of the original Long Island City Courthouse (1872–76), at that time the Queens County Court House (Queens Library, Long Island Division, Illustrations Collection)

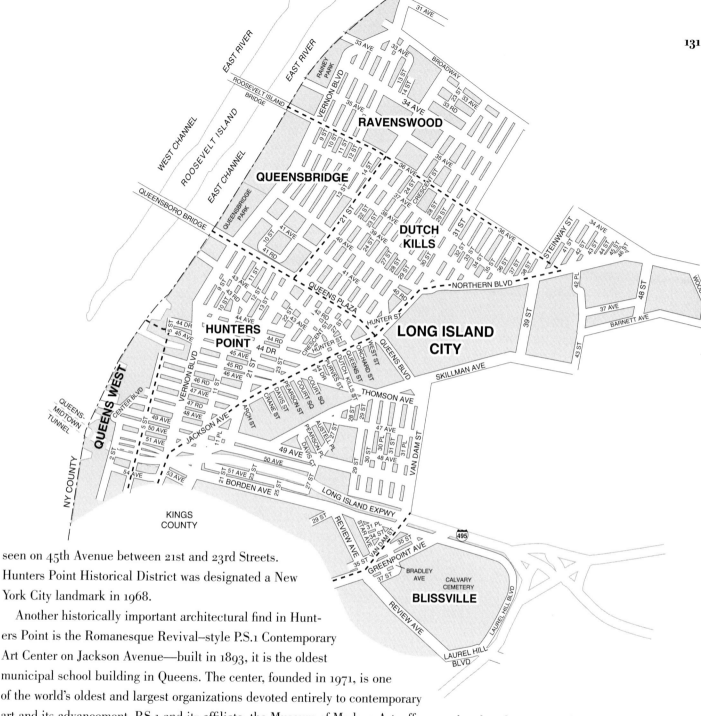

seen on 45th Avenue between 21st and 23rd Streets. Hunters Point Historical District was designated a New York City landmark in 1968.

Another historically important architectural find in Hunters Point is the Romanesque Revival–style P.S.1 Contemporary Art Center on Jackson Avenue—built in 1893, it is the oldest municipal school building in Queens. The center, founded in 1971, is one of the world's oldest and largest organizations devoted entirely to contemporary art and its advancement. P.S.1 and its affiliate, the Museum of Modern Art, offer extensive educational programs, exhibitions, and events in its nearly 125,000-square-foot facility. These landmarks may contrast starkly with the run-down warehouses and abandoned factories, but even those buildings are undergoing a renaissance. One example of the creative reuse of industrial space is the Chocolate Factory Theater, an arts center situated at 5-49 49th Avenue in an

abandoned commercial garage. Founded in 2003, the facility sponsors performance art, gallery exhibitions, and a visiting artist program of dance, theater, music, and multimedia performances.

The 7 line runs by Silvercup Studios

Two new luxury high rises, Avalonbay Riverview and Citylights, are bringing hope for additional growth along the waterfront, particularly in the southern region known as **Queens West,** an ongoing development that will eventually include nineteen of the high rises.

Citylights, a complex of residential high rises in Queens West

(Queens West was proposed as the site of the Olympic Village in New York's bid for the 2012 games, which went to London.) The beautiful 2.5-acre Gantry Plaza State Park at 48th Avenue, which features two historic Long Island Rail Road gantries and four piers, is certainly a draw for prospective residents.

Directly north of this section, along Vernon Boulevard, is the 20-acre Queensbridge Park, enjoyed by the largely African American residents of **Queensbridge,** the largest public housing development in New York City. Completed in 1940, it consists of twenty-six six-story buildings. A bit farther north is **Ravenswood,** home to Rainey Park, named after Thomas Rainey (1824–1910), an engineer who dedicated much of his life to lobbying for the construction of a bridge across the East River, which opened to traffic as the Queensboro Bridge in 1909 (see the Bridges photo spread). In its heyday, this area was home to opulent waterfront mansions; today it is known in part as the location of Ravenswood Houses, a New York City Housing Authority public housing complex built in 1951 along 34th to 36th Avenues. The Queensview cooperative apartments, built in 1951, are part of this residential neighborhood as well.

Also here is Socrates Sculpture Park. A dumpsite before its opening in 1986, the park was founded by sculptor Mark DiSuvero, along with other artists and city officials, and is one of the most acclaimed public art spaces in the country, serving as an outdoor studio for more than five hundred artists and presenting more than forty exhibitions of large-scale sculpture. Modern sculpture is also on display at the Isamu Noguchi Garden Museum, where visitors can view more than 250 works by the artist indoors or head outside to enjoy an open-air sculpture garden. The museum was created by the artist in an abandoned factory building.

Along the northern part of Long Island City is **Dutch Kills** (the name is known primarily to locals), where the earliest European settlements were located and where British soldiers set up camps between 1776 and 1783 during their occupation of New York. Largely

NEIGHBORHOOD PROFILE

Boundaries: <u>Long Island City:</u> <u>north border:</u> 31st Avenue to Vernon Boulevard to Broadway to 31st Street to 36th Avenue to Steinway Street to 34th Avenue to Northern Boulevard; <u>east border:</u> Woodside Avenue to Barnett Avenue to 43rd Street to Skillman Avenue to Van Dam Street to Long Island Expressway to Laurel Hill Boulevard; <u>south border:</u> Kings County line; <u>west border:</u> New York County line (East River); <u>Hunters Point:</u> <u>north border:</u> Queens Plaza South; <u>east border:</u> Jackson Avenue to Vernon Boulevard; <u>south border:</u> Kings County line; <u>west border:</u> 5th Street to 45th Avenue to New York County line; <u>Queens West:</u> <u>north border:</u> 45th Avenue; <u>east border:</u> 5th Street; <u>south border:</u> Kings County line; <u>west border:</u> New York County line (East River); <u>Queensbridge:</u> <u>north border:</u> 36th Avenue; <u>east border:</u> 21st Street; <u>south border:</u> Queens Plaza North; <u>west border:</u> New York County line (East River); <u>Ravenswood:</u> <u>north border:</u> 31st Avenue to Vernon Boulevard to Broadway; <u>east border:</u> 31st Street; <u>south border:</u> 36th Avenue; <u>west border:</u> New York County line (East River); <u>Dutch Kills:</u> <u>north border:</u> 36th Avenue; <u>east border:</u> Northern Boulevard to Queens Plaza East; <u>south border:</u> Queens Plaza North; <u>west border:</u> 21st Street; <u>Blissville:</u> <u>north border:</u> Long Island Expressway; <u>east border:</u> Laurel Hill Boulevard; <u>south border:</u> Kings County line; <u>west border:</u> Greenpoint Avenue to Van Dam Street

Subway and Train: <u>7 train:</u> Vernon Boulevard/Jackson Avenue, Hunters Point Avenue, 45th Road/Court House Square, Queensboro Plaza/Queensboro Bridge; <u>E, V, G trains:</u> 21st Street, 45th Road/Court House Square; <u>N, W trains:</u> Queensboro Plaza/Queensboro Bridge, 39th Avenue, 36th Avenue; <u>LIRR:</u> Hunters Point Avenue, Long Island City

Bus: <u>B61:</u> Jackson Avenue; <u>Q103:</u> Vernon Boulevard; <u>Q39:</u> Thomson Avenue/48th Avenue; <u>Q67:</u> Borden Avenue/21st Street; <u>Q19A:</u> 21st Street; <u>Q101:</u> Steinway Street; <u>Q101R:</u> Queensboro Plaza to 21st Street; <u>Q32:</u> Queens Boulevard/Queensboro Bridge; <u>Q102:</u> 31st Street; <u>Q66:</u> Northern Boulevard; <u>Q104:</u> Broadway; <u>Q60:</u> Queens Boulevard

Libraries: Queens Library, Court Square Branch (25-01 Jackson Avenue); Queensbridge Branch (10-25 41st Avenue); Ravenswood Branch (35-32 21st Street)

Museums: P.S.1 Contemporary Art Center (22-25 Jackson Avenue); Museum for African Art (36-01 43rd Avenue); Isamu Noguchi Museum (32-37 Vernon Boulevard); Fisher Landau Center for Art (38-27 30th Street); Sculpture Center (44-19 Purves Street), Socrates Sculpture Park (32-01 Vernon Boulevard); Outsider Gallery (26-25 Jackson Avenue)

Theaters: La Guardia Performing Arts Center (31-10 Thomson Avenue); Ravenswood Theater (42-16 West Street); Mass Transit Street Theater (10-23 Jackson Avenue); The Chocolate Factory Theater (5-49 49th Avenue)

Community Board: Nos. 1, 2

Police Precinct: 108th Precinct (5-47 50th Avenue); 114th Precinct (34-16 Astoria Boulevard, Astoria)

Fire Department: Engine 258, Battalion 45 (10-40 47th Avenue); Engine 259, Battalion 45 (33-51 Greenpoint Avenue); Engine 260, Battalion 45 (11-15 37th Avenue); Engine 261, Battalion 45 (37-20 29th Street); Ladder 128, Battalion 45 (33-51 Greenpoint Avenue); Ladder 115, Battalion 45 (10-40 47th Avenue); Ladder 116, Battalion 45 (37-20 29th Street)

Hospitals and Clinics: Queensbridge Geriatric Center Division of Wyckoff Heights Hospital (10-25 41st Avenue); New York Foundling Hospital (22-11 47th Avenue); Lutheran Medical Center (150 55th Avenue); New York Presbyterian Hospital Community Center (36-11 21st Street); Mount Sinai Hospital of Queens (25-10 30th Avenue); Hospice of New York (45-18 Court Square)

Beautiful brownstones are a surprising discovery in Hunters Point, a largely industrial area

farmland in its early years, Dutch Kills began to be developed residentially and commercially in the mid-nineteenth century. It was targeted as an industrial area in 1961, when new city zoning was enacted to keep present manufacturing in the district and encourage new industry. The initiative was largely unsuccessful, and the area declined, but recently, with the development of Queens Plaza and the area's easy access to the Queensboro Bridge, Dutch Kills has been staging a comeback. Another lesser-known enclave is **Blissville,** at the eastern edge of the neighborhood. Mostly made up of industrial buildings, the area has only about seven hundred residents—although Calvary Cemetery, founded in 1848, is a resting place for generations of families that once lived in the borough.

The commercial heart of Long Island City is Queens Plaza, a mass-transit hub where the Queensboro Bridge and Northern Boulevard meet. On Queens Plaza North stands the Brewster Building (1911), originally a factory that supplied horse-drawn carriages, automobiles (including Rolls Royces for a while), and fighter planes. The restored six-story brick building today houses the Metropolitan Life Insurance Company.

Another important structure—the fifty-story Citicorp building, at 1 Court Square—is located in the largely industrial area east of Jackson Avenue and Northern Boulevard. Built in 1989 by Skidmore, Owings and Merrill, the Citicorp Building is the tallest in Long Island. Also in this area is La Guardia Community College, at 31-10 Thomson Avenue, which opened its doors in 1971. With students hailing from 160 countries, it is no wonder that La Guardia proudly refers to itself as "The World's Community College." But like the rest of Long Island City, this area is undergoing a transition, perhaps spurred by the presence from 2002 to 2004 of the Museum of Modern Art, which took over an abandoned Swingline factory on Queens Boulevard just across the border in neighboring Sunnyside (the mailing address was Long Island City) while its Manhattan site was being renovated. Among the new artistic ventures drawn here in 2002 is Flux Factory, at 38-38 43rd Street. Founded in Brooklyn by students at Manhattan's New School for Social Research, Flux Factory sponsors innovative and collaborative art events and performances.

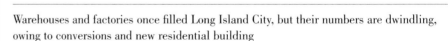

Warehouses and factories once filled Long Island City, but their numbers are dwindling, owing to conversions and new residential building

THE BRIDGES

Queens has four major motor-vehicle bridges connecting it to the other boroughs—the Queensboro (59th Street), the Triborough, the Bronx-Whitestone, and the Throgs Neck. (For the Hell Gate, a railroad bridge, see Astoria.)

The oldest bridge in the borough is the Queensboro Bridge (1901–9), which

---

Queensboro Bridge

Robert Moses posing at the Bronx-Whitestone Bridge, 1965 (Courtesy of the Queens Library, Long Island Division, Portraits Collection)

136

View of the Throgs Neck Bridge from Bay Terrace

spans the East River between 59th Street in Manhattan and Long Island City. Designed by Gustav Lindenthal, the rail and motor-vehicle bridge was the first bridge to connect the two boroughs and served for years as the gateway to Long Island for Manhattanites. Today the bridge, with nine lanes for motor traffic and one lane for pedestrians and bicycles (the elevated railroad and trolley lines were

removed in 1957), is one of the most traveled bridges in the world, carrying some 200,000 vehicles a day. It was designated a national historic landmark in 1973.

Lindenthal also submitted designs for a Hell Gate crossing, hoping to prevent the needed new structure from spoiling the view of his recently com-

Construction of the Tower Chord of Queensboro Bridge, 1907 (Courtesy of the Queens Library, Long Island Division, Chamber of Commerce of the Borough of Queens)

pleted Hell Gate Bridge. But the Triborough (1929–36), along with the later Bronx-Whitestone (1937–39) and the Throgs Neck (1957–61), which took thousands of people years to build, largely owe their creation to the vision of two men: Othmar Ammann, who designed them, and Robert Moses, head of the Triborough Bridge Commission and Commissioner of Parks and Recreation for the City of New York, who wielded the power to build them, even in the depth of the Depression. (Ground for the Triborough was broken on October 25, 1929, the day after "Black Thursday," when the Stock Market crashed.)

The Triborough Bridge actually consists of the three bridges, a viaduct, approach roads, and a network of parks connecting Manhattan, Queens, and the Bronx that together make up the Triborough Bridge and Tunnel Author-

ity. More than just a bridge, in the grim days of the Depression the Triborough represented the future: in the words of Robert Moses, "The Triborough is not just a bridge nor yet a crossing . . . but a general city improvement, reclaiming dead areas and providing for residence along its borders, esplanades, play facilities, landscaping and access to the great new parks." The longest span, a suspension bridge, connects Astoria to Ward's Island as part of Interstate 278; the entire network now serves about 200,000 vehicles a day.

Following the Triborough came the rush construction of the Bronx-Whitestone, which was completed in just twenty-three months, opening on April 29, 1939, the day before the 1939 New York World's Fair opened in Flushing Meadows–Corona Park, which—along with the proposed new airport (La Guardia)—it had been built to serve. The elegant Art Deco suspension bridge spans the East River, connecting the Queens neighborhood of Whitestone with Unionport and Schuylerville in the Bronx as part of Interstate 678, and carries about 110,000 vehicles a day.

But even these three bridges were not enough to serve the traffic needs of the rapidly expanding borough, and in 1955 a new six-lane suspension bridge over the East River was proposed. The Throgs Neck (the name derives from John Throckmorton, who settled in the area in 1643) connects Bay Terrace with Locust Point, Fort Schuyler, Throgs Neck, and Edgewater Park in the Bronx as part of Interstate 295; it carries some 105,000 vehicles a day. Queens's newest bridge opened in 1961—in time to bring the world flocking to the borough for yet another World's Fair.

View of Triborough and Hell Gate Bridges, with Astoria Park in the foreground, 1946 (Courtesy of the Queens Library, Long Island Division, Postcard Collection)

Maspeth

Modern-day Maspeth is really two neighborhoods in one. On the eastern side, quiet, well-maintained attached and semi-attached brick row houses sit on pleasant, tree-lined streets. Long-time residents, of Italian, German, Irish, Lithuanian, and especially Polish descent, mingle comfortably with more recent arrivals from Korea and Latin America. The rest of the neighborhood is highly commercial and industrial and is flanked or intersected by busy roadways: the Long Island Expressway, Metropolitan Avenue, Grand Avenue, and Queens Boulevard.

Two cemeteries lie within the neighborhood to the north and south. Mount Olivet, on Grand Avenue, was incorporated in 1850 and designed with winding, landscaped roads and an abundance of trees and shrubbery. Some twenty-five veterans of the Civil War are buried here. And Mount Zion, on 54th Avenue, is a historic Jewish cemetery. Nathan Wallenstein Weinstein, better known as Nathanael West, author of *Miss Lonelyhearts* and *The Day of the Locust,* is buried there.

The Mespat Indians, for whom this neighborhood is named, long ago settled to the east of this cemetery, and the first formal English colony put down roots back in 1642 under the Newtown Patent. A year later an Indian attack dismantled the settlement, and the colonists ventured farther east into what eventually came to be called Elmhurst. But because the area that is now western Maspeth is situated along Newtown Creek, which leads into the East River, and at the head of Maspeth Creek, a tributary of Newtown Creek, it became a convenient center of commerce. Farmers could ship their crops into Manhattan, and after the Revolutionary War the area flour-

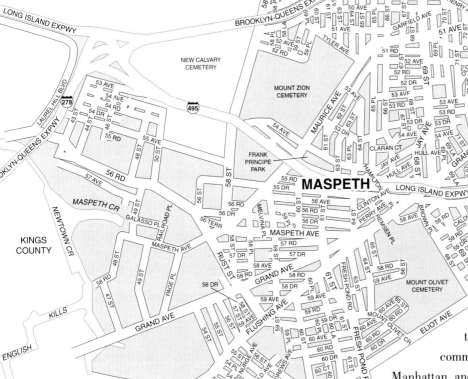

ished, with roads built from crushed oyster shells (as well as more conventional wooden planks) to facilitate further trade. By the 1850s, industries had sprung up along the waterway, creating jobs and the need for dwellings for local laborers. Among the earliest businesses were a glue factory, a rope works, and a tin factory. The first kerosene refinery in the nation and the first modern oil refinery were built here as well.

With this economic growth came an undesirable side effect: pollution. For years, a sewage treatment plant, factories, and refineries along the creeks were virtually unregulated regarding the dumping of byproducts. Today's Newtown Creek is polluted, with littered banks, and the half-mile-long Maspeth Creek is no better. But environmental groups such as Riverkeeper are bringing attention to these two historic creeks and lobbying for cleanups.

The corner of Grand Avenue and 69th Street offers a good view of nearby Manhattan

Cleaning up other sorts of undesirable activities in the neighborhood, such as crime, has been the task of a group called Communities of Maspeth and Elmhurst Together (COMET). And

NEIGHBORHOOD PROFILE

Boundaries: <u>North border:</u> Long Island Expressway to 48th Street to 54th Avenue to 50th Street to 55th Avenue to 58th Street to Queens Boulevard; <u>east border:</u> 74th Street; <u>south border:</u> Eliot Avenue to Fresh Pond Road to Metropolitan Avenue; <u>west border:</u> Kings County line to Laurel Hill Boulevard

Bus: <u>Q59:</u> Grand Avenue; <u>Q58:</u> Grand Avenue; <u>Q54:</u> Metropolitan Avenue; <u>B57:</u> Flushing Avenue; <u>Q39:</u> 59th Street to 61st Street; <u>B24:</u> 48th Street; <u>Q45:</u> Calamus Avenue; <u>Q18:</u> 69th Street

Libraries: Queens Library, Maspeth Branch (69-70 Grand Avenue)

Theaters: Polish Theater Group of New York (73-54 53rd Avenue, Suite 4)

Community Board: Nos. 2, 5

Police Precinct: 104th Precinct (64-2 Catalpa Avenue, Ridgewood)

Fire Department: Engine 288, Battalion 46 HazMat Unit (56-29 68th Street)

This 69th Street Irish pub is a local gathering place

concerned citizens have taken action on preservation matters as well: Maspeth locals are keenly proud of their place in borough history, and in 1971 they united to save Maspeth Town Hall, located at 53-37 72nd Street. Built in 1898 by the early Dutch Brinkerhoff family, the gathering place, which was never used as an official village or town hall, was home to a one-and-a-half-story schoolhouse until 1932, when it became a girls' club. During the Depression, the Works Project Administration took control of

Clinton House, home of De Witt Clinton, in 1852 (Queens Library, Long Island Division, Illustrations Collection)

the building, and it housed the 112th Precinct. In 1971, concerned about the building's state of disrepair, citizens formed a coalition of private, business, and government interests to save the historic structure. Today the Maspeth Town Hall Community Center offers all types of cultural and recreational activities for the Maspeth community.

Residents seeking to save St. Saviour's Church, a Carpenter Gothic structure on Rust and 57th Streets, may be able to come up with a similar compromise. The 1847 redwood building, designed by noted church architect Richard Upjohn, was due to be razed to make way for three-family homes. Maspeth residents, led by the Juniper Park Civic Organization's Committee to Save St. Saviour's, have managed to delay the demolition, and they are bringing their case to the mayor, the New York City Landmarks Preservation Commission, and their local community board in the hope of finding a way to preserve the elegant structure.

One of those fighting to save St. Saviour's is Lee James Principe, son of legendary Maspeth community leaders Frank and Virginia Principe. Among his many neighborhood services, Frank Principe, affectionately known as "Mr. Maspeth," helped found Maurice Park, an 8.9-acre green space between Maurice Avenue and 63rd Street that was created in 1940 and renovated in 1996, largely due to Principe's efforts as head of Community Board 5. Originally named for James Maurice, a U.S. Congressman and resident of Maspeth, the park was renamed Frank Principe Park in 2005 at the request of the community. Unusually, the park also honors Frank's wife, Virginia Principe, a founding member of the Maurice Park Civic Association, which maintained the park for children when the city did

NEIGHBORHOOD FACTS

■ The Polish-American National Hall, at 61-60 56th Road, was erected in 1934 to house the Polish National Home, an organization founded in 1921 to preserve the heritage of the Polish immigrants who began arriving in the neighborhood around 1890. The large Polish population played an important part in Maspeth, and members of the organization even took part in the opening of the 1939 World's Fair. A new wave of Polish immigrants began arriving in the 1990s, and storefronts along Grand and Maspeth Avenues still sport Polish signs.

■ Transfiguration Church, a Roman Catholic church at 64-14 Clinton Avenue, was founded in 1908 to serve Maspeth's Lithuanian immigrants. The current structure, which dates from 1962, is decorated with Lithuanian folk motifs and has a replica of a Lithuanian roadside shrine in the churchyard. The church offers Lithuanian-language masses every weekend.

■ Hagstrom Map Company, based at 46-35 54th Road, publishes street maps and road maps of the New York City area, from Manhattan to Long Island, New Jersey, and Connecticut.

■ De Witt Clinton, mastermind of the Erie Canal and New York City mayor (1803–15) as well as governor of New York State (1817–23), had a mansion in Maspeth, which burned down in 1933.

■ Maspeth residents were starstruck in 2003 when the HBO hit *The Sopranos* filmed scenes there for two days. A seven-vehicle car chase—which included lead character Tony Soprano's white Cadillac Escalade SUV—was shot along Grand Avenue and Flushing Avenue.

■ On September 11, 2001, Maspeth was one of the hardest-hit neighborhoods in Queens: nineteen firefighters from Maspeth lost their lives during the terrorist attack on the World Trade Center, the greatest number lost from a single firehouse in the city.

dent of the Cosmopolitan Soccer Club, came to the rescue: he launched the Metropolitan Oval Foundation to pay the tax debt and, with help from Nike, brought the field back to life for soccer fans throughout New York.

not have sufficient resources. In 2000 Maurice Playground, a recreational space within the park, was renamed Virginia Principe Playground.

Another favorite recreational space that has been preserved for local residents is the Metropolitan Oval, one of the most popular soccer fields in New York. Located at 60-58 60th Street (hidden away behind a private home), the arena was built in the 1920s and was originally the home of the German-Hungarian Soccer Club. But although major soccer stars such as Werner Roth played here, the Oval began to decline, and by 1997 it owed $250,000 in back taxes. Jim Vogt, presi-

Middle

Imagine living a half-hour by train from midtown Manhattan in a friendly, attractive neighborhood that feels more like a suburban enclave. Middle Village, a quiet corner of Queens that is surrounded on three sides by hushed cemeteries and a beautiful, recently renovated park, is just the sort of peaceful home base that many commuters dream of—and that current residents hope to preserve with thoughtful community planning.

Middle Village, which began as a hamlet of families of English descent, was named for its location at the midpoint of the Williamsburgh (now Williamsburg, Brooklyn) & Jamaica Turnpike, which became Metropolitan Avenue after 1860. The neighborhood has strong ties to several churches, and its initial development had a lot to do with

In business since 1889, Niederstein's was a neighborhood fixture until it closed in 2005 (Queens Library, Long Island Division, Illustrations Collection)

Village

A two-family attached home on 83rd Place

a decision by the Common Council of New York City prohibiting any further burials in Manhattan: as a result of that ruling, cemeteries sprang up throughout the borough and in particular around Middle Village and neighboring Glendale. In 1852 the St. Matthews and St. Marks Lutheran congregations in Manhattan bought several farms north and south of Metropolitan Avenue to create a cemetery and a chapel that was to become home to the first Lutheran Congregation in Queens—signaling an increasing German population in Middle Village by 1860.

The All Faiths Lutheran Cemetery on Metropolitan Avenue also was important to the Lutheran church, and has a particular historical significance: buried here are most of the more than 1,000 victims of the *General Slocum* steamboat ferry disaster of 1904, in which more people were killed than on the *Titanic*. Three monuments at the cemetery commemorate the horrific burning of the boat on its way to a picnic from Manhattan to Long Island. The boat's passengers were mostly women and children from an area on the Lower East Side then known as Little Germany. To commemorate the disaster, every year on the Saturday before June 15 the *General Slocum* Memorial Association holds an ecumenical memorial service at Trinity Lutheran Church (63-70 Dry Harbor Road) and a wreath-laying ceremony at the Slocum monument in All Faiths Cemetery.

Another early cemetery is St. John. Operated by the Roman Catholic Diocese of Brooklyn and founded in 1879, it covers some 200 acres on Metropolitan Avenue, bordering the neighborhood to the east. This is where mobster John Gotti was laid to rest in 2002.

It was the thriving burial grounds that made Middle Village a popular stopping point, because visitors to the cemeteries required flower shops, monuments, food, and lodging. These businesses sprang up along Metropolitan Avenue, which cuts across the two burial grounds, dividing the 225 acres of All

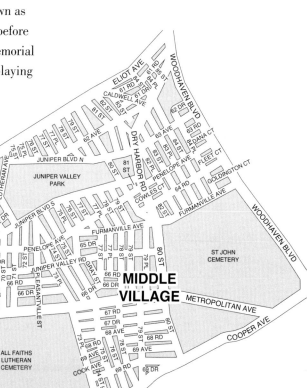

■ Racketeer Arnold Rothstein, who was accused of being the brains behind the "Black Sox" scandal (the 1919 World Series fixing), created a phantom village of flimsy houses on property he owned in what is today Juniper Valley Park to increase property values. He then proposed selling the site for a municipal airport or for a civic center. The Parks Department didn't buy into this scheme and in the early 1930s instead acquired the land to settle $225,000 in back taxes against the Rothstein estate (Rothstein died in 1928).

■ The first Methodist Church on Long Island was established in 1768 on Dry Harbor Road in what is now Middle Village. The leader of the congregation was Joseph Harper, a local farmer, whose sons James and John in 1817 started the publishing firm J. and J. Harper (the name was changed to Harper & Brothers in 1833 after their brothers Joseph Wesley and Fletcher Harper joined the firm), a predecessor of today's HarperCollins.

■ For over a hundred years, between 1889 and 2005, Niederstein's Restaurant on Metropolitan Avenue was the place to go for authentic German American cuisine.

Faiths Lutheran Cemetery roughly in half. Today, Metropolitan Avenue continues to serve shoppers with the Metro Mall, which houses chain and local retailers.

Today's residents include descendants of the Germans who first settled here, as well as Italians, Jews, Russians, Poles, Hispanics, and recent immigrants from the former Yugoslavia. They all are drawn to this community for its stability—a word frequently used to describe this neighborhood comprised mostly of one- and two-family

attached and semi-attached houses.

Avoiding overcrowded streets and schools, and working to maintain and improve the look of the community, are serious endeavors for neighborhood organizations, which have not always been successful in slowing aggressive development. One of the most active civic groups in the neighborhood is the Juniper Park Civic Association, founded in 1938 to protect Juniper Valley Park, a beautiful and historically important resource for the entire community. Originally a swamp surrounded by juniper and white cedar trees, the more than 55-acre park was transformed in the early 1940s to include playgrounds, benches, athletic fields, a wading pool, and strolling paths.

The park also houses one of the last remaining farm burial grounds in the city: the Pullis Farm Cemetery at North 63rd Avenue near 81st Street. Dating back to 1846, the remains of landowner Thomas Pullis, Sr., and at least eight other family members were buried there when family-only burial

Florist shops like these photographed in 1901 clustered on what is now Mount Olivet Crescent to serve visitors to the local cemeteries (Queens Library, Long Island Division, Illustrations Collection)

St. John Cemetery, founded in 1879

NEIGHBORHOOD PROFILE

Boundaries: <u>North border:</u> Eliot Avenue; <u>east border:</u> Woodhaven Boulevard; <u>south border:</u> Cooper Avenue to Long Island Rail Road tracks; <u>west border:</u> Long Island Rail Road tracks to Fresh Pond Road

Subway and Train: <u>M train:</u> Middle Village/Metropolitan Avenue/ 67th Avenue

Bus: <u>Q54:</u> Metropolitan Avenue; <u>Q11:</u> Woodhaven Boulevard; <u>Q53:</u> Woodhaven Boulevard; <u>Q38:</u> Eliot Avenue to Metropolitan Avenue to Penelope Avenue; <u>Q67:</u> 69th Street to Fresh Pond Road; <u>Q58:</u> Fresh Pond Road; <u>Q29:</u> Dry Harbor Road

Libraries: Queens Library, Middle Village Branch (72-31 Metropolitan Avenue)

Community Board: No. 5

Police Precinct: 104th Precinct (64-2 Catalpa Avenue, Ridgewood)

Fire Department: Engine 319, Battalion 46 (78-11 67th Road)

plots on private land were common. But the historically significant site would have gone by the wayside were it not for Ed Shusterich, a Middle Village resident living nearby who took an interest in the dilapidated landmark in 1993. Shusterich formed a group of like-minded citizens who have lovingly cleaned the grounds and planted gardens at the historic cemetery, renamed the Pullis Farm Cemetery Historical Landmark, located in one of the quietest and most peaceful parts of the park in this quiet and peaceful neighborhood.

Playing bocce in Juniper Valley Park

Ozone Park

It could just as easily have been named Breezy Park or Airy Park. But in 1880, music publisher and developer Benjamin W. Hitchcock and his partner Charles C. Denton decided to call their newly formed development Ozone Park because of the gentle, fresh air currents that blew unobstructed from Jamaica Bay and the Atlantic Ocean.

In the late nineteenth century, there was still no development in Howard Beach, which lies just south of this neighborhood, and *ozone* had no connection to air pollution. Even so, today's negative connotation of the word does not seem to have dampened the appeal of this residential area, which is composed mostly of working-class families, origi-

nally of Italian, Irish, and German descent—the Italian influence is still strong, especially visible along the commercial strip of 101st Avenue, which has a number of Italian American businesses—and now including African Americans and immigrants from Latin America, the Philippines, India, and the Caribbean. In fact, overcrowding is currently one of the main issues facing Ozone Park.

An abundance of modest detached and semidetached one- and two-family frame houses built mostly in the 1920s and 1930s make up most of Ozone Park's homes. There is little room for development here. One exception is Magnolia Court, an upscale gated townhouse condominium complex at 95th Street and Albert Road that was constructed in 2003. Its modern style is quite a contrast to Tudor Village, another enclave in Ozone Park established in 1929. Located in the southwestern section of the neighborhood, just off Pitkin Avenue on 81st to 87th Streets, the area is attractively laid out with tree-lined

Aqueduct Racetrack draws residents with a three-day-a-week year-round flea market

streets and nearly four hundred meticulously maintained Tudor-style homes. An adjacent park honors the late congressman Joseph P. Addabbo, a lifelong resident, who served in the House of Representatives from 1961 until his death in 1986. (Addabbo's son Joseph P. Addabbo, Jr., another lifelong resident of the neighborhood, currently serves on the city council.)

Ozone Park's most notorious citizen was mobster John Gotti, head of the Gambino crime family. Gotti, who died in prison in 2002 from throat cancer, lived in

NEIGHBORHOOD FACTS

■ The Beat writer Jack Kerouac lived with his parents sporadically at their apartment at 133-01 Cross Bay Boulevard in Ozone Park from 1943 to 1950. There he wrote his first novel, *The Town and the City*, and his most famous, *On the Road*, which was composed on a single 120-foot roll of telegraph paper. A letter to him from his friend Allen Ginsberg was addressed to "The Wizard of Ozone Park."

■ The album notes on *At Last*, Cyndi Lauper's 2003 release, state: "*At Last* finds [Lauper] revisiting the music she heard growing up in [the] Ozone Park section of Queens." And Ozone Park claims another singer as its own: Bernadette Lazzara, better known to fans as Bernadette Peters, was born there.

neighboring Howard Beach, but he ran his operations from the now infamous Bergen Hunt and Fish Club on 101st Avenue. It was here too that for years Gotti hosted an annual neighborhood Fourth of July fireworks show.

Ozone Park is also known for racing—horseracing, that is. The first racetrack in Queens, Centerville Race Track, located near the junction of

Centerville Playground, between 96th Street and 96th Place, was named after a former racetrack

• Vanished Racetracks of Queens

Today, Aqueduct Racetrack, bordering Ozone Park in South Ozone Park, is the only horseracing venue in Queens. But as the past two centuries reveal, the area that constitutes modern-day Queens has a long and intimate history with the sport.

Horse racing made its debut in New York City with the arrival of English settlers in the 1600s. By the 1820s two racetracks had opened in the area that today makes up Ozone Park and neighboring Woodhaven: Union Course, built in 1821 for thoroughbred racing, and Centerville Race Track, built four years later for a new craze, trotting racing. (Another trotting course, the short-lived National Race Course—renamed Fashion Race Track after a famous racehorse—opened in Newtown, in today's Corona, in 1854.)

Union, the first racetrack to use dirt for its course, was considered particularly cutting-edge, and on May 27, 1823, it hosted one of the sport's most famous match races, a pre–Civil War battle between North and South featuring American Eclipse, representing the North, and Sir Henry, championing the South. More than 60,000 spectators, including most of the members of Congress, the vice president, future president Andrew Jackson, and former vice president Aaron Burr, gathered to watch the two fight it out in three grueling four-mile heats. After losing the first heat—and causing a panic in the New York Stock Exchange—American Eclipse won the next two and was declared the victor, saving the Stock Market from collapse but causing several southerners, who had bet their plantations on Sir Henry, to commit suicide on the spot. Both Union and Centerville continued to draw huge crowds, although neither facility had grandstands, which meant that the spectators—sometimes as many as 70,000—were forced to spread out along the track. Daniel Webster, the famous Whig politician from New England, was a regular at Union—and at the nearby Snedicker's Hotel, where he was known to retire for refreshments.

In the aftermath of the Civil War, new courses sprang up, including Aqueduct and tracks at Coney Island, Brighton Beach, and Jamaica. Architects increasingly turned to European models for inspiration, opting to construct elaborate clubhouses and roomy grandstands for their American spectators. By the end of the century, however, the racing boom was over. A flood of anti-gambling legislation, passed by the federal government, forced the closure of hundreds of tracks. One of the venues to fail was Union Course, which in 1939 was converted to a freight station for the Long Island Rail Road. Jamaica Race Track, a thoroughbred course built in 1903, fell victim to the housing boom; it was torn down in 1960 to make way for the Rochdale Village apartments. But two famous parks, fortunately, did survive: Aqueduct, and its neighbor Belmont Park, in Nassau County.

Magnolia Court condominiums, 95th Street and 150th Road

Rockaway and Woodhaven Boulevards, no longer exists, but the name survives in Centerville Playground, at 96th Street and Albert Road. And Ozone Park residents still flock to the "Big A," Aqueduct Racetrack, which sits on the border of Ozone Park in South Ozone Park, at 108th Street and Rockaway Boulevard (see South Ozone

A dairy wagon in 1910 (Queens Library, Long Island Division, Illustrations Collection)

Park). When it isn't hosting races, Aqueduct is the site of a three-day-a-week, year-round flea market featuring dozens of vendors selling pastries, perfume, and everything in between.

Shopping is also available along Cross Bay Boulevard near Howard Beach, where national chains are squeezed in among smaller merchants. But closer to the area is Atlantic Avenue, which separates Ozone Park from

Woodhaven to the north, and just south of that 101st Avenue, where residents can conveniently find delis, laundromats, and other establishments.

This neighborhood is just fourteen miles from Manhattan via the A subway line, but locals needn't commute far for jobs—Aqueduct Racetrack and nearby John F. Kennedy International Airport provide ample employment opportunities for those wishing to stay close to home and enjoy the ocean breezes.

NEIGHBORHOOD PROFILE

Boundaries: <u>North border:</u> Atlantic Avenue; <u>east border:</u> 108th Street to Aqueduct Racetrack to Race Track Road; <u>south border:</u> North Conduit Avenue; <u>west border:</u> Kings County line (75th Street to Liberty Avenue to Drew Street to 95th Avenue to Eldert Lane)

Subway and Train: <u>A train:</u> 80th Street, 88th Street, Rockaway Boulevard, 104th Street, Aqueduct Racetrack, North Conduit Avenue

Bus: <u>Q24:</u> Atlantic Avenue; <u>Q8:</u> 101st Avenue; <u>Q7:</u> Sutter Avenue; <u>Q11:</u> Woodhaven Boulevard to Pitkin Avenue to Centerville Street; <u>Q21:</u> Cross Bay Boulevard; <u>Q41:</u> Woodhaven Boulevard; <u>Q53:</u> Woodhaven Boulevard; <u>B15:</u> South Conduit Avenue

Libraries: Queens Library, Ozone Park Branch (92-24 Rockaway Boulevard)

Community Board: Nos. 9, 10

Police Precinct: 102nd Precinct (87-34 118th Street, Richmond Hill); 106th Precinct (103-51 101st Street)

Fire Department: Engine 285, Ladder 142, Battalion 51 (103-17 98th Street); Engine 303, Ladder 126, Battalion 50 (104-12 Princeton Street)

Hospitals and Clinics: Medisys Family Center (91-20 Atlantic Avenue)

Queens

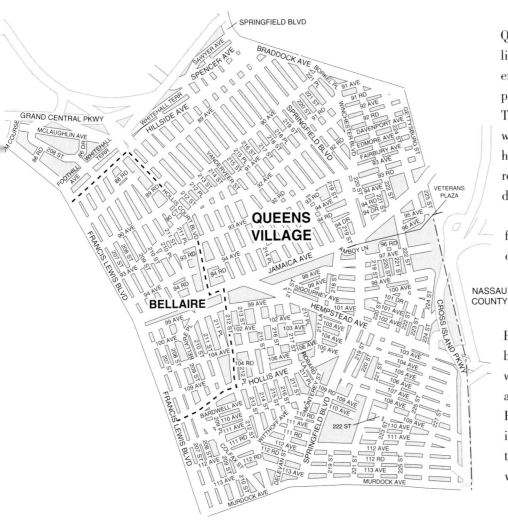

Queens Village is where young families can jump into first-time home ownership. It's also an affordable, relaxed place for those settling into retirement. This eastern Queens neighborhood, with its modest but well-tended row houses, features an unusual history—remnants of which still intrigue residents and visitors.

The neighborhood has been named four times, reflecting the area's development over the years. In colonial days it was known as Little Plains because of the treeless plain to the west that extended toward Wantagh. But starting in 1824, several small businesses along Springfield Boulevard were opened by one Thomas Brush, and the hamlet came to be called Brushville. Thirty or so years later, residents voted to change the name again to Queens, after the county in which it was located. Extensive development

Village

This neighborhood was simply called Queens in 1854 (Queens Library, Long Island Division, Illustrations Collection)

followed, along with a railroad station. After several years, to avoid confusion with the county name, the Long Island Rail Road added "Village" to the station name and the neighborhood followed suit, becoming Queens Village.

Queens Village inhabitants have long regarded their neighborhood as a solid starting point for young families seeking an affordable first home. With a smattering of cooperative apartments among a majority of one- and two-story

NEIGHBORHOOD PROFILE

Boundaries: <u>Queens Village:</u> <u>north border:</u> Grand Central Parkway to Springfield Boulevard to Braddock Avenue; <u>east border:</u> Gettysburg Street to 225th Street to Nassau County line; <u>south border:</u> Murdock Avenue; <u>west border:</u> Francis Lewis Boulevard to Epsom Course; <u>Bellaire:</u> <u>north border:</u> Hillside Avenue; <u>east border:</u> Hollis Court Boulevard to Jamaica Avenue to 212th Street; <u>south border:</u> Hollis Avenue; <u>west border:</u> Francis Lewis Boulevard

Subway and Train: <u>LIRR:</u> Queens Village, Belmont Park

Bus: <u>Q1</u>: Hillside Avenue to Springfield Boulevard to Braddock Avenue; <u>Q43, x68, N22A, N22, N26, Q36</u>: Hillside Avenue; <u>Q110</u>: Jamaica Avenue to Hempstead Avenue; <u>Q2</u>: Hollis Avenue to Hempstead Avenue; <u>Q77</u>: Francis Lewis Boulevard; <u>Q3</u>: 190th Street; <u>N1, N2, N3, N6, N24</u>: Hillside Avenue to Francis Lewis Boulevard to Jamaica Avenue to Hempstead Avenue; <u>Q27, Q88</u>: Springfield Boulevard; <u>Q83</u>: Springfield Boulevard

Libraries: Queens Library, Queens Village Branch (94-11 217th Street)

Community Board: No. 13

Police Precinct: 105th Precinct (92-08 222nd Street)

Fire Department: Ladder 160, Battalion 53 (64-04 Springfield Boulevard); Engine 304, Ladder 162, Battalion 53 (218-44 97th Avenue)

frame houses, it is just west of Nassau County but has significantly lower property taxes, especially appealing to first-time homebuyers. In that respect, this community has not changed much since the housing boom of the 1920s, when hundreds of modest row houses were built to accommodate the working classes eager to leave the city behind for a simpler, more bucolic life. They found just what they were looking for in this rural neighborhood, which had long before been an oasis for shooting enthusiasts. The area had been home to the Creedmoor Rifle Range, established in 1873, which hosted numerous regional, national, and international competitions. When accommodations proved necessary for competitors, the Creedmoor Range Hotel was built, along with the Creedmoor Club House and Pavilion, which also served as headquarters for the National Rifle Association.

All these buildings are now gone, but remains of those days are reflected in some of the existing street names—Winchester Boulevard, for example, which runs north to Musket and Range Streets in Bellerose Manor, an area once part of Queens Village. And today Creedmoor Psychiatric Center lies where the massive rifle range once did. While this facility's zip code still falls under Queens Village, Creedmoor is geographically situated in Bellerose, to the northeast.

In the western section of Queens Village lies a small area called **Bellaire,** which once attracted shooting aficionados of another sort. In 1899 Interstate Park held a casino, a grandstand, and the National Pigeon Shooters Association. Fortunately for the

A peaceful respite welcomes residents and visitors to Queens Village

NEIGHBORHOOD FACTS

■ The American novitiate of Little Sisters of the Poor, an international organization founded in 1839 to care for the elderly poor, is located at 110-30 221st Street. Queens Village is also home to a number of churches. Among the oldest are Queens Reformed Church (1858) at 94-79 Springfield Boulevard and St. Joachim and Anne Church (1898) at 218-26 105th Avenue; the eighteenth-century parsonage of Embury Methodist Church is the oldest building in Queens Village.

■ Antun's Catering, at 96-43 Springfield Boulevard, in the former Commonwealth Hotel building (which before that was the old Creed farmhouse), has been providing catering services for more than fifty years. Indeed, the firm proudly boasts that it has catered both a couple's wedding and their Golden Anniversary.

■ Queens Village was the site of the notorious 1927 "Dumb-bell Murder" (so dubbed by Damon Runyon because "it was so dumb"), when Ruth Snyder and her lover Judd Gray murdered her husband, Albert Snyder, at their Queens Village home. After a clumsy attempt to make the murder look like an interrupted robbery, Snyder and Gray were quickly arrested. The juicy details of their relationship and their immediate attempts to blame one another helped turn their trial into a media sensation: mystery writer Mary Roberts Rinehart, director D. W. Griffith, and evangelists Billy Sunday and Aimee Semple McPherson all attended. Snyder and Gray were electrocuted in 1928, and new headlines were made when a reporter smuggled a camera into the execution chamber and photographed the moment of Snyder's death. James M. Cain's best-seller *Double Indemnity* and Sophie Treadwell's play *Machinal* are both based on the case.

The old Community movie theater in Bellaire

birds, gunning down pigeons was outlawed in 1902, and five years later a development company cleared the grounds for housing.

The relatively low taxes of Queens Village are attractive not only to new home-buyers but to the many older people who have been here since the 1950s. At that time, Queens Village was populated mostly with German, Italian, and Irish families, but as in other borough neighborhoods, this area is now a fusion of cultures: Hispanic, Asian, Indian, and other nationalities, with African Americans predominating.

Modest but well-maintained houses attract first-time homebuyers to 217th Street

Residents of Queens Village shop, dine, and find entertainment along Jamaica Avenue, Springfield Boulevard, and Hillside Avenue. And mass-transit options are plentiful, including the Long Island Rail Road at Springfield Boulevard, which offers a half-hour ride to Manhattan, as well as a number of buses that run to Manhattan and connect with the subway.

Rego Park

Brick Tudor-style homes like this one on Fitchett Street are common in the Crescents

Yuabov. Izgelov. Fuzailov. These exotic-sounding surnames and thousands more can be found in the telephone directory of Rego Park, a neighborhood that is home to an impressive concentration of Bukharian Jews from Central Asia. Some are Soviet Jews who settled here in the 1970s, though many emigrated after the 1991 collapse of the Soviet Union. Consequently, to walk through one of the neighborhood's main commercial centers along Queens Boulevard and 63rd Drive is to see vendors peddling everything from fruits and vegetables to beauty products and fish, all from the former Soviet republics of Uzbekistan, Lithuania, Georgia, and Ukraine. And in a perfect example of original and adopted cultures blending to make a new community, alongside these vendors are run-of-the-mill all-American chains in Rego Park Center on Queens Boulevard, site of the former Alexander's department store, a longtime Queens landmark.

Rego Park developed swiftly once the seven-mile-long Queens Boulevard was expanded around 1936 from two lanes in each direction to the massive twelve-lane artery it is today. For years this "Boulevard of Death," as residents called it, was considered extremely hazardous to pedestrians, particularly senior citizens, but there have been fewer fatalities in recent years, and in 2004 a variety of safety improvements were put into place for pedestrians, including longer intervals for crossing.

Such improvements are good news for the vast number of Rego Park businesses that rely on customers who walk. But Queens Boulevard is not just a retail center. It is also lined with residential buildings, many erected in the 1920s by the Real Good Construction

The original site of Alexander's department store, a long-time landmark, which now houses the Rego Park Shopping Center

Company, from which the neighborhood's name was derived (*Real Good*). The developers also built an abundance of single- and multifamily houses that drew Irish, German, Italian, and Jewish families who wanted to leave crowded Manhattan. The opening of a Long Island Rail Road station in 1928 and the Independent subway line in 1936, the expansion of Queens Boulevard, and the 1939 World's Fair in nearby Flushing Meadows–Corona Park spurred even more growth. It was during that time that Rego Park acquired its famous landmark Lost Battalion Hall on Queens Boulevard. Built to commemorate the service of the U.S. Army's 77th Division, which refused to surrender during the World War I Battle of Argonne Forest and lost more than half its 550 members, the hall is now an active community center and home to the city's only dedicated Olympic weightlifting program.

During the 1940s further construction occurred in this neighborhood, with one example of an outstanding development just south of the railroad in a neatly arranged section of semicircular blocks known as the Crescents. These six unique streets run alphabetically, from Asquith to Fitchett, and feature mock-Tudor and Colonial houses.

NEIGHBORHOOD FACTS

- Graphic novelist Art Spiegelman grew up in Rego Park, and his Pulitzer Prize–winning *Maus: A Survivor's Tale* juxtaposes the story of his father's experiences in Poland during the Holocaust with the family's later life in the neighborhood.
- The Bukharian Jewish Museum, at 60-05 Woodhaven Boulevard, contains more than two thousand artifacts and features exhibits on the 2,500-year-old culture of the Bukharian Jews.
- She was just a faceless voice on the airwaves, but "Doris from Rego Park" was one of the best-known callers to an overnight sports show on WFAN-AM radio hosted by Joe Benigno. Doris Bauer's chronic cough, raspy voice, and encyclopedic knowledge of all things Mets made her a favorite among listeners for years.
- The Remsen family cemetery, located between Alderton Street and Trotting Course Lane, was designated a New York City landmark in 1981. The Remsens, originally from Germany, settled in Queens in the late 1600s. Among the most famous of the clan was Jeromus Remsen, a veteran of the French and Indian War and a colonel in charge of the 7th New York Regiment during the Revolution.

Queens Boulevard and 63rd Drive, Rego Park's commercial hub

N E I G H B O R H O O D
P R O F I L E

Boundaries: <u>North border:</u> Long Island Expressway; <u>east border:</u> 102nd Street to Queens Boulevard to 67th Avenue to Thornton Place to Fleet Street to Selfridge Street; <u>south border:</u> Metropolitan Avenue; <u>west border:</u> Cooper Avenue to Woodhaven Boulevard

Subway and Train: <u>R,G,V trains:</u> Woodhaven Boulevard, 63rd Drive/Rego Park, 67th Avenue

Bus: <u>Q88:</u> Horace Harding Expressway; <u>x51:</u> Horace Harding Expressway; <u>Q38:</u> 63rd Drive to Woodhaven Boulevard; <u>Q53:</u> 63rd Drive to Woodhaven Boulevard; <u>Q11:</u> Woodhaven Boulevard

Libraries: Queens Library, Rego Park Branch (91-41 63rd Drive)

Museums: Bukharian Jewish Museum (60-05 Woodhaven Boulevard)

Community Board: No. 6

Police Precinct: 112th Precinct (68-40 Austin Street, Forest Hills)

Fire Department: Engine 292, Battalion 46 (64-18 Queens Boulevard); Engine 324, Battalion 46 (108-01 Horace Harding Expressway)

With its clean, quiet residences, abundant shopping, and easy access to Manhattan (a mere seven miles away), Rego Park has long been recognized as an ideal place to live—not only by the general public but also by a host of celebrities such as burlesque star Gypsy Rose Lee, former Miss America Bess Myerson, Knicks center Willis Reed, and television producer Fred Silverman. In 1947 Sid Caesar moved to Rego Park from Manhattan with his wife, Florence, and their infant daughter. Three years later, having become a television phenomenon with *Your Show of Shows* (the precursor to today's *Saturday Night Live*), Caesar returned to Manhattan. But other Rego Park newcomers of his era stayed; today nearly 20 percent of the population is age sixty-five and older.

The neighborhood offers its large Jewish population a variety of houses of worship, from the conservative Rego Park

Stores along 63rd Drive reflect the increasing Russian-speaking population

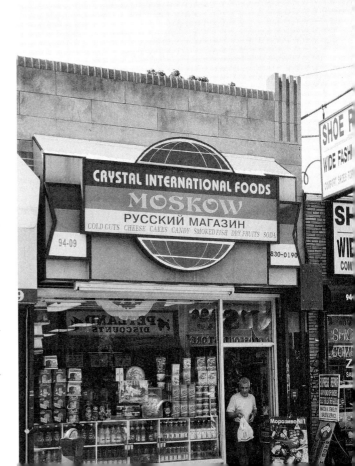

Apartment buildings along Saunders Street

Ben's Best, a Jewish delicatessen on Queens Boulevard near 63rd Drive, features sandwiches named after local dignitaries

Jewish Center, built in 1939 on Queens Boulevard, to the Chabad of Rego Park, a Hasidic synagogue on 99th Street, to the Beth-El Messianic Congregation at 63rd Drive and Wetherole Street, while Our Saviour Lutheran Church, also on 63rd Drive, has been serving the Rego Park Christian community for more than seventy-five years. In addition to ministering in English, the church offers services in Chinese, Russian, and some African languages. And a visit to Rego Park is not complete without a meal at Ben's Best, a landmark kosher deli on Queens Boulevard that has been serving the neighborhood's Jewish—and non-Jewish—residents for more than fifty years.

Richmond

Established in 1897 and in Richmond Hill since 1923, Jahn's Old Fashion Ice Cream still delights on a hot day

gingerbread trim, wraparound porches, balconies, porticos, dormers, and turrets still line the airy streets in the northern section of the neighborhood.

Once home to acres of farmland, Richmond Hill was founded in 1867 by Manhattan attorney Albon P. Man, who teamed up with landscape architect Edward Richmond to lay out the residential area, which is bounded to the north by a portion of the lush 538 acres that make up Forest Park (the rest of the park is in Woodhaven). A small section of the land was known as Morris Park until 1894, when it was absorbed into the village of Richmond Hill. (The name lingered in a separate railroad station, which closed down in 1940.) Stately homes were built by Manhattan professionals on streets that were designated by name: Waterbury Avenue (now 105th Street), Garfield Avenue (106th Street), and Herald Av-

Some neighborhoods host Renaissance fairs, others hold craft fairs; Richmond Hill offers "Restoration Fairs." Every two years, craftsmen, artisans, and professionals in plasterwork, woodwork, upholstery, quilting, gardening, painting, and other disciplines share their skills with neighborhood homeowners wanting to maintain and decorate their dignified Victorian and Queen Anne–

style houses, many of which were built at the turn of the century.

The fair is hosted by the Richmond Hill Historical Society, which is determined to maintain the neighborhood's character. The idea was conceived to encourage homeowners to protect, preserve, and appreciate the historical value of their homes. Dozens of charming structures featuring ornamental

Hill

posed the evils of tenement living in New York City. The Republican Club, across from the Richmond Hill library on Lefferts Boulevard, was built in 1908 and is now a New York City landmark.

Today Myrtle Avenue, Lefferts Boulevard, and Jamaica Avenue are this neighborhood's main shopping boulevards, and where the three meet stands the famous Triangle Hofbrau (originally Doyle's Hotel, built in 1864) at 117th Street. Currently closed to business, this was formerly the oldest running restaurant in Queens, in operation from 1893 to 1999, frequented by the likes of Mae West, Babe Ruth, and Senator Robert Wagner, Sr. It was reportedly here that composer Ernest R. Ball, a Richmond Hill resident, wrote "When Irish Eyes Are Smiling." Another long-established eatery—opened in 1923 and still active—is Jahn's Old Fashion Ice Cream and Restaurant on Hillside Avenue, which features a working nickelodeon piano and other memorabilia of days gone by.

Richmond Hill's population was largely Irish, as well as German and Italian, until the 1970s, when Hispanics began settling there as well. During that time, realtors attempted to induce white property owners to

Richmond Hill has one of the largest Sikh communities in the United States

enue (107th Street). Around 1915 the names were changed to emulate Philadelphia's numerical street system.

Several historic buildings still recall the elegance of those days. The Church of the Resurrection, on 118th Street between Hillside Avenue and 85th Avenue, was the first church in Richmond Hill. Built in 1874, it is listed on the National Register of Historic Places. A plaque in the church commemorates the visit of Governor Theodore Roosevelt to attend the June 1, 1900, wedding of Clara Riis, daughter of famed newspaperman and Richmond Hill resident Jacob Riis, whose *How the Other Half Lives* (1890) ex-

160

The famed Triangle Hofbrau restaurant around the turn of the century (Queens Library, Long Island Division, Illustrations Collection)

"Little Guyana," featuring such retailers as West Indian Halal Meat, Madhu Beauty Salon, and Kaieteur Express Restaurant.

A true melting pot, Richmond Hill also boasts one of the largest Sikh communities in the United States. The

sell hastily and at a loss, instilling fears of reduced property values once minorities began moving in. By 1973, however, the Richmond Hill Block Association had been established, and was hard at work trying to counteract this blockbusting.

South Richmond Hill, essentially the area between Atlantic Avenue and Linden Boulevard, has its own zip code, and houses here are much closer together because developers built new houses between older ones or demolished large homes to make way for a multitude of smaller ones. Many of these are multifamily dwellings housing Trinidadians, Colombians, Ecuadorians, and Indians who relocated here in the 1980s from their home countries. The area was also discovered by Guyanese, primarily of East Indian descent, who immigrated to Richmond Hill during the same time period. With its exotic aromas and colorful wares, Liberty Avenue is a virtual

NEIGHBORHOOD PROFILE

Boundaries: Richmond Hill: north border: Union Turnpike to Park Lane to Forest Park Drive to Babbage Street to 85th Avenue to Metropolitan Avenue to 127th Street to Kew Gardens Road to 86th Road to 135th Street to 87th Avenue; east border: Van Wyck Expressway; south border: Linden Boulevard to Rockaway Boulevard; west border: 108th Street to Atlantic Avenue to 98th Street to Park Lane to Freedom Drive to Myrtle Avenue to Forest Park to Pedestrian Way; South Richmond Hill: north border: Atlantic Avenue; east border: Van Wyck Expressway; south border: Linden Boulevard to Rockaway Boulevard; west border: 108th Street
Subway and Train: J train: 104th Street, 111th Street, 121st Street; Z train: 104th Street, 121st Street; A train: 111th Street/Liberty Avenue, Lefferts Boulevard/Liberty Avenue
Bus: Q56: Jamaica Avenue; Q37: 111th Street; Q24: Atlantic Avenue; Q8: 101st Avenue; Q41: 111th Street to 127th Avenue; Q112: Liberty Avenue; Q10: Lefferts Boulevard; Q7: Rockaway Boulevard; Q9: 135th Street; Q55: Myrtle Avenue
Libraries: Queens Library, Lefferts Branch (103-34 Lefferts Boulevard); Richmond Hill Branch (118-14 Hillside Avenue)
Community Board: Nos. 9, 10
Police Precinct: 102nd Precinct (87-34 118th Street)
Fire Department: Engine 270, Battalion 50, Division 13 (91-45 121st Street); Engine 308 (107-12 Lefferts Boulevard)
Hospitals and Clinics: Women's Health Center (133-03 Jamaica Avenue); Jamaica Hospital Medical Center (8900 Van Wyck Expressway)

N E I G H B O R H O O D
F   A   C   T   S

■ Jamaica Hospital Medical Center, at 8900 Van Wyck Expressway, was founded in 1891 by a group of philanthropic women known as the United Circle of the King's Daughters. Launched in a rented four-bedroom home, Jamaica Hospital Medical Center today is a 387-bed, not-for-profit teaching hospital serving a population of more than half a million in Queens and eastern Brooklyn.

■ In the 1920s, during the time that the Marx Brothers were performing on Broadway, they lived in a house on 134th Street.

■ The corner of Park Lane and Myrtle Avenue is the site of a monument erected by neighborhood residents to commemorate soldiers who fought and died in World War I. Sculpted by Joseph Pollia, the bronze statue of an infantryman at the grave of his fallen comrade was titled by the artist *My Buddy* but is popularly known as "The Doughboy."

■ Scenes from *White Lies, Goodfellas, In & Out*, and *Big Night* were shot at various locales throughout Richmond Hill.

Sikh religion originated in the Punjab region of India, and in the 1980s and early 1990s, after a failed attempt to achieve independence from the Indian government, Sikhs fled widespread persecution in their homeland. A large number of survivors established roots in Richmond Hill, where the Sikh Cultural Society gurdwara (temple) was built in 1972 on 118th Street. The gurdwara was the oldest in North America and the center of the 150,000-member Sikh community in the Tri-State area as well as the repository of an extensive library of Sikh cultural and religious materials. It was destroyed in a fire in 2002, but plans are under way to rebuild it, with donations coming in from around the world. To help educate their neighbors about the Sikh religion the community hosts the festive Sikh Pride Parade each year.

Ridgewood

Ridgewood is a piece of living history. Considered primarily a modest, working-class neighborhood on the Brooklyn border, as a Multiple Historic Resource Area, Ridgewood is in fact one of the largest historic districts in the United States, with more than 2,900 buildings in eighteen districts listed on the National Register of Historic Places.

Residents and visitors can't help but notice the turn-of-the-century two- and three-story Romanesque Revival and Renaissance tenements, brick row houses, and brownstones that dominate this neighborhood—a substantial portion of which are in mint condition, with original ironworks, front stoops, carvings, cornices, and other intact architectural elements. These noble structures of Ridgewood were built mostly by Germans, who not only worked as laborers to create this neighborhood but also settled here with their families in the late 1800s and early 1900s.

The neighborhood became famous for its German beer gardens and breweries, and by 1905 five major brewing companies spanned a five-block area. Knitting mills and other light manufacturing also flourished, providing ample job opportunities for locals. Descendants of those first German residents still live in Ridgewood, and a number of German stores and restaurants can be found along the neighborhood's main shopping street, Myrtle Avenue. The 165-foot tower of St. Aloysius Catholic Church at 382 Onderdonk Avenue, built more than a hundred years ago by German immigrants, is still a neighborhood landmark.

Although today's retail and residential environment is also influenced by the arrival of Hispanics, Italians, Asians, Koreans, and Romanians, among others, many Ridgewood residents maintain a strong sense of German nationalism, with a number of clubs and organizations, among them the German American School (founded in 1892 and incorporated in 1911 by the Regents of the University of the State of New York) and the national headquarters of the Steuben Society of America (established in 1919 in the aftermath of World War I to educate the public about the positive roles that German Americans have played in American society), both on Fresh Pond Road.

During the seventeenth and eighteenth centuries, the area of today's Ridgewood was farmland, owned primarily by Dutch settlers, including the Onderdonk family, whose house, the Vander Ende–Onderdonk farmhouse, built around 1709 and

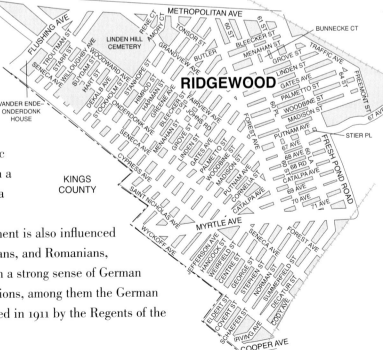

acquired in the 1820s by Adrien Onderdonk, remained a family home until 1905. English settlers began arriving in the early eighteenth century, and it was they who named the area Ridgewood, after its main topographical features. As transportation to Brooklyn improved, with a horsecar line along Myrtle Avenue and, later, elevated train and trolley lines, the area began to grow. At the turn of the twentieth century, Gustav Mathews acquired the remaining farmland and began building housing for Ridgewood's largely German working class.

The population of Ridgewood has changed since then, with a large influx of Hispanics and other immigrants, but residents are united in their commitment to preserving the neighborhood's historic structures. Credit for obtaining the national landmark designation for much of Ridgewood goes to the Greater Ridgewood Restoration Corporation, a nonprofit housing consultant founded in 1975 to stabilize and improve the neighborhoods of Ridgewood, Glendale, Middle Village, and Maspeth.

Residents also banded together in 1975 to form the Greater Ridgewood Historical Society, which saved the notable Vander Ende–Onderdonk Dutch farmhouse from demolition. Situated at 18-20 Flushing Avenue, the house is listed on the National Register of Historic Places and is on the state register of historic sites.

NEIGHBORHOOD FACTS

■ Fans of polka dancing will find a great party at Gottscheer Hall on Fairview Avenue, a popular German social club where members of the dance group Die Erste Gottscheer Tanzgruppe meet. Also here are the Gottscheer Bowling Club and the Gottscheer Rod and Gun Club.

■ In a continuation of the Queens-Brooklyn boundary dispute, a portion of what is now Ridgewood spread into the neighborhood of Bushwick. Residents organized to disassociate themselves from what they considered a less-than-desirable neighborhood, and in 1979 they were granted a Queens zip code, which they share with Glendale.

■ Stockholm Street is the only brick road in Queens.

■ James Cagney and Yankee Phil Rizzuto both attended Public School 71 in Ridgewood.

The house operates as a museum, with the society holding guided tours, slide lectures, workshops, and other special events there throughout the year.

The grounds of the Onderdonk

Vander Ende–Onderdonk House (ca. 1709), with Covert House (ca. 1786) at right, 1922 (The Queens Library, Long Island Division, Eugene Armbruster Collection)

164 house hold another significant piece of local history: Arbitration Rock, half of which at one time lay in Bushwick, Brooklyn, and the other half in Ridgewood. In 1769, after the settlement of a boundary dispute between Queens and Brooklyn that began in 1660, the rock was placed as a boundary marker, but over the years it all but disappeared from view—that is, until 2000, when representatives of the

• Mathews Model Flats

Most famous among the Romanesque Revival and Renaissance tenements and brick row houses that grace Ridgewood are the Mathews Model Flats. Built around 1905 by the G. X. Mathews Company, the complex features more than eight hundred six-family row houses of three stories each—a four-and-a-half-mile row if all the homes were placed side by side. One reason the complex is so attractive is that although each home follows a consistent overall design (including beautiful arched windows on the third floor), they all have unique flourishes—for example, in the area above each doorway.

Gustav Mathews was famous for his attention to detail. He insisted on only the best workmanship and planned the homes literally down to the last brick: the row houses use alternating light and dark brickwork, and most of the glazed bricks came from the kilns of the Kreischerville Brick Works on Staten Island, which was known for its speckled or iron-spotted bricks that sparkle in the light. Mathews's multiple-family dwelling concept was so inventive that it was exhibited at the Panama Pacific Fair of 1915 as one of the most significant accomplishments in New York City housing. Residents today honor Mathews's achievement by living in, and carefully maintaining, these distinctive, lovingly crafted homes.

Brick homes on Seneca Avenue and Summerfield Street

NEIGHBORHOOD PROFILE

Boundaries: <u>North border:</u> Metropolitan Avenue; <u>east border:</u> Long Island Rail Road tracks to 67th Avenue to Fresh Pond Road to Long Island Rail Road tracks; <u>west border:</u> Kings County line (Irving Avenue to Eldert Street to Wyckoff Avenue to Gates Avenue to Saint Nicholas Avenue to Menahan Street to Cypress Avenue to Flushing Avenue to Onderdonk Avenue)
Subway and Train: <u>M train:</u> Seneca Avenue, Forest Avenue
Bus: <u>B20:</u> Decatur Street/Summerfield Street; <u>Q58:</u> Fresh Pond Road; <u>Q39:</u> Forest Avenue; <u>B38:</u> Woodward Avenue to Seneca Avenue; <u>B13:</u> Gates Avenue to Fresh Pond Road; <u>B54:</u> Madison Street; <u>Q54:</u> Metropolitan Avenue
Libraries: Queens Library, Ridgewood Branch (20-12 Madison Street)
Museums: Vander Ende–Onderdonk House Museum (18-20 Flushing Avenue)
Community Board: No. 5
Police Precinct: 104th Precinct (64-2 Catalpa Avenue)
Fire Department: Engine 291, Ladder 140, Battalion 45 (56-07 Metropolitan Avenue)

Gottscheer Hall is a neighborhood meeting place for Ridgewood's German American population

New York City Department of Environmental Preservation and Queens Borough Hall found it buried under a portion of Onderdonk Avenue. After much dispute, it was agreed that the rock would be moved to its current home, where it was ceremoniously placed in June 2002.

The

NASSAU
COUNTY

NASSAU
COUNTY

FAR
ROCKAWAY

SEAGIRT
BLVD

B 31 ST

WAVECREST

SURF RD

ROCKAWAY INLET

Legal surfing is back, and here come the Rocka-ways—riding a wave of new interest in New York City's only oceanfront community. In April 2005, a "surf access zone," designated by the New York City Parks and Recreation Department and championed by the citizen group Surfrider NYC, was opened, allowing residents and visitors to score some swells in the Atlantic without breaking the law. It is a sign of good things to come for this promising—and long-neglected—area. Bordering Nassau County's Five Towns area, the Rocka-ways is an eleven-mile penin-

Rockaways

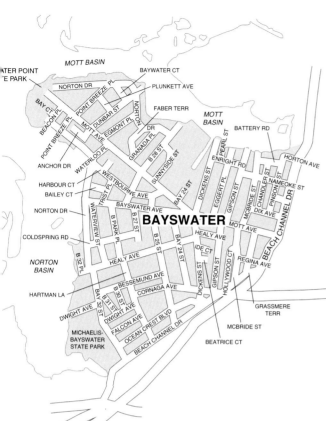

BAYSWATER

(map labels: MOTT BASIN, WATER POINT STATE PARK, NORTON DR, BAY CT, BEACON PL, POINT BREEZE PL, ANCHOR DR, HARBOUR CT, BAILEY CT, NORTON DR, COLDSPRING RD, NORTON BASIN, HARTMAN LA, MICHAELIS-BAYSWATER STATE PARK, WATERLOO PL, TRISH PL, WESTBOURNE AVE, WATERVIEW ST, B PARK PL, B 27 ST, B 25 ST, B 30 ST, B 31 ST, B 32 ST, B 32 PL, DWIGHT AVE, FALCON AVE, OCEAN CREST BLVD, BEACH CHANNEL DR, BAYSWATER AVE, HEALY AVE, BESSEMUND AVE, CORNAGA AVE, DWIGHT AVE, BAY 24 ST, BAY 25 ST, IDE CT, DICKENS ST, GIPSON ST, HOLLYWOOD CT, REGINA AVE, MCBRIDE ST, BEATRICE CT, GRASSMERE TERR, DICKENS ST, EGGERT PL, GIPSON ST, MCBRIDE ST, CHANDLER ST, DIX AVE, PINSON ST, NAMEOKE ST, ENRIGHT RD, PEARL ST, BATTERY RD, HORTON AVE, MOTT BASIN, FABER TERR, DUNBAR ST, GRANADA PL, SUNNYSIDE ST, BAY 24 ST, B 28 ST, MOTT AVE, EGMONT PL, NORTON DR, PLUNKETT AVE, BAYWATER CT)

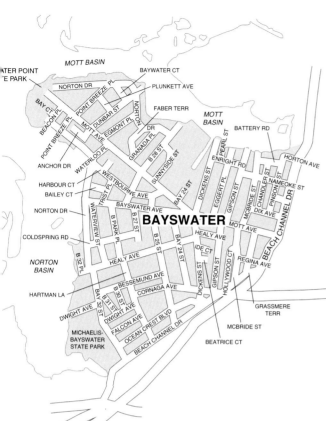

The revitalized Rockaways draw people from all over the city to the boardwalk at Rockaway Beach

Today's Edgemere is mostly apartment complexes, but traces of the past remain, such as these houses from the early 1900s

sula stretching to the west. The original landholders, the Native American Canarsie Indians, called this peninsula "Rechouwacky," which translates to "the place of our people." White settlers changed the name to Rockaway and in the 1800s and early 1900s developed it as a thriving vacation spot for wealthy Manhattanites and the working classes, replete with hotels, board-

EDGEMERE

(map labels: GRASS HASSOCK CHANNEL, EDGEMERE PARK, NORTON BASIN, COUCH BASIN, CONCH RD, HOUGH PL, REINHART RD, ALMEDA AVE, ALMEDA AVE, ELIZABETH AVE, HANTZ RD, NORTON, B 51 ST, B 54 ST, B 58 ST, B 56 ST, BEACH CHANNEL DR, ARVERNE BLVD, ROCKAWAY BEACH BLVD, ROCKAWAY BEACH BLVD, B 56 PL, B 55 ST, B 54 ST, B 53 ST, B 52 ST, B 51 ST, B 50 ST, B 49 ST, B 48 ST, ROCKAWAY FWY, EDGEMERE AVE, B 47 ST, B 46 ST, B 45 ST, B 44 ST, B 43 ST, B 42 ST, B 41 ST, B 40 ST, B 39 ST, B 38 ST, B 37 ST, B 36 ST, B 35 ST, B 34 ST, B 33 ST, B 32 ST, EDGEMERE RD, SPRAY VIEW AVE, SEAGIRT BLVD, NORTON AVE, BEACH CHANNEL DR, B 48 WAY, B 48 WAY, B 46 WAY, B 46 PL, B 47 WAY)

ATLANTIC OCEAN

167

Rockaways' Playland, 1970 (Courtesy of the Queens Library, Long Island Division, Postcard Collection)

KINGS
COUNTY

JAMAICA BAY

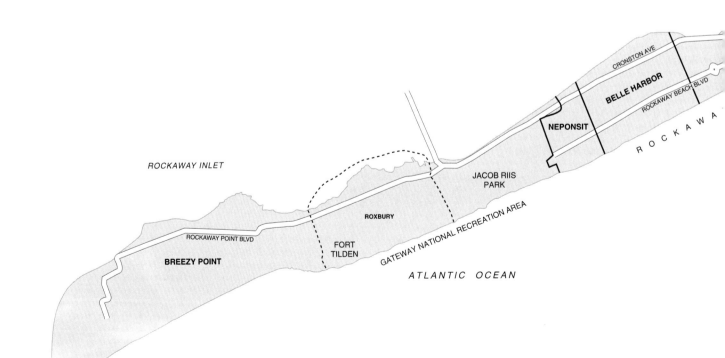

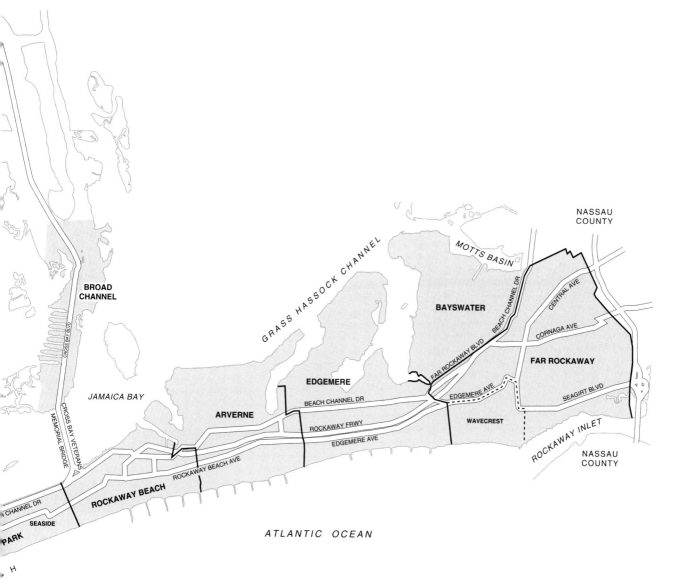

walks, concession stands, grand estates, and an amusement park. Jewish, German, Russian, and Irish immigrants settled in the peninsula, and a variety of tiny communities sprang up.

The tide started to turn after World War II when the city began dotting the area with public housing projects, causing many of the white residents to leave for the suburbs in the 1950s and 1960s. As advances in transportation made distant summer resort areas increasingly accessible, too, this beachfront playground rapidly lost its appeal. Corroded and abandoned beach bungalows and cottages in once thriving areas painted a dismal landscape, and large tracts of land, bulldozed in urban-renewal plans that never came to fruition, remained vacant for years.

Until now, that is. The Rockaways, accessible via the A train and the Long Island Rail Road, are undergoing a resurrection. Eager developers are seizing even

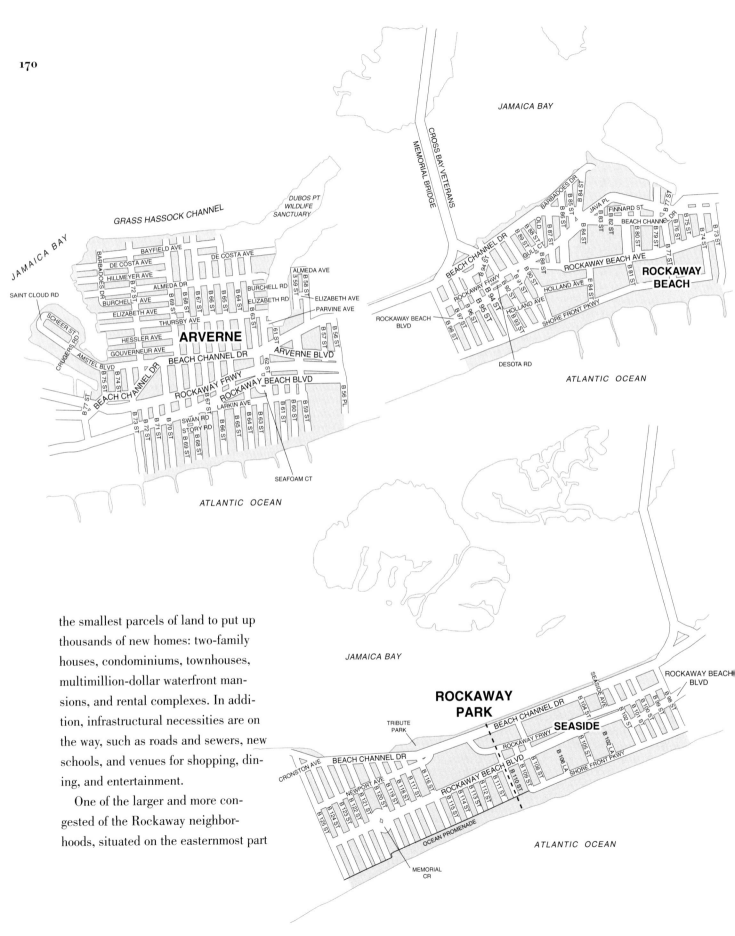

170

the smallest parcels of land to put up thousands of new homes: two-family houses, condominiums, townhouses, multimillion-dollar waterfront mansions, and rental complexes. In addition, infrastructural necessities are on the way, such as roads and sewers, new schools, and venues for shopping, dining, and entertainment.

One of the larger and more congested of the Rockaway neighborhoods, situated on the easternmost part

Summer visitors flock to Seaside

of this peninsula, is **Far Rockaway.** Among the earliest of those putting roots down here was Captain John Palmer, who sold his grant of land in 1690 to a Richard Cornell. Cornell built a large house near what is today Beach 19th Street between Plainview Avenue and Seagirt Boulevard. When he died a few years later, he left his vast property holdings to his children. (Cornell and his descendants are buried in the historic Cornell Cemetery.) In 1833 the first hotel in the Rockaways, the Marine Pavilion, opened around these grounds, drawing the first wave of out-of-towners to the ocean breezes.

Today Far Rockaway is struggling with increasing development. Almost Paradise, a popular beachfront scuba

NEIGHBORHOOD FACTS

■ In the mid-1800s, the largest hotel in the world, the Rockaway Beach Hotel, in what is now Rockaway Park, stretched from Beach 110th Street to Beach 116th Street. Today there are no hotels in the Rockaways at all.

■ Among the spectacular parks situated along the Rockaways (including Michaelis-Bayswater Park, Edgemere Park, and the Jamaica Bay Wildlife Refuge) are Jacob Riis Park and Fort Tilden, both part of the Gateway National Recreation Area, a 26,000-acre resource that stretches through three New York City boroughs and parts of northern New Jersey. Jacob Riis Park, named after the famed newspaperman (and Queens resident) who was an advocate of the urban poor, was completed in 1938, the brainchild of Robert Moses. In addition to the sprawling beach and boardwalk, visitors can enjoy basketball and handball courts, a golf course, and hiking and bicycle trails. To the immediate west is the military base Fort Tilden (and the Rockaway Naval Air Station), built in 1917 to defend New York Harbor during World War I. (In 1919, the nation's first transatlantic flight took off from the Rockaway Naval Air Station.) The fort was named after Samuel J. Tilden, who was governor of New York in 1874 and a presidential contender in 1876. The 317-acre facility was decommissioned in 1974, and is now a public park with dunes, trails, and recreational facilities.

■ The Rockaways lost seventy-seven residents in the September 11, 2001, attack on the World Trade Center. To honor them Tribute Park was created on the spot between Jamaica Bay and Beach Channel Drive in Rockaway Park where locals watched in horror as the twin towers burst into flames and then collapsed. Rockaway residents have found other ways to pay tribute to American heroes as well: on July 14, 2006, retired firefighter Flip Mullen and his Rockaway neighbors organized a homecoming parade for wounded Iraq veterans. The thirty or so veterans were driven into the neighborhood on antique fire trucks and provided with host families for a warm welcome back.

■ *The Wave of Long Island*, a daily newspaper located at 88-08 Rockaway Beach Boulevard that has been serving the Rockaways since 1893, began as an information broadsheet headlined "Wave of Fire Sweeps Rockaway" following the Great Seaside Fire of 1892. The headline name stuck when the newspaper was founded the following year.

■ Famous residents of the Rockaways include talk show host Richard Bey and Dr. Joyce Brothers.

■ The Bayswater Players, a nonequity community theater group, has been producing one or two shows a year for almost fifty years.

pit-stop next to the legendary Atlantic Ocean diving spot at Beach 9th Street, gave way in 2003 to a housing development. And townhouses and one- and two-family houses are sprouting up throughout the neighborhood seemingly overnight. Far Rockaway's high-rise apartment buildings and houses—Colonials, Tudors, and ranches, mixed in with much older, ramshackle cottages —make for an eclectic residential area.

The population is equally diverse, with African Americans and immigrants from Guyana, Jamaica, and Central and South America, including a large population of elderly people, and a growing Orthodox Jewish community. This demographic shift is especially noticeable on Saturdays, during which

Breezy Point, a secluded respite from the clamorous boardwalk.

there is very little car and truck traffic in certain parts of this neighborhood, because Talmudic law prohibits the driving of vehicles on the Sabbath. The building of new yeshivas (Jewish schools) is also fueling the construction of hundreds of houses specifically for the Orthodox community.

The **Wavecrest** section, at the lower western corner of Far Rockaway, has also seen its share of recent construction. It was first developed in 1880 by an association of wealthy investors from Manhattan who built themselves lodges and estates. By the 1920s, beachfront bungalows also dotted the waterfront. After World War I, the estates were broken up, streets were laid out in their place, and buildings were erected. More recent

NEIGHBORHOOD
PROFILE

Boundaries: <u>The Rockaways:</u> <u>north border:</u> Jamaica Bay; <u>east border:</u> Nassau County line; <u>south and west borders:</u> Atlantic Ocean; <u>Far Rockaway:</u> <u>north and east borders:</u> Nassau County line; <u>south border:</u> Rockaway Inlet; <u>west border:</u> Beach 32nd Street to Seagirt Boulevard to Beach Channel Drive; <u>Wavecrest:</u> <u>north border:</u> Seagirt Boulevard to Edgemere Avenue to Fernside Place to Elk Drive; <u>east border:</u> Beach 20th Street to Seagirt Boulevard to Beach 19th Street; <u>south border:</u> Rockaway Inlet; <u>west border:</u> Beach 32nd Street; <u>Bayswater:</u> <u>north border:</u> Mott Basin; <u>east border:</u> Beach Channel Drive; <u>south and west borders:</u> Norton Basin; <u>Edgemere:</u> <u>north border:</u> Grass Hassock Channel; <u>east border:</u> Norton Basin to Beach Channel Drive to Seagirt Boulevard to Beach 32nd Street; <u>south border:</u> Atlantic Ocean; <u>west border:</u> Beach 56th Place to Beach 56th Street to Beach Channel Drive to Beach 58th Street to Almeda Avenue; <u>Arverne:</u> <u>north border:</u> Jamaica Bay to Grass Hassock Channel; <u>east border:</u> Almeda Avenue to Beach 58th Street to Beach Channel Drive to Beach 56th Street to Beach 56th Place; <u>south border:</u> Atlantic Ocean; <u>west border:</u> Beach 73rd Street to Beach Channel Drive to Beach 77th Street; <u>Rockaway Beach:</u> <u>north border:</u> Jamaica Bay; <u>east border:</u> Beach 77th Street to Beach Channel Drive to Beach 73rd Street; <u>south border:</u> Atlantic Ocean; <u>west border:</u> Beach 98th Street; <u>Rockaway Park:</u> <u>north border:</u> Jamaica Bay; <u>east border:</u> Beach 98th Street; <u>south border:</u> Atlantic Ocean; <u>west border:</u> Beach 125th Street; <u>Seaside:</u> <u>north border:</u> Jamaica Bay; <u>east border:</u> Beach 98th Street; <u>south border:</u> Atlantic Ocean; <u>west border:</u> Beach 110th Street; <u>Belle Harbor:</u> <u>north border:</u> Jamaica Bay; <u>east border:</u> Beach 125th Street; <u>south border:</u> Atlantic Ocean; <u>west border:</u> Beach 142nd Street; <u>Neponsit:</u> <u>north border:</u> Jamaica Bay; <u>east border:</u> Beach 142nd Street; <u>south border:</u> Atlantic Ocean; <u>west border:</u> Jacob Riis Park; <u>Breezy Point:</u> <u>north border:</u> Rockaway Inlet; <u>east border:</u> eastern boundary of Jacob Riis Park; <u>south and west borders:</u> Atlantic Ocean; <u>Roxbury:</u> <u>north border:</u> Rockaway Inlet; <u>east border:</u> Beach 169th Street; <u>south border:</u> Atlantic Ocean; <u>west border:</u> Beach 193rd Street; <u>Broad Channel:</u> <u>north border:</u> Gateway National Recreation Area; <u>east, south, and west borders:</u> Jamaica Bay

Subway and Train: <u>A train:</u> Far Rockaway/Mott Avenue, Beach 25 Street, Beach 36th Street, Beach 44th Street, Beach 60th Street, Beach 67th Street; <u>A, S trains:</u> Broad Channel, Beach 90th Street, Beach 98th Street, Beach 105th Street, Beach 116th Street; <u>LIRR:</u> Far Rockaway

Bus: <u>Q22, N33:</u> Seagirt Boulevard; <u>N31, N32:</u> Beach 20th Street to Central Avenue; <u>Q113:</u> Beach 9th Street to Beach Channel Drive; <u>Q22A:</u> Bayswater Avenue to Mott Avenue; <u>Q22:</u> Beach Channel Drive, Rockaway Beach Boulevard, Jacob Riis Park; <u>Q21, Q53:</u> Rockaway Beach Boulevard across Cross Bay Bridge, Cross Bay Boulevard; <u>Q35:</u> Newport Avenue, Jacob Riis Park

Libraries: Queens Library, Far Rockaway Branch (16-37 Central Avenue); Arverne Branch (312 Beach 54th Street); Peninsula Branch (92-25 Rockaway Beach Boulevard); Seaside Branch (116-15 Rockaway Beach Boulevard); Broad Channel Branch (16-26 Cross Bay Boulevard)

Museums: Rockaway Museum (88-08 Rockaway Beach Boulevard)

Theaters: Rockaway Park Playhouse (160 Beach Street and 116th Avenue); The Bayswater Players (2355 Healy Avenue)

Community Board: No. 14

Police Precinct: 101st Precinct (16-12 Mott Avenue); 100th Precinct (92-24 Rockaway Beach Boulevard, Rockaway Beach)

Fire Department: Engine 264, Battalion 47 (16-15 Central Avenue); Engine 265, Ladder 121 (58-03 Rockaway Beach Boulevard, Arverne); Engine 266, Battalion 47 (92-20 Rockaway Beach Boulevard); Engine 268, Ladder 137, Battalion 47 (257 Beach 116th Street); Engine 328, Ladder 134 (16-19 Central Avenue); Engine 329, Battalion 47 (402 Beach 169th Street, Roxbury, Breezy Point); Broad Channel Volunteer Fire Department and Ambulance Corps (15 Noel Road)

Hospitals and Clinics: St. John's Episcopal Hospital South Shore (327 Beach 19th Street); Neponsit Health Care Center (149-25 Rockaway Beach Boulevard); Horizon Care Center (64-11 Beach Channel Drive); Lawrence Health Care Center (50 Beach 54th Street); Resort Nursing Home (430 Beach 68th Street)

• Rockaways' Playland

The now-defunct Rockaways' Playland, built in 1901 along Rockaway Beach, was Coney Island's chief rival for the first half of the twentieth century. Its brightly colored lights stayed lit until 1987—well past its heyday—when financial pressures and urban redevelopment finally forced the park's closure.

The idea behind Rockaways' Playland sprang from the mind of LaMarcus Thompson, an enterprising patent collector, who in 1884 erected the world's first roller coaster at Coney Island. Seeking to replicate his success, Thompson turned to Rockaway Beach, "the most famous watering place in America," according to one of his contemporaries, historian William W. Munsell. A prominent beachside arcade was built along the Atlantic, and rides and games followed soon thereafter: among them, a Fun House, Shooting Gallery, and Skee-ball ramp. The park's first roller coaster, Playland Coaster, opened in 1925. Several other coasters came and went, including the 3,000-foot-long, 70-foot-high Atom Smasher (also known as the Cinerama Coaster), which was featured prominently in the 1950s film *This Is Cinerama.*

Key to Playland's early popularity were the surrounding towns—Edgemere, Arverne, Rockaway Park—that offered visitors affordable summer accommodations. By the 1950s, however, that dynamic had begun to change. Public housing projects, popular with New York City planners, introduced thousands of low-income housing units to the area. In 1969, a large section of the Rockaways was bulldozed for future construction. Attendance at the park declined, a trend from which Playland never recovered. All that remains of the amusement park once dubbed "the playground of New York" is a collection of artifacts housed along with other local memorabilia in the Rockaway Museum on Rockaway Beach Boulevard.

In recent years, the Playland site has begun to show new life. A modern condominium complex owned by Rockaway Estates now sits on the ground the park once occupied.

developments include the 2004 complex of two- and three-family semi-attached houses at Lewmay Road, between Beach 29th and Beach 32nd Streets.

But not everyone is happy with the new construction, especially those who cherish the last of the quaint bungalows in this tiny neighborhood. In 1984, because developers were threatening to raze these bungalows, a group of concerned citizens formed the Beachside Bungalow Preservation Association of Far Rockaway, which continues to fight to save the cottages. The remaining bungalows, between Beach 24th and Beach 26th Street, are especially distinctive against the backdrop of Wavecrest Gardens on Seagirt Boulevard, a six-story, thirty-eight-building apartment complex built in 1999 for low- to moderate–income families. Wavecrest II, also for low to moderate–

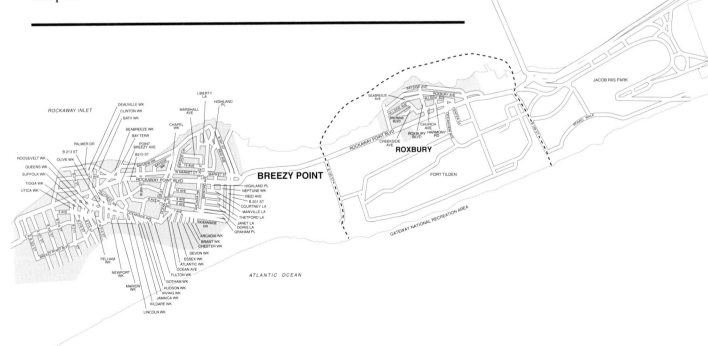

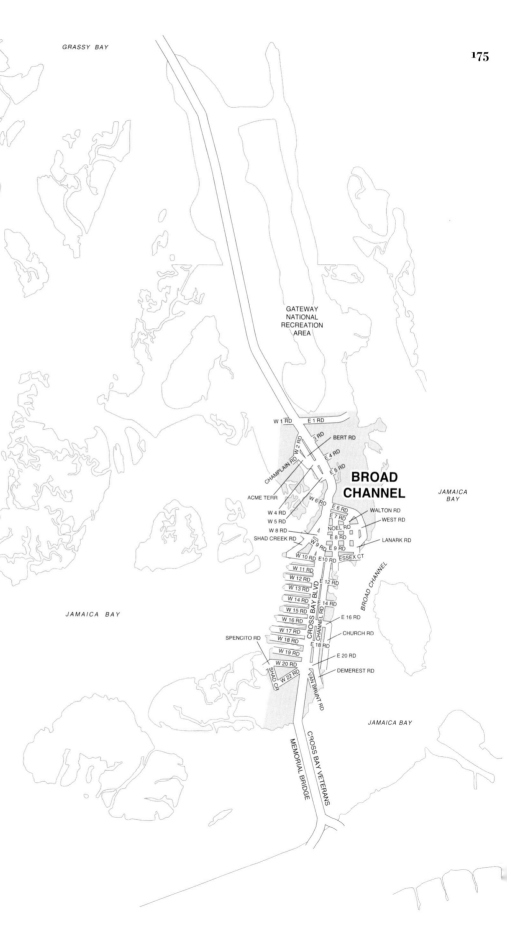

income households, followed in 2001 on Beach 24th Street.

Additional affordable housing can be found directly north of Wavecrest in the more secluded **Bayswater** neighborhood. Here, Ocean Pointe on Beach Channel Drive features attached one-family and semi-detached two-family townhouses geared toward lower-income buyers. There are also free-standing one- and two-family homes here and, in a nod to the past, well-maintained mansions, such as the former residence of the influential Mott family, who first acquired land in the Rockaways beginning in the seventeenth century and remained into the twentieth, and for whom Mott Avenue and Mott Basin are named. Point Breeze Place features a lovely assortment of these older structures dating back to the late 1800s, when this neighborhood was developed as a summer resort for the elite.

Heading west, turn-of-the-century travelers would have come across what was then called New Venice. Of course, there are no canals in **Edgemere,** renamed in Anglo-Saxon for its proximity to the ocean on one side and the bay on the other. Today this neighborhood is known primarily for the Edgemere Houses, a New York City Housing Authority project built in 1961. Directly west of it is what was previously known as Arverne Houses, another Housing Authority complex,

Broad Channel, a rustic fishing village off
the coast of New York City

built in 1951. Collectively, they are today called Ocean Bay Apartments. On
Beach 41st Street is yet another housing project, and the Housing Authority
has launched a multifaceted overhaul
of these complexes, which have been
plagued with crime.

Arverne is not only having its public housing revitalized; it is also undergoing massive development of other
sorts that has been a long time coming.
Like its counterparts in the Rockaways, Arverne was a trendy summer
resort in its heyday. It was named for its developer Remington Vernam, who
would sign checks "R. Vernam." The Arverne, a magnificent hotel, stood here
among hundreds of cottages by the sea. The boardwalk thrived. But when the
peninsula as a whole lost its appeal to tourists, the neighborhood went into a
downward spiral. By the 1960s, the area was so decrepit that most of it was bulldozed by city officials. Plan after plan for rebuilding was rejected, and for decades
more than 300 barren acres designated the Arverne Urban Renewal Area made a
dismal, blighted backdrop to the stunning views of water to the north and south.

Today an exciting oceanfront development project is under way. When completed, Arverne by the Sea will include a mix of one- and two-family homes, mid-
rise rental apartment buildings, and condominiums that are designed for middle-
to upper-income households and will be sold by lottery with preference to
Queens residents. The plans include retail space, a YMCA, a new school, a
transportation center, and 10 acres of parkland. These follow earlier and much
smaller developments, Waters Edge and Waters Edge II, erected in 1999 and
2001 by another private builder.

An entirely different sort of house—a fun house—used to be located in **Rockaway Beach,** home of Rockaways' Playland, an amusement park that opened in
1901 and rivaled Coney Island, attracting thousands of visitors annually, until it
closed down in 1987. This neighborhood was originally called Hammels after its
developer, and the name is now associated with Hammel Houses, a public housing complex built in 1955 along Beach 81st and Beach 86th Streets. The punk
group the Ramones recorded their song "Rockaway Beach" about this area in the
1970s, while it was still a popular at-
traction. Today, the neighborhood attracts surfers, who venture with their
boards via the A train for one of the
best wave-riding spots in the state.

Seasonal renters also come here and
to nearby **Seaside,** a section of **Rockaway Park** that developed as a resort
after the New York, Woodhaven and
Rockaway Railroad opened a station at
Beach 102nd and Beach 103rd Streets
in 1880. Bathhouses, bars, and hotels
were built, most of which were destroyed in the Great Seaside Fire of
1892. The area was rebuilt in the boom
following the fire, and amid the smattering of public housing projects, one
can still find small colonies of rustic
beach houses and wooden summer
bungalows—although if development
extends to this central part of the peninsula in the coming years, they could
disappear. Rockaway Beach is the

home of the Rockaway Artists Alliance, on Beach 116th Street, which engages residents of the Rockaways, particularly younger residents, in the arts and other cultural activities.

The possible loss of Rockaway Park's bungalows may not sit well with residents of adjacent **Belle Harbor,** a charming middle-class neighborhood where house styles range from Colonials to Capes to the occasional bungalow. Developed in 1907 by the West Rockaway Land Corporation, the area expanded to incorporate the Belle Harbor Yacht Club. For the most part the neighborhood consists of single-family homes, although there are cooperatives and some two-family homes. An overall sense of community predominates in Belle Harbor, one which was especially keen after neighbors lost loved ones in the September 11, 2001, attack on the World Trade Center, and just two months later, when shortly after takeoff from Kennedy Airport, a plane crashed into several homes on Beach 131st Street with deadly results for both residents and passengers—265 fatalities in all. In the spirit of the times, the Briarwood Organization, one of the new developers involved in the peninsula's recent growth, offered to rebuild the destroyed houses at no cost.

Belle Harbor's next door twin is **Neponsit,** a quiet, upscale beachfront community that was laid out around 1911, when stores and hotels were prohibited. Durable single-family houses, each required to cost over $3,000, were built for year-round residence. To ensure that this enclave remained a secluded, well-to-do neighborhood, the Neponsit Property Owners Association was formed in 1919. As a result, it remains a tight-knit community of immaculate homes just steps from the beach.

Equally exclusive, though less affluent, is the westernmost neighborhood in the peninsula—**Breezy Point,** a gated cooperative of year-round cottages, and its adopted sister, **Roxbury** (which became part of Breezy Point in 1962). The area includes Jacob Riis Park and Fort Tilden, which together make up Gateway National Recreation Area. There has been no shortage of development proposals for Breezy Point, but for the most part the generally all-white communities here have remained immune to new construction. For years, this area was dubbed the Irish Riviera, but Italian and German families are also moving in. The cooperative maintains strict guidelines for home purchases.

On the other side of the Cross Bay Veterans Memorial Bridge lies **Broad Channel,** the only populated island in Jamaica Bay, but one still rather isolated from mainland Queens. For years a remote fishing village, this largely working-class, white neighborhood grew up after Cross Bay Boulevard was opened in 1924. Most of the neighborhood residents, known as "Channelites," have lived here for generations, with deep family ties and strong national pride. Houses are humble, with a good number of them built on stilts. New York City retained title to the land here, offering households renewable ten-year leases until 1982, when the city finally allowed residents to purchase their homes. Motorboats are as common in this remote island as one-car garages are elsewhere. Cross Bay Boulevard is not only the commercial hub of this tiny community; it is also the gateway to Rockaway Beach and the rest of Queens.

Despite the congested residential housing in Far Rockaway, there's ample space on the beach

Rosedale

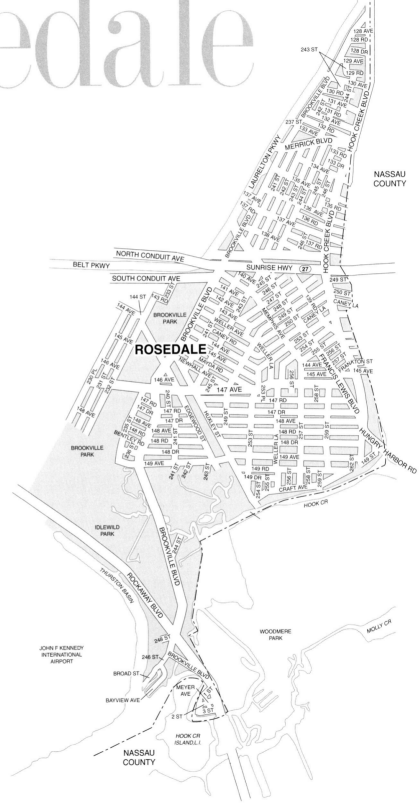

Rosedale is a success story. During the 1970s, as the borough battled racial discrimination, the neighborhood was in the headlines—for all the wrong reasons. But today this sought-after middle-class community is reaping the benefits of strong local organizations that were launched then and continue their positive work today. Rosedale, a place where neighbors of all back-grounds work together, is once again a welcoming, attractive place to call home.

Rosedale was originally called Fos-ter's Meadow, after the brothers Chris-topher and Thomas Foster, who settled the area in 1647. A railroad station that opened in 1870 led to development, and some twenty years later the Stan-dard Land Company changed the com-munity's name to Rosedale, perhaps for the wild roses that were growing there. The area later became populated with Irish and German families fleeing the crowded inner city in the 1920s and 1930s. After World War II, Italian and Jewish families also moved into these attractive, quiet streets.

Like other southeastern Queens neighborhoods such as St. Albans, Cambria Heights, and Laurelton, Rose-

dale was at that time an all-white enclave of working- and middle-class homeowners. During the early 1970s, black families began moving in as well, attracted by the low taxes and suburban feel of the neighborhood. Rosedale became a hotbed of racial tensions. Violent incidents against African Americans were frequently reported in the press, placing Rosedale in a highly undesirable limelight.

Most neighborhood residents denounced the violence, but many still left the neighborhood. To counterbalance the racial polarization and encourage citizens of all races to stay, the Rosedale Block Association was formed, welcoming newcomers. In addition, the Rosedale Civic Association, which had been founded in 1946, launched into action: in collaboration with the 113th police precinct, its members formed a volunteer civilian security patrol that quickly stabilized the neighborhood.

Today a majority African American population mingles easily with the whites, Haitians, Jamaicans, Hispanics, and others who make their home here. Rosedale, a neighborhood of one- and two-family houses, duplexes, and townhouses, today aptly bills itself as "a model integrative community" and "a strong community of harmony." A visible sign of this is the Derek Dilworth Tennis Courts, dedicated in 2001

to honor a local man who was the first African American to hold the job of air traffic control supervisor at John F. Kennedy International Airport, and a longtime youth volunteer. Before his death in 1999, Dilworth spent his spare time offering free tennis lessons to local youngsters.

The courts are located in Brookville Park, a source of pride for residents of Rosedale and neighboring Springfield Gardens, who share it. Brookville abounds in beautiful natural and humanmade features including Majestic Lake, a playground, grill sites, baseball fields (more than four hundred children play baseball in Rosedale's Little League), bocce courts, basketball courts, picnic tables, handball courts, and tennis courts.

In keeping with Dilworth's example, volunteers are essential to the park's maintenance. On one day in October 2005, for example, the new community group Friends of Brookville Park, in coordination with the nonprofit New York City's Partnership for Parks, organized volunteers on an "It's My Park Day" to paint the volleyball courts and footbridges, plant bulbs, remove debris from the lakeshore, and do general cleanup. After the hard work was finished, participants and their families celebrated with face painting and arts and crafts. The dynamic group plans to expand their park advocacy with a community garden and a park Family Day each fall.

Residents have come together on other issues as well, among them alleviating noise pollution in local classrooms affected by aircraft at nearby JFK Airport.

Two schools, Public School 195 and St. Pius, were designated "noise-affected areas" and in 2003 received soundproofing from the Port Authority of New York and New Jersey.

Another pressing issue involves the state of Idlewild Park, a part of Brookville Park that spans more than 100 acres across Rockaway Boulevard, stretching between Rosedale and neighboring Springfield Gardens. The park was once part of the grounds that make up the airport (which was originally named Idlewild Airport). Many Rosedale residents live within walking distance of the marshes and tidal creeks that form Idlewild, but unfortunately the park has become polluted with litter. The area is overseen by the City of New York Parks and Recreation Department, which a few years ago allowed development of an air cargo complex on parts of the site. But environmentally minded residents want the rest of Idlewild to be preserved with a massive cleanup and continue to press for its improvement.

Such a cleanup would probably be a welcome change for those living in Meadowmere, a tiny hamlet on the southernmost tip of Rosedale, surrounded by Hook Creek, that is home to about fifty-five people. There are no street sewers here yet, and potholed streets are paved only rarely. A bait-and-tackle shop is the only retail establishment found in this rural little waterfront community of weathered houses.

In 1975 police joined with neighbors to guard and stabilize the neighborhood. Here policemen stand watch outside the home of an African American family that was firebombed (AP Images, courtesy of Queens Library, Long Island Division, Rosedale)

NEIGHBORHOOD PROFILE

Boundaries: <u>North border:</u> Intersection of Brookville Boulevard and Hook Creek Boulevard; <u>east border:</u> Nassau County line (includes Hook Creek Boulevard); <u>south border:</u> Thurston Basin to Rockaway Boulevard; <u>west border:</u> across Brookville Park to 230th Place to 144th Avenue to 144th Street to 232nd Street to 143rd Road to 233rd Street to North Conduit Avenue to Laurelton Parkway

Subway and Train: <u>LIRR:</u> Rosedale

Bus: <u>x63:</u> Merrick Boulevard to Hook Creek Boulevard to Francis Lewis Boulevard; <u>Q5:</u> Merrick Boulevard to Hook Creek Boulevard to Brookville Boulevard; <u>Q77:</u> Springfield Boulevard; <u>Q85:</u> North Conduit Avenue to 243rd Street; <u>Q113:</u> Brookville Boulevard; <u>Q111:</u> 147th Avenue

Libraries: Queens Library, Rosedale Branch (144-20 243rd Street)

Community Board: No. 13

Police Precinct: 105th Precinct (92-08 222nd Street, Queens Village)

Fire Department: Engine 314, Battalion 54 (142-04 Brookville Boulevard)

Game time in Rosedale

Equally remote is the slightly more populated Warnerville. Here, beach-bungalow-style houses are set on marshland along Broad Street, on the easternmost boundary of JFK Airport. Its one commercial street includes a boatyard and a single seafood restaurant. And like their neighbors in Meadowmere, the residents complain that their secluded community is sorely lacking in city services. That is destined to change, however: in response to neighborhood complaints the Department of Environmental Protection announced in 2005 that it will extend the New York City sewer system to both Meadowmere and Warnerville by 2009. In the meantime, there is a fanciful appeal to this sleepy pocket on the water: rumor has it that Warnerville was once the summer destination of the Warner Brothers of Hollywood.

Many of Meadowmere's streets are still unpaved

NEIGHBORHOOD FACTS

■ The land between Edgewood and Huxley Streets was once part of the Cedarhurst Cutoff, a spur of the Long Island Rail Road that ran from Cedarhurst, Long Island, to Rockaway Junction and was intended to provide service to the Rockaways. The line, built in 1872, was in use for only a few years, and though periodic plans were suggested to revive it, it was torn up during World War I so that the rails could be reused; built again after the war, it was torn up for good following the Depression.

■ Civil War buff Patrick Falci of Rosedale served as a historian for the 1992 Turner Network Television film *Gettysburg* and the 1996 Warner Brothers release *Gods and Generals*.

■ Actor and director John Turturro grew up in Rosedale, and in 2004 he shot scenes from his film *Romance and Cigarettes* a few blocks from his childhood home.

South

$6.00 Per Month will Buy a 4-Room Cottage

LOT $9.00 CASH and $1.00 per WEEK

South Ozone Park

$15.00 Per Month will Buy a 17-Room House

LOTS, $220

THIS OFFER FOR 30 DAYS ONLY

FREE EXCURSION EVERY DAY

Title Perfect—Guaranteed by the Lawyers' Title Insurance Co.

HOW TO GO

Brooklyn Bridge, Manhattan end. Take Fulton St. City Line "L" or Bergen St. surface cars. Williamsburg Bridge (Delancey St.). Take Hamburg Ave. or Ralph Ave. cars and transfer to Bergen St. cars. Leave cars at end of line, 1158 Liberty Ave., Brooklyn, where our representatives, wearing Blue South Ozone Park badges, will meet you.

David P. Leahy Realty Co.

80 William St.   1158 Liberty Ave.
New York City   Brooklyn, N. Y.

64 TWOMBLY PLACE
Opposite Long Island Depot, Jamaica, L. I.

92

A 1908 advertisement for the new development (Queens Library, Long Island Division, Illustrations Collection)

South Ozone Park is roaring. Whether it's fans cheering on a favorite horse at Aqueduct Racetrack or planes taking off and landing at nearby John F. Kennedy International Airport, the sounds of this lively, energized neighborhood proclaim its new spirit of vitality.

The early developers of the neighborhood, which is actually southeast of Ozone Park, may have recognized its potential—by the time developer David P. Leahy began laying out his affordable, modest houses for working-class families on land that had primarily held truck farms, at the turn of the twentieth century, Aqueduct Racetrack had already opened and was drawing crowds to the area. By the 1920s the neighborhood was thriving, with a large Italian and Irish population.

Today the ethnic composition is quite different. Almost half of the residents are African American, and immigrants have been settling from such far-flung points of origin as Latin America, Asia, Trinidad and Tobago, and Guyana. To serve this diverse neighborhood, the South Ozone Park branch of the Queens Library has special collections in Haitian Creole, French, and Spanish, as well as a collection on the black experience.

But the main feature of the neighborhood is Aqueduct Racetrack, one of the premier racetracks in the country, which draws fans to South Ozone Park for two seasons of exciting racing. The track is busy in the off-season as well, hosting a year-round flea market that brings in shoppers from throughout the borough. The racetrack is accessible by bus from various locations throughout Queens and Brooklyn, and via the A train. (The Old Aqueduct Station was actually built by

Ozone Park

At the starting gate, Aqueduct Racetrack (Adam Coglianese, NYRA track photographer)

Mayor Robert F. Wagner and Governor Nelson A. Rockefeller (third and fifth from left) join state and N.Y. Racing Authority dignitaries for Opening Day at Aqueduct Racetrack, 1959 (Courtesy of the Queens Library, Long Island Division, Chamber of Commerce of the Borough of Queens)

NEIGHBORHOOD PROFILE

Boundaries: <u>North border:</u> Rockaway Boulevard to Linden Boulevard; <u>east border:</u> Van Wyck Expressway to Rockaway Boulevard to 150th Street; <u>south border:</u> Nassau Expressway; <u>west border:</u> Race Track Road along border of Aqueduct Racetrack

Subway and Train: <u>A train:</u> Aqueduct Racetrack, North Conduit Avenue

Bus: Q7: Rockaway Boulevard; Q37: 114th Street to 133rd Avenue to 116th Street; Q10: Lefferts Boulevard

Libraries: Queens Library, South Ozone Park Branch (128-16 Rockaway Boulevard)

Community Board: Nos. 10, 12

Police Precinct: 106th Precinct (103-51 101st Street, Ozone Park); 113th Precinct (167-02 Baisley Boulevard, Jamaica)

Fire Department: Engine 302, Ladder 155, Battalion 54 (143-15 Rockaway Boulevard)

the New York Racing Association.) The Belt Parkway and North Conduit Avenue, which cross South Ozone Park in an east-west direction, also offer access by car.

South Ozone Park residents, of course, have the luxury of simply walking to the track, located in the western portion of the neighborhood on Rockaway Boulevard. (The racetrack borders Ozone Park.) Lefferts Boulevard cuts through the area in a southeasterly direction, but except for Cross Bay Boulevard in nearby Ozone Park, there is no significant commercial presence here. South Ozone Park is essentially a residential neighborhood with unassuming one- and two-family houses.

And then there is John F. Kennedy Airport. Although the airport provides

• Aqueduct Racetrack

Aqueduct Racetrack, a 192-acre facility operated by the New York Racing Association, got its name from its proximity to a conduit from the Brooklyn Water Works. The only remaining racetrack of the many that once dotted Queens County (see Ozone Park), the "Big A," as it is affectionately termed, opened in 1894, with a new clubhouse and track offices built in 1941. In 1959 the New York Racing Association renovated the track, and in 1975 a one-mile inner dirt track was added to the existing seven-eighths-mile Turf Course and the one-and-one-eighth-mile Main Course. In all, Aqueduct has an attendance capacity of 40,000.

Feeding so many potentially hungry spectators was a challenge until 1981, when Equestris opened as the largest restaurant in New York City, with a seating capacity of 1,600. Fifteen concession stands are also standing by for those who prefer to eat while watching the horses.

Because Aqueduct's fall and winter seasons do not offer the best conditions for racing, the track does not host many important races, although it was the site of the second Breeder's Cup, and the Jockey Gold Cup was held there for many years. But Man o' War, Seabiscuit, and Cigar have all raced there, as well as legendary jockeys Eddie Arcaro, Bill Shoemaker, and Angel Cordero, Jr. The track's most distinguished race is the Wood Memorial, a one-and-one-eighth-mile race run in early April that serves as a major run-up to the Kentucky Derby. Triple Crown winners Gallant Fox (1930), Count Fleet (1943), Assault (1946), and Seattle Slew (1977) all won the Wood, although the most famous Triple Crown winner—Secretariat (1973)—came in a surprising third. Aqueduct Racetrack is also the site of the only triple dead heat in stakes history. On June 10, 1944, Brownie, Bossuet, and Wait a Bit all finished in a tie for first place in the Carter Handicap.

already soundproofed several neighborhood public schools and is working on doing the same for other public buildings in the area. And despite the assault on their eardrums, neighborhood residents appreciate the job opportunities afforded by both airport and racetrack.

Meanwhile, the spiritual and family life of the community continues to flourish. At least nine churches serve the community, as well as eight public schools and four private schools. After school and on holidays, families enjoy Lefferts Playground, bounded by North Conduit Avenue and 120th and 122nd Streets. It was conceived by Robert Moses long ago but reconstructed in 2001 to include a new playground area,

Jacob Bergen barns, Old South Road (now Conduit Avenue) on line of 130th Street, 1922 (The Queens Library, Long Island Division, Eugene Armbruster Collection)

essential jobs to area residents, the planes that take off and land there are noisy. (In 1949 there were some 80,000 airplanes using the airport; today that number has increased to almost 300,000.) Consequently, municipal, civic, and neighborhood organizations have been working hard to insulate the neighborhood from noise pollution. The Port Authority of New York and New Jersey, operator of the airport, has

N E I G H B O R H O O D
F   A   C   T   S

■ In 1908 a four-room house could be purchased for $9 down payment and $6 monthly installments.

■ Celebrities from South Ozone Park include members of the rap group Lost Boyz, who attended John Adams High School, and Debra Wilson, a cast member of *Mad TV*.

■ Actor and World War II veteran Aaron Boddie fled his native Alabama for Manhattan in 1946, settling in South Ozone Park in 1953. Boddie was not only seeking better employment opportunities, he was also escaping Alabama's iniquitous poll tax and like measures that kept blacks from voting, of which he was an outspoken critic—a dangerous position for blacks to take in the Jim Crow South. Boddie still lives in South Ozone Park, but he had the last word in the struggle for Alabama voting rights: he is the model for a life-size statue that is part of a voter registration exhibit at Birmingham's Civil Rights Institute.

game tables, a refurbished basketball court, and a water-lily-shaped sprinkler that is refreshing and fun on a hot day.

Planes are a constant in South Ozone Park

THE AIRPORTS

Test of the world's most powerful all-weather lights at New York International Airport, Idlewild, 1948 (Courtesy of the Queens Library, Long Island Division, Chamber of Commerce of the Borough of Queens)

La Guardia Airport, ca. 1970 (Courtesy of the Queens Library, Long Island Division, Postcard Collection)

Queens is not only a destination for tourists and those seeking a place to raise their families; it is arguably the nation's leading gateway to the world. Its two major airports, La Guardia and John F. Kennedy, in 2005 carried more than 20 million international passengers—and that's not counting the more than 46.5 million domestic travelers who passed through their doors! (La Guardia, though generally considered a domestic airport, also offers service to Canada and the Caribbean.)

La Guardia Airport was built on land that began as an amusement park before being turned into a

private flying field in 1929. One of the many Works Progress Administration projects undertaken by Robert Moses, the airport was dedicated as New York City Municipal Airport in October 1939. A month later "La Guardia Field" was added to the name, honoring New York's charismatic Mayor Fiorello La Guardia, and in 1947 the airport officially became La Guardia Airport. The current Central Terminal Building opened in 1964. The 680-acre airport sits in East Elmhurst, bordering Astoria, jutting out into Flushing and Bowery Bays.

Construction of John F. Kennedy International Airport began in 1942. Originally called Idlewild Airport because it was built on the site of the former Idlewild Golf Course, it was officially given the name New York International Airport in 1948—thirty days after flights began taking off and

landing there. It was rededicated John F. Kennedy International Airport on December 24, 1963, to honor the recently assassinated president. Covering 4,930 acres, the airport is bordered by South Ozone Park, Howard Beach, Springfield Gardens and Rosedale. The JFK AirTrain, a new light-rail transit system, links the airport's Central Terminal Area with the Long Island Rail Road and with city subways and buses.

Although Queens residents have complained about the noise, congestion, and pollution generated by the two airports, most agree that the benefits of having them in the borough outweigh these problems. The airports employ some 43,000 people and generate close to $37 billion in economic activity to the New York–New Jersey region.

Nikita Khrushchev arrives at New York International Airport for an appearance at the United Nations, 1959 (Courtesy of the Queens Library, Long Island Division, Chamber of Commerce of the Borough of Queens)

Springfield

■ Until it was phased out in 2007, Springfield Gardens High School worked to keep its disadvantaged students in school by some unusual programs, like a veterinary science program in which students took care of exotic animals, including tropical fish, pythons, cockatoos, and capuchin monkeys, and a vocational course in culinary arts whose graduates could go on to study at the French Culinary Institute or the New York Restaurant School. The high school has been replaced by George Washington Carver High School, Excelsior and Queens Preparatory Academies, and the Preparatory Academy for Writers.

■ Old Springfield Cemetery, a nonsectarian, 5.5-acre cemetery on Springfield Boulevard, is one of the oldest in Queens, with a tombstone dating back to 1761. The cemetery is surrounded on three sides by Montefiore Cemetery, which is in neighboring Cambria Heights.

■ The First Presbyterian Church of Springfield Gardens at 216-02 137th Avenue began in a borrowed room in a schoolhouse in 1860. By 1867 the congregation had established itself and the church was built at its present location. Although fire destroyed the church's lecture room and auditorium in 1927, it continues to serve the community of Springfield Gardens.

Springfield Gardens is a community in full flower. A middle-class enclave of tidy one- and two-family frame homes, this neighborhood bordering John F. Kennedy International Airport and Jamaica Bay is flourishing from the efforts of a creative and engaged civic leadership—and as a result of receiving some long-needed municipal services.

When it was first settled around 1660, Spring Field (as it was known then) was largely farmland, replete with brooks, creeks, streams, and a pond, where a sawmill and gristmill operated as far back as 1750. During the American Revolution, local farmers were required to supply firewood for the British army, although no troops were actually stationed there. The Samuel Higbie house, on Springfield Boulevard and 141st Road, built in 1770 for an area family, is a remnant of that era.

Gardens

The reclaimed Springfield Park is now a source of community pride

The land remained mostly farmland until 1906, when a housing development called Springfield Gardens was completed, and the post office adopted the name for the neighborhood in 1927. The Long Island Rail Road, which had opened a station there at the turn of the century, followed suit by taking on the new name.

Springfield Gardens grew swiftly in the early twentieth century as people fled crowded Brooklyn: the population increased from 3,046 to 13,089 in the 1920s alone. Although the neighborhood benefited from the city's installation of gas pipes, electric lines, and sanitary sewers, it was never equipped with storm sewers. Instead, developers relied on seepage wells, which turned out to be insufficient for this low-lying area surrounded by wetlands.

In fact, it took years of perilous basement and street floods from massive rainstorms, as well as the declaration of the area as a state and federal disaster zone at least twice in 1996, for the city to undertake the

building of storm sewer systems. After some thirty years of planning, the Department of Environmental Protection came up with a viable strategy for alleviating flooding, and in 2003, much to the relief of neighborhood residents, Mayor Michael Bloomberg implemented a multiphased reconstruction plan, which is still ongoing.

In addition to storm sewers, for years Springfield Gardens was missing another basic neighborhood staple—a supermarket. Today the corner of Springfield and Merrick Boulevards, roads that were once served by small merchants like L. E. Decker's General Store and Henry Furthoffer's Springfield Hotel, is home to a Pathmark,

Springfield Gardens was a desirable neighborhood as early as 1912 (Queens Library, Long Island Division, Illustrations Collection)

NEIGHBORHOOD PROFILE

Boundaries: <u>Springfield Gardens:</u> <u>North border:</u> 121st Avenue to Lucas Street to 122nd Avenue to Nashville Boulevard to 121st Avenue; <u>east border:</u> Springfield Boulevard including Old Springfield Cemetery to Long Island Rail Road tracks to North Conduit Avenue to 233rd Street to 143rd Road to 232nd Street to 144th Street to 144th Avenue to 230th Place through Brookville Park at 230th Place; <u>south border:</u> Rockaway Boulevard to Nassau Expressway; <u>west border:</u> JFK Expressway to South Conduit Avenue to Farmers Boulevard; <u>Brookville:</u> <u>north border:</u> South Conduit Avenue; <u>east border:</u> Farmers Boulevard; <u>south border:</u> Nassau Expressway; <u>west border:</u> JFK Expressway

Subway and Train: <u>LIRR:</u> Laurelton

Bus: <u>Q3:</u> Farmers Boulevard; <u>Q77:</u> Springfield Boulevard; <u>Q85:</u> North Conduit Avenue to Springfield Boulevard to 140th Avenue; <u>Q111:</u> 147th Avenue; <u>Q113:</u> Guy R. Brewer Boulevard; <u>N4:</u> Merrick Boulevard; <u>Q5:</u> Merrick Boulevard; <u>x63:</u> Merrick Boulevard

Community Board: Nos. 12, 13

Police Precinct: 103rd Precinct (168-02 P.O. Edward Byrne Avenue, Jamaica); 105th Precinct (92-08 222nd Street, Queens Village); 113th Precinct (167-02 Baisley Boulevard, Jamaica)

Fire Department: Engine 311, Ladder 158, Battalion 54 (145-50 Springfield Boulevard)

Hospitals and Clinics: Medisys Family Center (130-20 Farmers Boulevard)

Single-family homes on 147th Avenue

which provides jobs for local residents. The store, originally opposed by merchants and residents who feared competition and increased traffic congestion, has also boosted Springfield Gardens' retail climate; several other national chains, encouraged by Pathmark's success, have launched stores in the area. Neighborhood residents, who are predominantly African American but also include people of Jamaican, Haitian, Guyanese, and Hispanic backgrounds, find both goods and increased employment opportunities at the new businesses.

They also enjoy the amenities of Springfield Park, at 147th Avenue and Springfield Lane, once an unsightly and dangerous area that has been cleaned up by activist groups. It is now a place for picnicking and relaxing for local families.

A small hamlet just north of Kennedy Airport, **Brookville,** was lately embroiled in its own changes when more than eighty blocks made up of one- and two-family homes were under a proposal for rezoning. Since 1961 the area had been governed by zoning that allows for the construction of multifamily units. But in an effort to maintain the neighborhood's small-town character, residents persuaded the Department of City Planning in 2004 to offer a proposal to rezone the area to permit only one- and two-family detached and semidetached houses. The proposal was accepted, preserving the neighborhood feel of this tiny middle-class community.

St. Albans

St. Albans, a draw for middle-class African American families since the 1940s, has been home to many of the world's best jazz musicians. Today it often resonates with the voices of parishioners attending the area's many houses of worship.

The neighborhood was established

Jamaican fare in central St. Albans, Linden Boulevard and Everitt Place

St. Albans Congregational Church

when a syndicate of developers from Manhattan laid out streets and building lots in 1892, after purchasing a farm on Linden Boulevard. A railroad station and post office soon followed, and by 1899 the population had grown to six hundred. St. Albans was named by its early residents after the town in Hertfordshire, England, which was in turn named for the first martyr of Britain.

In its early years the population was largely middle-class whites, but today St. Albans is home predominantly to African Americans. The neighborhood's ethnic composition began changing in the 1940s, when a who's who of musicians moved in, particularly to the prestigious **Addisleigh**

Park section, with its elegant Tudor-style homes on expansive plots. Fats Waller (whose home at Sayres Avenue and 174th Street had a built-in Hammond organ) was reportedly the first to arrive, followed by such greats as Lena Horne, Ella Fitzgerald, Milt Hinton, John Coltrane, and James Brown—many of whom are depicted in a colorful mural on the northern side of Linden Boulevard under the Long Island Rail Road. More recent musicians hailing from St. Albans are the rappers Q Tip and LL Cool J, who wrote about his youth in southeastern Queens in *I Make My Own Rules* (1997).

Addisleigh Park was developed in 1926 just off the St. Albans Golf Course, which was built in 1919. The

NEIGHBORHOOD FACTS

■ Back in the 1950s, the borders between St. Albans and Hollis were less clearly defined than today. The homes of many upwardly mobile black families who moved to Hollis, considered a good address, are now part of St. Albans.

■ The Black Spectrum Theatre, in Roy Wilkins Park, was founded in 1970 to engage issues of concern to the African American community. In addition to theater—including the Professional Theatre Company, the Youth Theatre Company, and the Theatre on Wheels, which tours the Tri-State area providing theater in the summer and renting its facilities out to local groups—Black Spectrum Theatre offers educational videos and a summer children's camp.

■ In addition to musicians, St. Albans has been home to some celebrated athletes: pro football player Will Poole grew up in the neighborhood, and Jackie Robinson, the Hall of Fame Brooklyn Dodger, moved to Addisleigh Park in 1949. And baseball great Babe Ruth used to play at the St. Albans Golf Course.

golf course itself was eventually sold to the government, which subsequently built the St. Albans Naval Hospital. World War II veterans were treated there, and in 1977 the Veterans Administration acquired the 100-acre property, half of which was donated to the city of New York. Today, an area between Linden and Baisley Boulevards serves as the Queens campus of the Veterans Administration New York Harbor Healthcare System.

Also on the site of the former golf course is the 53-acre Roy Wilkins Park, which features tennis, basketball, and handball courts, as well as baseball fields and a jogging path. St. Albans residents also enjoy the Roy Wilkins Family Center, with an Olympic-size pool and a 425-seat theater, complete with a piano lounge and film studio.

Tucked in among the many Baptist, Episcopal, and Christian churches that line Farmers and Linden Boulevards is the Beth Elohim Hebrew Congregation (189-31 Linden Boulevard), which caters to a congregation of black Jews. The synagogue was founded in 1968 by the late Levi Ben Levy, the chief rabbi of New York City's black Jews (or Israelites), from his St. Albans living room.

St. Albans Congregational Church was also created in a neighborhood living room, in 1953. In 1959 the congregation was established at its present location on Linden Boulevard by the late Rev. Robert Ross Johnson, a renowned clergyman who was also a

NEIGHBORHOOD PROFILE

Boundaries: St. Albans: north border: 109th Avenue to 178th Street to 110th Avenue to Dunkirk Street to Liberty Avenue to 104th Avenue; east border: Francis Lewis Boulevard to Springfield Boulevard; south border: 121st Avenue to Nashville Boulevard to 121st Avenue to Long Island Rail Road tracks to 120th Avenue to Roe Road to Irwin Place to Baisley Boulevard; west border: Merrick Boulevard; Addisleigh Park: north border: Sayres Avenue; east border: 180th Street; south border: Linden Boulevard; west border: Marine Place

Subway and Train: LIRR: St. Albans

Bus: Q77: Francis Lewis Boulevard; Q3: Farmers Boulevard; Q2: Hollis Avenue; Q83: Liberty Avenue to Murdock Avenue; Q5, Q85: Merrick Boulevard; Q42: Sayres Avenue; Q84: 120th Avenue to Merrick Boulevard; Q4: Linden Boulevard to Merrick Boulevard; x64: Liberty Avenue to Farmers Boulevard

Libraries: Queens Library, St. Albans Branch (191-05 Linden Boulevard)

Theaters: Black Spectrum Theatre (Roy Wilkins Park, 177th Street and Baisley Boulevard)

Community Board: No. 12

Police Precinct: 113th Precinct (167-02 Baisley Boulevard, Jamaica)

Fire Department: Engine 317, Ladder 165, Battalion 54 (117-11 196th Street), Ladder 133 (111-36 Merrick Boulevard)

Hospitals and Clinics: Medisys Family Center (111-20 Merrick Boulevard)

founder of York College in nearby Jamaica.

While St. Albans Congregational is a freestanding church, many storefronts in this community also serve as houses of worship, alongside meat stores, barbershops, printers, and luncheonettes. For major shopping, St. Albans residents head to Jamaica's bustling commercial district or the Green Acres Mall in Valley Stream, Long Island.

Restaurants on Linden Boulevard suit a variety of tastes

Addisleigh Park

Sunnyside

In the early 1920s, a savvy architect and a landscape designer came up with an unusual plan: they would develop part of the area that is now Sunnyside into a microcosm of pastoral village life. The idea of common gardens shared by private homes has had great appeal ever since. Today, the neighborhood is a dramatic example of how highly desirable residential areas are shaped by pressures to both conserve and adapt.

After the opening in 1909 of the Queensboro Bridge, which fed into Queens Boulevard, as well as the opening of the elevated line in 1917, the population of the previously tiny hamlet of Sunnyside grew rapidly. Sunnyside's earliest settlers were the Fitting, Gosman, Heiser, Lowery, and Van Buren families, who owned farms that were subdivided in the 1880s and 1890s, as well as the French Bragaw family, which owned the Sunnyside Hill Farm near the roadhouse-

Shopping on 46th Street off Queens Boulevard

style Sunnyside Hotel (situated on what is today the southwest corner of Northern Boulevard and 38th Street in Long Island City), which was built to accommodate visitors to Fashion Race Course in nearby Corona.

In 1850 a railroad station was built just across the street from the Sunnyside Hotel. But instead of locating its center there, the neighborhood shifted southward to make way for rail yards designed by the Pennsylvania Railroad in 1910. Development of rows of attached

houses and apartment buildings followed in the 1920s. One example is the Phipps Garden Apartments on 50th and 51st Streets and 39th Avenue. Built during the early 1930s as affordable apartments for working-class families, today these elegant buildings include immaculate landscaped gardens.

Back in the early 1900s, an athletic compound called Celtic Park (now an apartment complex) was the center of activity for a largely Irish population, which still exists in Sunnyside, visible in the shamrocks displayed on some doorways. Today German, South American, Middle Eastern, Korean, and other ethnic groups also call this neighborhood home. Their influence is most apparent in the abundance of in-

49th Street in Sunnyside Gardens, modeled after England's planned garden communities

NEIGHBORHOOD FACTS

■ The nonprofit Thalia Spanish Theatre, at 41-17 Greenpoint Avenue, is the only Spanish theater in Queens. Established in 1977, it is devoted to promoting and preserving Spanish and Latin American culture with bilingual productions.

■ Sunnyside and neighboring Woodside have been hosting the annual "St. Pat's for All" St. Patrick's Fair and Irish Parade since 2000. The only New York St. Patrick's Day Parade open to gays and lesbians, the event has drawn visitors from Ireland as well as non-Irish participants including Koreans, Caribbeans, Hispanics, and Native Americans, and politicians like Mayor Michael Bloomberg and Senator Hillary Rodham Clinton.

■ New Calvary Cemetery, on Queens Boulevard and 51st Street, is a Roman Catholic cemetery owned by the Archdiocese of New York. It is part of the 365-acre Calvary Cemetery (est. 1845), which spreads into neighboring Blissville and other locations, and is the largest cemetery in the United States.

ternational restaurants. On Queens Boulevard, which crosses Sunnyside, Dazies Restaurant serves Italian cuisine; Hemsin offers Turkish food; and Ariyoshi has Japanese fare, while El Comelon on Greenpoint Avenue features Salvadorian and Colombian dishes.

Skillman Avenue provides shopping; it is also the site of an annual street fair hosted each September by the Sunnyside Foundation for Community Planning and Preservation. Other commercial centers are Greenpoint Avenue and, of course, Queens Boulevard, which in just minutes takes drivers onto the Queensboro Bridge. The 46th

Street–Queens Boulevard subway station provides an approximately fifteen-minute trip to Manhattan. People are still drawn to Sunnyside for its close proximity to Manhattan—as well as its strong sense of community.

Sunnyside Gardens, an idyllic enclave of some fifteen hundred houses, is situated on 77 acres bordering Woodside south of the Sunnyside rail yard. Built by the visionary architects Clarence S. Stein and Henry Wright and the landscape architect Marjorie Sewell Cautley in 1924, this section of attached one-, two-, and three-family brick houses, each with a common courtyard and private yard, was modeled after England's planned garden communities and is considered one of the first garden apartment complexes in the United States. A 3-acre private park—one of only two private parks in

NEIGHBORHOOD PROFILE

Boundaries: Sunnyside: north border: Skillman Avenue to 43rd Street to Barnett Avenue; east border: Woodside Avenue to 39th Road to 52nd Street to Queens Boulevard to 58th Street; south border: 55th Avenue to 50th Street to 54th Avenue to 48th Street to Long Island Expressway; west border: Van Dam Street; Sunnyside Gardens: north border: Barnett Avenue; east border: Woodside Avenue to 39th Road to 52nd Street; south border: Skillman Avenue to 48th Street to Queens Boulevard to 47th Street to Skillman Avenue; west border: 43rd Street
Subway and Train: 7 train: 33rd Street, 40th Street, 46th Street
Bus: Q39: 48th Avenue; Q32: Queens Boulevard/Roosevelt Avenue; Q60: Queens Boulevard; B24: Brooklyn-Queens Expressway/Greenpoint; Q104: 48th Street; Q67: Calvary
Libraries: Queens Library, Sunnyside Branch (43-06 Greenpoint Avenue)
Theaters: Thalia Spanish Theatre (41-17 Greenpoint Avenue)
Community Board: No. 2
Police Precinct: 108th Precinct (5-47 50th Avenue, Long Island City)
Fire Department: Engine 325, Ladder 163, Battalion 49 (41-24 51st Street, Woodside)
Hospitals and Clinics: Department of Veterans Affairs Community Clinic (41-03 Queens Boulevard)

47th Avenue

New York City (the other is Manhattan's Gramercy Park)—was included in the development.

Aptly described as "Utopian," the area was originally designed for the benefit of low- and middle-income families. For more than a decade, until the mid-1930s, the influential writer and critic Lewis Mumford lived there. Other notable figures who settled in Sunnyside Gardens over the years include Rudy Vallee, Perry Como, and Judy Holliday, while the apartment building at 43-30 46th Street was the last residence of jazz legend Leon "Bix" Beiderbecke. Sunnyside Gardens today remains pretty much intact, thanks to the efforts of the Sunnyside Foundation for Community Planning and Preservation. In 1984 the area was added to the National Register of Historic Places.

Whitestone

NEIGHBORHOOD FACTS

■ In the 1840s Whitestone was re-named Clintonville in honor of New York City mayor (and later New York governor) De Witt Clinton, but the neighborhood reverted back to "Whitestone" in 1854.

■ Whitestone resident Vincent Santelmo is the author of *The Complete Encyclopedia of G.I. Joe* (3rd ed., 2001) and *G.I. Joe: Official Identification and Price Guide* (1999). One of Malba's best-known residents was country-and-western singer and yodeler Elton Britt, whose hit songs include "Chime Bells," "Rocky Mountain Lullaby," "Buddy Boy," and "Driftwood on the River." Britt was best known for his patriotic 1942 ballad "There's a Star Spangled Banner Waving Somewhere," the first country song awarded a gold record for selling more than a million copies.

To the west is a dazzling panorama of the Bronx-Whitestone Bridge; to the east, a dramatic view of the Throgs Neck Bridge. Situated in the northern part of the borough, Whitestone, with its gentle breezes from the East River, lovely clean and shady streets, and waterfront park, is a popular place to live, work, and visit.

Whitestone was settled by the English in 1643. Among the area's famous early residents was Francis Lewis, a member of the Continental Congress and signer of the Declaration of Independence. Lewis lived in Whitestone on a farm near the river off today's 7th Avenue; during the Revolutionary War, the British burned down his house. Today he is honored by the 16-acre Francis Lewis Park, situated on the East River waterfront between Parsons Boulevard and 147th Street. Walt Whitman also worked in the area for a short time in 1840 when a local philanthro-

The boulder that is said to have given the neighborhood its name, photographed in 1905 (Queens Library, Long Island Division, Illustrations Collection)

pist, Samuel Leggett, hired the poet to teach at a free school he had established for the area's children.

Whitestone remained largely farmland until the mid-1800s, when John D. Locke opened a tin and copper stamp-works factory there. Locke's Brooklyn workers relocated to Whitestone with him, and by 1860 the neighborhood's population had increased to eight hundred. When the Long Island Rail Road offered access soon thereafter (with a station that closed down in the early 1930s), this beautiful waterfront section of Queens was discovered by well-to-do Manhattanites, who enjoyed the summer resort amenities that had sprung up—halls, hotels, and park grounds—and built mansions along the highly desirable waterfront (the bridges did not yet exist).

In keeping with its long history, Whitestone boasts a number of historic buildings, many of which were awarded "Queensmark" plaques when the Queens Historical Society honored the neighborhood in 2003. Among them are the Grace Episcopal Church (1860) at 151-17 14th Road and three Tudor-style houses on 14th Avenue.

One famous mansion erected in the 1920s was the neo-Tudor "Wildflower," on a 4.5-acre estate belonging to the Broadway producer Arthur Hammerstein. Despite its 1982 New York City landmark designation, the renamed Hammerstein House,

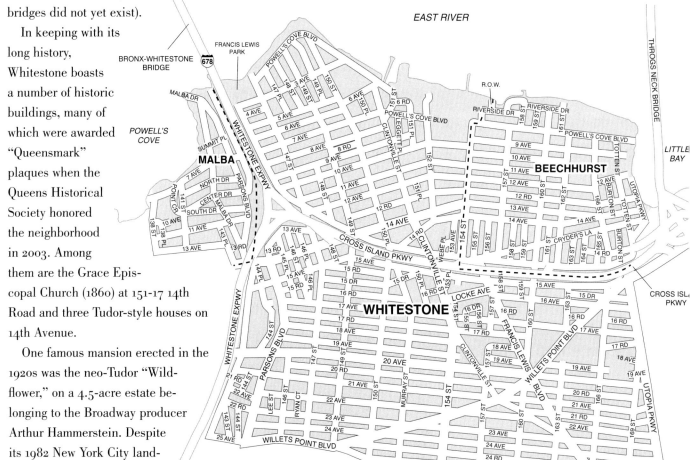

• Robert Moses

Praised by some, loathed by others, Robert Moses was New York City's "master builder" for more than thirty years, from the late 1920s through the early 1960s. During his reign, he was responsible, often single-handedly, for shaping the city's swelling metropolis into its present-day form. Although his influence can be felt throughout the five boroughs—from the Verrazano Bridge, which he promoted, to the Central Park Zoo, which he refurbished, and the more than 250 playgrounds he built—it is perhaps most apparent in Queens, whose topography was radically altered by such projects as the Bronx-Whitestone, Throgs Neck, and Triborough Bridges, with their attendant roadways and infrastructure, the Belt Parkway and Brooklyn-Queens Expressway, and Flushing Meadows–Corona Park, which he gave to the city in 1967.

Born in 1888 in New Haven, Connecticut, Moses attended Yale College, Oxford University, and Columbia University, from which he earned a Ph.D. He then stayed on in New York City, hoping to involve himself in reform politics. Through a mutual acquaintance he befriended Al Smith, a rising politician who later became governor of New York. When Smith gained power in 1928, Moses was his right-hand man, with an arsenal of ideas to centralize the state's infrastructure: granting commissions, building bridges, paving roads. These activities would later define the so-called Moses era.

Against the backdrop of the Great Depression, Moses undertook dozens of projects that radically altered the landscape of New York City: the construction of the Triborough Bridge complex to connect the Bronx, Manhattan, and Queens, completed in 1936; the creation of Jones Beach Park, on Long Island; the planning of the 1939 New York World's Fair; and the opening of ten massive public swimming pools, capable of holding 66,000 swimmers. Because of his foresight, New York City was able to secure more than a fifth of all New Deal funding.

Though Moses himself never learned to drive, he was a strong proponent of the automobile. In the aftermath of World War II, he lobbied for the construction of new highways and high-rise housing—at the expense of public transportation. He continued to order bridges, fought to bring the headquarters of the United Nations to New York (for a time it was housed in the New York City Building in Flushing Meadows–Corona Park), and later organized the second New York World's Fair, in 1964. By that time, however, his projects had begun to generate significant controversy, and Moses' power began to weaken in the early 1960s, when he lost his state appointments. When the Triborough Bridge and Tunnel Authority, of which he was commissioner, was merged into the Metropolitan Transportation Authority in 1968, Moses lost his last significant position.

Opinions about Moses' lasting impact on New York City, and its people, have been mixed. In 1976 Robert Caro's Pulitzer Prize–winning biography of Moses, *The Power Broker*, criticized the planner for championing projects that dislocated thousands of lower-class residents and undermined public transportation. Such anti-Moses sentiment peaked in the 1980s, as the city struggled with social problems. More recently, however, Moses' reputation has been receiving something of a make-over. In January 2007, the *New York Times* published a piece on Moses' legacy in which a number of scholars argued that history had judged the man too harshly. According to one, "Too little attention has been focused on what Moses achieved, . . . and the enormous bureaucratic hurdles he surmounted to get things done."

located on Powell's Cove Boulevard within the **Beechhurst** section of this neighborhood, fell into a state of disrepair and endured numerous fires until 1997, when a developer began converting the estate and its acreage into luxury townhouse condominiums. Sitting in the northeast corner of Whitestone, along with standard garden apartment complexes and private houses, the Beechhurst area boasts other upscale waterfront complexes, such as Beechhurst Shores, a gated townhouse community, and the massive Le Havre cooperative complex, featuring thirty-two eight-story buildings within 25 acres. Beechhurst was the recipient of Queensmark honors in 2002, along with a ten-square-block area called Robinwood.

Queens residents seeking even greater exclusivity and affluence can find it in **Malba,** where winding streets meet circular drives to stately homes. Unlike Whitestone, which was reportedly named for a large white stone in the area, and Beechhurst, named for the abundance of beech trees, Malba obtained its name from the last names of its five developers: George A. Maycock, Samuel Avis, George W. Lewis, Nobel P. Bishop, and David Alling, who built more than a hundred houses, a private beach, a pier for pleasure boats, a golf club, and a polo club here in the 1920s, intending the development to be part of Long Island's Gold Coast. (Although William Ziegler, president of the Royal Baking Powder Company, acquired the land in 1883 and began development in 1908 through a subsidiary, the Realty Trust Company, only thirteen houses had been built by the start of World War I.)

10th Avenue and 151st Place

NEIGHBORHOOD PROFILE

Boundaries: <u>Whitestone:</u> <u>north border:</u> East River, Bronx County line; <u>east border:</u> Little Bay to Utopia Parkway; <u>south border:</u> 25th Avenue to Willets Point Boulevard to 25th Avenue; <u>west border:</u> Whitestone Expressway to 14th Avenue to 143rd Place to 13th Avenue to 138th Street to Powell's Cove; <u>Beechhurst:</u> <u>north border:</u> East River, Bronx County line; <u>east border:</u> Little Bay to Utopia Parkway; <u>south border:</u> Cross Island Parkway; <u>west border:</u> 154th Street to Powell's Cove Boulevard to Riverside Drive; <u>Malba:</u> <u>north border:</u> East River; <u>east border:</u> Whitestone Expressway; <u>south border:</u> 14th Avenue to 143rd Place to 13th Avenue; <u>west border:</u> 138th Street to Powell's Cove
Bus: <u>QBx1:</u> Whitestone Expressway; <u>Q44:</u> Whitestone Expressway to Parsons Boulevard; <u>x32:</u> Whitestone Expressway to Parsons Boulevard; <u>Q20B,</u> <u>Q20A:</u> Parsons Boulevard; <u>Q14:</u> 149th Street to Willets Point Boulevard; <u>Q34:</u> Willets Point Boulevard; <u>Q15:</u> Powell's Cove Boulevard to 154th Street to 150th Street; <u>Q76:</u> Parsons Boulevard to 14th Avenue to Francis Lewis Boulevard; <u>Q16:</u> Willets Point Boulevard to Francis Lewis Boulevard to Utopia Parkway
Libraries: Queens Library, Whitestone Branch (151-10 14th Road)
Community Board: No. 7
Police Precinct: 109th Precinct (37-05 Union Street, Flushing)
Fire Department: Engine 295, Ladder 144, Battalion 52 (12-49 149th Street)

Today this tiny enclave of just over four hundred homes is touted as the borough's best-kept secret, and locals, generally professionals and business executives, prefer the anonymity. Consequently, there's no public transportation here: the closest bus stop is just south of this community, on 14th Avenue and the Whitestone Expressway. Malba also has no shopping areas, but stores can be found nearby, along 12th and 14th Avenues and 150th Street. The Malba Association, incorporated in 1908, helps maintain the beauty of the development—and its seclusion.

Woodhaven

Bridle paths and homemade chocolate. An all-volunteer ambulance corps and a historic clock tower. Woodhaven, with its convenient, big-city location between Brooklyn and Richmond Hill, is a neighborhood in transition, but it still retains some small-town charms.

Although two racetracks, Union Course and Centerville Race Track, drew people to the area in the 1820s (see Ozone Park), Woodhaven wasn't developed residentially until 1835, when John R. Pitkin decided that this was where he would build a manufacturing center. A year later he abandoned that plan, but he did begin promoting his village, then called Woodville. He persuaded the Long Island Rail Road to build a station and then launched a newspaper in 1853. (By then, villagers had voted to change the name to Woodhaven.) A shoe factory opened in 1854, but the neighborhood really took off in 1860, when Florian Grosjean and Charles Lalance opened a tinware factory and built housing for their employees—2,100 of them by the 1880s and 1890s, many of them French. Thousands of Irish and Italians moved in as well after elevated

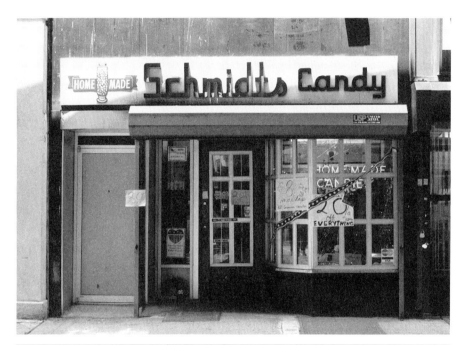

Schmidt's Candy, opened in 1925, is still a family-owned business

lines were extended through the neighborhood.

Comprised mainly of Irish, Italian, German, and Polish families through the 1950s and 1960s, the close-knit, working-class community was made up primarily of one- and two-family attached and semi-attached houses, many of which still sport inviting porches. A sprinkling of Victorians and small apartment buildings throughout

did not affect the small-town ambience of the neighborhood. Today, Woodhaven's centrality within the borough offers another appeal, with short rides to Rockaway Beach and the airports as well as convenient access to Manhattan via the A, J, and Z trains.

Old-timers remember that small-town atmosphere fondly, recalling not only their neighbors but the owners of the one-of-a-kind mom-and-pop stores along Woodhaven Boulevard, Jamaica Avenue, and Atlantic Avenue where they used to shop. Children were sent to Willie the butcher or Charlie's grocery to fetch the makings for dinner. Al's candy store was a welcome stop for errand-bound kids headed to Rosen's drugstore or the Senesa family tailor shop. Lewis's, an old-fashioned general store with two locations run by three generations of the Lewis family, recently closed down, as did Neirs Tavern (also known as Union Course) on 78th Street, which opened for business in 1838 and was the oldest (and possibly most notorious) neighborhood establishment.

Since the 1970s many of these original businesses have been replaced by a new generation of family stores, run by newcomers to this "Haven in the City" (the neighborhood slogan) from places such as Guyana, Jamaica, China, and Latin America. But remnants of Woodhaven's past remain. A clock tower, once part of the Lalance and Grosjean tinware factory, which closed down in 1955, is now part of a shopping center on the same site along 91st and 92nd Streets and Atlantic Avenue. And Schmidt's Candy, founded in 1925, is still a favorite at 94-15 Jamaica Avenue. The original Schmidt's granddaughter runs the candy store, famous for its homemade chocolate. The late–Gothic Revival St. Matthew's Episcopal Church at 85-45 96th Street, established in 1900, continues to welcome worshipers, while the Wyckoff-Snediker Family Cemetery behind it has plots dating back to 1750. The church and cemetery are both listed in the National Register of Historic Places, thanks to the work of the Woodhaven Cultural and Historical Society.

Despite their best efforts, however, the society was unable to obtain New York City landmark designation for St. Anthony's Hospital, opened in 1914 by the Franciscan Sisters of the Poor. Because the hospital treated tuberculosis patients, the five-story brick edifice included four solariums, which provided refreshing sunlight to patients. A chapel with stained-glass windows and

NEIGHBORHOOD FACTS

■ What were Babe Ruth and Lou Gehrig doing in Woodhaven on Columbus Day, 1928? Both were having fun playing with the semi-pro team the Bushwicks at Dexter Park, a ballfield near Franklin K. Lane High School. About twenty thousand fans attended the game, in which Gehrig hit a home run. The site of the ballpark is now a supermarket.
■ Strack Meadow, a portion of Forest Park, is named after Lawrence George E. Strack (1948–67), the first Woodhaven resident to die while serving in the Vietnam War.
■ Mae West is said to have lived for a time in an unassuming frame house on 88th Street and 89th Avenue.
■ Trotting Course Lane received its name from the neighborhood racetrack. In the mid-1930s, it became the mammoth Woodhaven Boulevard. Reminders of the quaint street name can still be found on signs along small portions of the boulevard.

vaulted ceilings was also part of the facility, which took up an entire square block bounded by 89th and 91st Avenues and Woodhaven Boulevard and 96th Street. St. Anthony's was demolished in 2001 to make way for Woodhaven Park Estates, a new development of semi-attached two-family houses.

Woodhaven's cultural needs—and those of the entire borough—are served by the Queens Council on the Arts, at 1 Forest Park, which was established in 1966 as a nonprofit organization to support, promote, and develop the arts in Queens. The council also educates schoolchildren, with programs like "High School to Art School" (which awards grants to artists), and produces exhibits and workshops. And to fill a void in emergency medical services, in 1965 some two dozen Woodhaven residents launched the Woodhaven Volunteer Ambulance Corps (today the Woodhaven–Richmond Hill Ambulance Corps), which provides its services without charge to the surrounding communities.

Not far from the Queens Council on the Arts is 85-34 Forest Parkway, the house where Betty Smith reportedly penned her classic *A Tree Grows in Brooklyn,* published in 1943. Brooklyn is actually a skip and a hop from Woodhaven; in fact, Franklin K. Lane High School sits on the border of

NEIGHBORHOOD PROFILE

Boundaries: <u>North border:</u> Jackie Robinson Parkway to Forest Park to 83rd Drive to Forest Park to Woodhaven Boulevard to Myrtle Avenue; <u>east border:</u> Freedom Drive to Park Lane to 98th Street; <u>south border:</u> Atlantic Avenue; <u>west border:</u> Kings County line (Eldert Lane to Jamaica Avenue to Dexter Court to west border of Forest Park)

Subway and Train: <u>A train:</u> 104th Street; <u>J train:</u> 75th Street, 85th Street/Forest Parkway, Woodhaven Boulevard; <u>Z train:</u> 75th Street, Woodhaven Boulevard

Bus: <u>Q56:</u> Jamaica Avenue; <u>Q24:</u> Atlantic Avenue; <u>Q53, Q11:</u> Woodhaven Boulevard

Libraries: Queens Library, Woodhaven Branch (85-41 Forest Parkway)

Museums: Queens Council on the Arts (1 Forest Park)

Community Board: No. 9

Police Precinct: 102nd Precinct (87-34 118th Street, Richmond Hill)

Fire Department: Engine 293, Battalion 51 (89-40 87th Street); Engine 294, Ladder 143, Battalion 51 (101-02 Jamaica Avenue)

Hospitals and Clinics: St. Anthony's Hospital Division of Catholic Medical Center of Brooklyn and Queens (89-15 Woodhaven Boulevard)

Woodhaven and Cypress Hills, along Dexter Court. Just north of that is perhaps what Woodhaven today is best known for—Forest Park, which cuts across Richmond Hill. There, the huff of horses still resonates, not from the race tracks of days gone by but from passing trotters taking in the natural forestry along seven miles of bridle paths.

The Woodhaven Avenue (now Boulevard) entrance to the Grosjean Mansion, ca. 1890 (Queens Library, Long Island Division, Illustrations Collection)

• **Forest Park**

The third-largest park in Queens, covering more than 500 acres, Forest Park is the only major Queens park that is not part of the Corridor—the nickname given to Flushing Meadows–Corona, Kissena, Cunningham, and Alley Pond Parks, which are all connected. Forest Pond Park was established in 1898 after a state-authorized search discovered it as the perfect location for a large recreational area for city residents. Although it was managed in its early days by the Brooklyn Parks Department, as soon as Queens had its own parks administration, in 1911, it assumed responsibility for the unique area; in fact, the Overlook, the current administration building for all of Queens's parks, is located on-site.

The current park is graced with the largest continuous red- and white-oak forest (413 acres) in Queens, 150-year-old plant specimens, and a rocky terrain that points to its glacial past. In addition to its natural features, Forest Park boasts a 110-acre, eighteen-hole golf course (expanded from the original nine holes), a bandshell, softball and basketball fields, tennis courts, hiking trails, bridle paths, and the old-fashioned wooden Daniel C. Mueller Carousel, which was built in 1903. It also is the site for many memorable events throughout the year, including a Victorian Christmas, Nature Trails day, orienteering, and battle reenactments.

For those interested in track and field events, the Victory Field sports complex is available. The 13.5-acre outdoor athletic facility dedicated to the veterans of World War I opened in the eastern park in 1927 and features a 400-meter track, handball courts, and facilities for pole vaulting, long jumping, shot putting, and discus throwing. The park can be explored on foot as well as on horseback (horses are available at two private stables), but even those who never leave their cars will have a beautiful view: Forest Park Drive was designed by Frederick Law Olmsted as an inviting way to access this lush park with its "knob and kettle" hills.

Woodside

A bustling working-class neighborhood, Woodside has long been a commercial, industrial, and residential hub for the borough, as well as a comfortable home for many families. But it wasn't always this way. Woodside had a much quieter, more aristocratic beginning, as noted by newspaperman John Andrew Kelly, who in the 1850s penned a series of articles, "Letters from Woodside," describing the area. His father, John Kelly, along with several others, had settled there and built mansions. Soon thereafter, however, Benjamin W. Hitchcock saw the area's broader potential: in 1867, the developer laid out streets and sold lots, creating a livable village, albeit a rural one, with swamps and woods that stretched for miles.

In 1915 the area was still quite rural. For instance, 3.5 acres were taken up by a "wild ani-

The 61st Street Station, Woodside's commuting hub

mal farm" owned by Louis Ruhe. Among the inhabitants: a Tasmanian devil named Buddy, a three-year-old camel named Hashish, and Jeff, a boxing kangaroo. Even after the elevated line came to the neighborhood in 1917, Woodside was still filled with open fields and empty lots on unoccupied land. Now those lots are long gone, replaced by private homes, multifamily houses, and residential build-

NEIGHBORHOOD FACTS

■ Winfield, a hamlet built in 1854 in a part of Woodside, was named after General Winfield Scott, a hero in the War of 1812 and a commander in the army during the U.S.-Mexican War of 1846–48. In 1852 he moved to New York City and ran for president. The center of this neighborhood lay on what is now 45th Avenue and Queens Boulevard. Singer sewing machines were built in a factory there that years later became the Moisant aircraft factory. After World War II, however, the town became part of the neighborhood, and the name all but disappeared.

■ Since its founding in 2000 by composer and visual artist Todd Richmond and choreographer Paz Tanjuaquio, Topaz Arts, at 55-03 39th Avenue, has been supporting artists and the arts throughout Queens. In addition to hosting four art exhibitions annually to showcase emerging and established artists and providing studio rentals and technical support for individual artists, Topaz Arts collaborates with other arts organizations to offer programs of contemporary dance, including "Dance in Queens," an annual dance residency program and performance series (with the Queens Museum of Art), residencies for choreographers (with Dance Theater Workshop), and free workshops (with Queens Theater in the Park). Richmond and Tanjuaquio also stage multidisciplinary dance productions.

■ The Jackson Social and Field Club on Northern Boulevard was established in 1902 by thirteen members of the Jackson Baseball Club of Woodside. Minutes of club meetings dating back to 1903 still survive. The club bar, situated in the lower level, was constructed out of wood from a casket.

■ The Moore-Jackson Cemetery, at 54th Street near 31st Avenue, dates back to 1733. This colonial family burial plot fell into neglect over the years, until a surviving family member transferred ownership of the grounds in 1998 to the Queens Historical Society, which has restored it.

which borders Woodside, and Northern Boulevard, which cuts across it, Roosevelt Avenue stretches for miles as one of this neighborhood's main commercial thoroughfares, featuring side-by-side mom-and-pop stores owned or operated by Irish, Hispanic, Indian, Korean, and Chinese immigrants. Roosevelt Avenue and 61st Street, for instance, includes Shane's Bakery and Toucan Tommy's bar. Stanley's hardware store has been a fixture near here, as has Maxwell Furniture, which has been on 64th Street for some fifty years. Donovan's Pub, on 57th Street, is legendary. Laundromats, delis, grocery stores, pharmacies, and restaurants also line this busy avenue, which lies below the No. 7 elevated train (the Woodside Long Island Rail Road station is also here).

During the 1920s, Woodside experienced a flurry of development that brought in a number of Irish families who had been living in cramped quarters in Manhattan. In later years, ethnic groups such as Italians and Germans, and later still Asians and Hispanics, settled here too, but the

Roosevelt Avenue is the heart of Woodside's commercial district

ings such as the Cosmopolitan apartments, a complex of sixteen five-story houses built in 1923 on 49th Street, and the Big Six Towers, on Queens Boulevard and 60th Street.

Along with Queens Boulevard,

neighborhood still has a large Irish component. The Emerald Isle Immigration Center (EIIC) at 59-26 Woodside Avenue welcomes recent Irish immigrants, as well as those from other countries, with employment placement, accommodations, citizenship inquiries, computer training, and other services. Founded in 1988, the center assists several thousand arrivals each year.

Other vital community organizations

There is still a strong Irish presence in Woodside

include Woodside on the Move, a nonprofit social services agency for residents and businesses, whose executive director, Jack Martin, relocated to this neighborhood from Long Island but whose ancestors were living in Woodside for generations. Roosevelt Avenue is kept clean and appealing for local patrons thanks to Ready, Willing and Able, a program that provides jobs to the homeless in exchange for meals, social services, and shelter, through which four formerly homeless men keep these sidewalks trash free by sweeping them and collecting debris five days a week.

Woodside was critical to the operation of the New York and Queens County Railway trolley in the early 1900s, and it is on Northern Boulevard, on the corner of Woodside Avenue, that you can still see the two towers marking the former site of the trolley terminal, built in 1896. Trolleys from various parts of Queens were serviced here, and commuters would change cars for other routes at this juncture. By the late 1930s, the trolley system gave way to the elevated subway line, the Independent Subway System, motorized buses, and cars, but Tower Square remains as evidence of those days long gone. In fact, the historic clock on one of the towers still marks the passing of time.

N E I G H B O R H O O D   P R O F I L E

Boundaries: <u>North border:</u> 31st Avenue; <u>east border:</u> Brooklyn-Queens Expressway West to Northern Boulevard to 69th Street to Amtrak tracks to Roosevelt Avenue to 74th Street; <u>south border:</u> Queens Boulevard; <u>west border:</u> 52nd Street to 39th Road to Woodside Avenue to Northern Boulevard to 49th Street
Subway and Train: <u>7 train:</u> 52nd Street, Woodside/61st Street, 69th Street; <u>R, V, G trains:</u> Northern Boulevard; <u>LIRR:</u> Woodside Station
Bus: <u>Q18:</u> 30th Avenue; <u>Q32:</u> Roosevelt Avenue; <u>Q45:</u> 69th Street; <u>Q60:</u> Queens Boulevard; <u>Q53:</u> Roosevelt Avenue/Broadway; <u>Q66:</u> Northern Boulevard; <u>Q104:</u> Broadway
Libraries: Queens Library, Woodside Branch (54-22 Skillman Avenue)
Museums: Topaz Arts, 55-03 39th Avenue
Community Board: Nos. 1, 2
Police Precinct: 108th Precinct (5-47 50th Avenue, Long Island City); 114th Precinct (34-16 Astoria Boulevard, Astoria)
Fire Department: Engine 325, Ladder 163, Battalion 49 (41-24 51st Street)
Hospitals and Clinics: Woodside Family Health Center (57-18 Woodside Avenue); Woodside Houses Child Health Clinic (50-53 Newtown Road); Woodside Senior Assistance Program–Builders for Family and Youth (61-20 Woodside Avenue)

Queens Timeline

JAMES DRISCOLL, PRESIDENT, QUEENS HISTORICAL SOCIETY

ca. 7,000 B.C.	Climatic changes following the last Ice Age force the borough's earliest inhabitants, Paleolithic hunters, to leave in search of disappearing large game
ca. 4,500 B.C.	Native American settlers speaking a Delaware language dialect who call themselves Lenapes start settling in the New York City area; over the centuries their culture evolves from one based on hunting and foraging to fishing and farming: a group called the Matinecocs occupies the north shore area of today's Queens, another group, the Rockaways, occupies southern Queens, and the Mespats, possibly a subdivision of the Rockaways, live in central Queens
1609	Henry Hudson explores the New York area, including what is now Coney Island
1614	Adriaen Block and the crew of his ship the *Onrust* are probably the first Europeans to see the area we now call Queens when they sail through the Hell Gate Channel on their way to the Long Island Sound; the Dutch establish a colony between the Connecticut and Delaware Rivers and call it New Netherland
1626	Peter Minuit, an official with the Dutch West Indies Company, purchases Manhattan Island from the Native Americans: the Dutch call this new settlement New Amsterdam
1636–39	Dutch authorities begin awarding grants of land in Queens to various individuals, the first Europeans to settle in western Queens, whose earliest dwellings may have been built in the Dutch Kills area of Long Island City
1637	Thomas Foster settles in the area of Bayside known as the Alley: much of this area is now covered by the intersections of the Cross Island and Grand Central Parkways and the Long Island Expressway
1642	The first organized European settlement in Queens built on land granted by the Dutch to the Reverend Francis Doughty, an English clergyman, in the Maspeth area near Newtown Creek
1643	New Netherland governor Willem Kieft's mishandling of Indian affairs provokes a war with Native Americans that destroys the Maspeth settlement
1645	Governor Kieft charters the town of Flushing: the charter is granted to a group of English settlers from New England and guarantees freedom of religion to the extent it is practiced in Holland (the name Flushing is probably an English corruption of the original Dutch name for the area, Vlissingen); William Lawrence settles in what is now College Point and builds the first house there
1652	The Maspeth colony is revived and relocated further inland: the settlement is called Middleburgh (changed to Newtown in 1665)

1655   English settlers from Hempstead, Long Island, establish the town of Rustdorp (later Jamaica): it is chartered by Peter Stuyvesant in 1656

1656   Settlers of Spring Field (now Springfield Gardens) obtain permission from Dutch authorities to purchase lands and build a town; Thomas Hicks settles the area known as Little Madnan's Neck (now Douglaston)

1657   The people of Flushing issue the Flushing Remonstrance to protest Governor Stuyvesant's persecution of the Quakers: one of first public statements on freedom of religion issued in the North American colonies, it argues that Stuyvesant violated rights granted to the colonists in their town charter

1661   John Bowne, a Quaker, builds his home in Flushing: now the oldest house in Queens, it is still standing on Bowne Street

1662   Peter Stuyvesant orders the expulsion of John Bowne from the colony for allowing Quakers to hold meetings in his home: Bowne travels to Holland to plead his case before the directors of the Dutch West India Company, who accept his arguments and order Stuyvesant to allow Quakers to worship in the colony; the First Presbyterian Church of Jamaica holds its first services: still in existence, it is the longest continuously worshiping Presbyterian congregation in America

1664   The Dutch surrender New Netherland to the English

1672   George Fox, founder of the Society of Friends, speaks to Quakers in Flushing beneath two oak trees near the Bowne House (a monument, Fox Stone, now marks the spot)

1683   The British colony of New York is divided into ten counties, one of which is Queens (the name is probably chosen to honor Catherine of Braganza, wife of Charles II): at this time Queens County includes all of the current Nassau County

1684   The town of Flushing signs its last deed with the Matinecocs

1685   Captain John Palmer purchases land from the Native Americans in what is now Far Rockaway; Governor Dongan confirms town charters and boundaries of Flushing, Newtown, and Jamaica, the three Queens County townships

1690   Richard Cornell purchases land in Far Rockaway from Captain John Palmer and establishes the first European settlement in the Rockaways (Cornell is buried in the Cornell Cemetery in Far Rockaway)

1694   Quakers in Flushing build a meetinghouse on Broadway (now Northern Boulevard): it is still being used by the Society of Friends and is the oldest house of worship in New York City

1702   Anglicans establish Grace Church, whose minister conducts services in the three Queens towns: eventually three separate parishes emerge, Grace Church in Jamaica, St. George in Flushing, and St. James in Newtown; the Dutch Reform Church is established in Jamaica, the first of that denomination in Queens

1703   The colonial legislature enacts a law providing for a highway from the East River ferry in Brooklyn through Queens and Suffolk counties to Easthampton (the route, which follows the old Indian trail, later becomes Jamaica Avenue)

1708   In Hallett's Cove (now Hallets Cove in Astoria), William Hallett and his family are murdered by his two slaves, an African American man and his Native American wife (who are tried and executed): this event increases the fear of slave rebellions throughout the New York area

ca. 1735   Robert Prince and his son William establish the first commercial nursery in North America in Flushing: the Prince family will continue to operate nurseries on land near Flushing Creek until the late 1860s

1735   St. James Episcopal Church of Newtown completed in what is now Elmhurst (the building, still owned by the church but no longer used for services, is still standing, the oldest Episcopal church building in New York City)

1768   Captain Thomas Webb, a Methodist missionary, establishes the first Methodist church on Long Island on Dry Harbor Road in what is now Middle Village: the congregation's leader is a local farmer named Joseph Harper, whose sons later start the publishing firm Harper and Brothers

1769   An ancient dispute between the towns of Bushwick in Brooklyn and Newtown in Queens over their borderline is settled: Arbitration Rock serves as one of the boundary markers (it can be seen today on the grounds of the Vander Ende–Onderdonk House in Ridgewood)

1774   The New York Yearly Meeting of the Society of Friends meets in Flushing and rules that Quakers in New York Colony may no longer own slaves; Elias Hicks and other Quaker leaders start visiting meetings throughout Long Island to persuade Quakers to manumit their slaves

1776   Francis Lewis of Whitestone signs the Declaration of Independence; in the Battle of Long Island, the British defeat General Washington's forces in Brooklyn, forcing him to retreat to Manhattan (no significant fighting takes place in Queens); American general Nathaniel Woodhull captured by the British in present-day Hollis (wounded and held on a prison ship in New York Harbor, he later dies in New Utrecht in British hands); British forces burn the Francis Lewis home in Whitestone and arrest his wife, who is thrown into a common New York City jail and not released until General Washington arrests the wives of two British officials in Philadelphia; the British garrison troops in Queens (remaining throughout the Revolution)

1783   The Treaty of Paris signed, ending the Revolution: British troops evacuate Queens, along with many Loyalists; Patriots who fled Queens after the Battle of Long Island start returning home

1789   George Washington visits Prince's Nursery in Flushing

1790   First U.S. Census taken: Queens County has 5,393 total population, including 1,095 slaves

1792	Union Hall Academy founded in Jamaica
1801	Nursery owner William Prince finances the building of the first bridge over Flushing Creek; wealthy Manhattan businessmen start building country estates in the Flushing area
1805	Rufus King purchases a farmhouse in Jamaica, which he greatly expands and lives in until his death in 1823 (King is buried in the Grace Church Cemetery; the house is today a museum)
1809	The Brooklyn and Jamaica Turnpike, a toll road, is completed from the Brooklyn ferry to what is now 168th Street in downtown Jamaica
1811	The Macedonia African Methodist Episcopal Church established in Flushing: still in existence, it is the oldest African American congregation in Queens
1814	The Penny Bridge, connecting Brooklyn and Queens, built over Newtown Creek, near the site of the Kosciuszko Bridge; Jamaica becomes an incorporated village (within the township of Jamaica), the first in Queens County; as part of the War of 1812 defenses, Fort Stevens is erected in the Hallets Cove area of Astoria (decommissioned in the early 1820s)
1814–16	The Williamsburg and Jamaica Turnpike constructed, the forerunner of today's Metropolitan Avenue
1821	The Union Course Race Track opens in Woodhaven: within a few years it becomes one of the leading thoroughbred tracks in the Northeast; *The Long Island Farmer*, a Jamaica newspaper and the first paper published in what is now Queens, is established (in 1920 it becomes the *Long Island Daily Press*, and later the *Long Island Press*)
1824	Thomas Brush starts Brushville, a hamlet west of Jamaica; Wyant Van Zandt of today's Douglaston finances the building of a road and bridge that traverse the wetlands south of Little Neck Bay: part of today's Northern Boulevard, the road made it possible to travel along the north shore to the East River uninterrupted from points east of Flushing (previously travelers had to detour south on the road to Alley Pond and then travel back north to Northern Boulevard); the Alley, the village around the Alley Pond, begins to decline
1825	Centerville Race Track opens in Woodhaven
1827	As of July 4, slavery is no longer legal in New York State, although most slaves in New York have been manumitted by this time
1833	The Marine Pavilion Hotel opens in Far Rockaway (burned down in 1864): this enormous seaside hotel establishes the area as a seaside resort, particularly for the wealthy
1834	The Brooklyn and Jamaica Railroad Company builds a line from Brooklyn to Jamaica; the Long Island Rail Road (spelled Long Island Railroad, 1901–44; Long Island Rail Road after 1944) established: it takes over the Brooklyn-Jamaica line; the Allen African Methodist Episcopal Church established as the first black church in Jamaica

1835   Scottish immigrant George Douglas purchases the Wyant Van Zandt house in Douglaston

1836   John Pitkin lays out a village he calls Woodville (changed to Woodhaven in 1853)

1837   Village of Flushing incorporated as a village within the township of Flushing

1838   Samuel Parsons establishes the Parsons's Nursery in Flushing: after his death in 1841, his two sons, Samuel Bowne and Robert Bowne Parsons, turn it into one of the most important nurseries in the Northeast (many of the original trees that Frederick Law Olmsted and Calvert Vaux plant in Manhattan's Central Park and Brooklyn's Prospect Park come from this nursery)

1839   Village of Astoria chartered by the state, the first new village in Queens to be chartered since the mid-seventeenth century: founded by Stephen Halsey, it is named to honor John Jacob Astor; the Reverend William Muhlenberg opens St. Paul's College, from which what is now called College Point takes its name (the college closes by the late 1840s, a victim of the long economic depression)

1840   In Whitestone, local philanthropist Samuel Leggett hires Walt Whitman (at the time an itinerant teacher) to teach at a "free school" he has established for the children of the area

1840–42 Catholic churches built in the villages of Flushing (St. Michael's), Astoria (Our Lady of Mount Carmel), and Jamaica (St. Monica's) to provide for the growing number of Catholics, mostly Irish, in Queens

1840–44 The hamlet of Middle Village springs up halfway between Jamaica and Williamsburg, Brooklyn, along the connecting turnpike, the future Metropolitan Avenue, when hotels and inns are built to accommodate farmers who want to spend the night before continuing on the long journey to markets in Brooklyn and Manhattan

1841   Neziah Bliss of Greenpoint lays out the village of Blissville on the shore of Newtown Creek across from Greenpoint, west of what would become Calvary Cemetery

1843   Ferry service begins between the village of Astoria and East 92nd Street in Manhattan

1844   The Long Island Rail Road completes the line from Brooklyn through Queens to Greenport, Long Island, part of a land and ferry route to Boston; completion of the New Haven Line's all-land route to Boston makes this older route cumbersome and the Long Island Rail Road evolves into a commuter railroad

1845–49 Irish Potato Famine leads to mass immigration to the United States: the number of Irish Catholics in Queens grows rapidly

1847   The state enacts a rural cemetery law that encourages the building of cemeteries in suburban areas and leads to the establishment of immense burial grounds in western and central Queens; Samuel Bowne Parsons imports the first weeping beech tree in America from Belgium and plants it in his Flushing nursery

1848   The first burials in Calvary Cemetery take place in land purchased by the New
        York Roman Catholic Archdiocese in 1846 from the Alsop family (the diocese
        expands the cemetery by purchasing neighboring farms until 1889); Cypress
        Hills and Evergreen Cemeteries established; first mansions erected in the Ra-
        venswood area of Astoria along the East River on the former estate of Colonel
        George Gibbs

1849   The American Anti-Slavery Society sends the abolitionist Abby Kelley Foster
        and her husband, Stephen Foster, on a lecture tour of Long Island, but angry
        crowds in Flushing and Hempstead, Long Island, force them to stop

1851   Lutheran Cemetery laid out in Middle Village, organized by two Manhat-
        tan Lutheran parishes, St. Matthew's and St. Mark's: this and other nearby
        cemeteries foster local business, including hotels and restaurants; the chapel
        in the Lutheran Cemetery becomes home to the first Lutheran congregation in
        Queens, a sign of increasing German immigration (Middle Village is a mostly
        German community by 1860)

1852   August Rapelje lays out the village of Laurel Hill, east of Calvary Cemetery:
        cemetery workers start moving into this community and Blissville

1853   In August a West Indian Emancipation Day celebration held at St. Ronan's
        Well Picnic Ground on Flushing Bay: the event commemorates the abolition of
        slavery in the British West Indies on August 1, 1834, and among the speakers
        are abolitionists William Lloyd Garrison and Horace Greeley, publisher of the
        New York Tribune

1854   Conrad Poppenhusen opens a hard-rubber factory in College Point, one of
        the first large-scale manufacturing plants in Queens, employing hundreds of
        workers, mainly German immigrants; real estate developers begin selling lots
        in a development called West Flushing, a stop on the newly opened Flush-
        ing Railroad line connecting Flushing with Long Island City (West Flushing
        renamed Corona in 1870); National Race Course opens in West Flushing (name
        changed to Fashion Race Course shortly after its opening to honor a famous
        race horse of the day; Corona's National Street was near the site of the original
        track); village of Winfield laid out in building lots: most of its residents work at
        a metal casket factory in what is now Woodside; Dr. William Valk of Flushing
        elected to Congress as a candidate of the Know Nothing Party (the following
        year the party's candidate for Flushing town supervisor is elected); the new St.
        George's Episcopal Church opens on Main Street in Flushing (now a New York
        City landmark)

1857   The name of the village of Brushville changed to Queens: residents start calling
        the area Queens Village to avoid confusing the village name with the county
        name; John Alsop King of Jamaica, son of Rufus King, becomes the governor
        of New York State (the former congressman serves a single two-year term and
        is well known for his anti-slavery sentiments)

1858 An all-star baseball game between the best players of Manhattan and Brooklyn is held at Fashion Race Course (the track was chosen as a neutral site), the first baseball game in the country to which admission is charged (50 cents a ticket; the Brooklyn team won, twenty to eighteen); prehistoric remains, identified as bones of a mastodon, found when Baisley Pond in today's South Jamaica is cleaned

1859 Ferry service established between Hunters Point (later Long Island City) and East 34th Street in Manhattan

1860 Florian Grosjean and Charles Lalance begin buying property in Woodhaven with the goal of the moving their kitchenware factory out of Manhattan (after their original 1863 wooden factory buildings burn down, they open a much larger factory along Atlantic Avenue in 1876); despite the strong anti-slavery sentiments of many of its residents, particularly in the Flushing area, Republican Abraham Lincoln fails to carry Queens in the 1860 election: Democrat Stephen Douglass carries the county

1861 The Long Island Rail Road opens a terminal in Hunters Point; the first hospital in Queens opened in Long Island City by a group of Catholic nuns

1861–65 The Civil War: the only populated areas of Queens capable of sending large numbers of volunteers and, later, draftees are Jamaica, Flushing, and College Point

1862 Construction of a fort at Willets Point in Bayside begun by the U.S. government: the fortress section, intended to be part of the New York City area's coastal defense, is built opposite Fort Schuyler in the Bronx (this style of defense is quickly outmoded by changes in warfare, and the fortress is never completed), and throughout the Civil War many local volunteers are trained on the grounds, which also hold a large military hospital (name changed to Fort Totten in 1898); Flushing Town Hall built

1863 Draft riots in Jamaica cause some property damage but no injuries or loss of life (the rioters threaten to burn down King Manor, home of the former governor John Alsop King); 20th Regiment of U.S. Colored Troops billeted on Rikers Island: the regiment was formed by members of the Union League Club of New York as a response to the draft riots

1865 Frederick Douglass delivers a speech at the Flushing Town Hall on the role of African Americans in post–Civil War America; the Brooklyn and Rockaway Railroad completed; day-trippers from the city start coming to Rockaway Beach; a Jewish congregation in Manhattan establishes the Bayside Cemetery in what is now Ozone Park

1866 Jamaica Avenue horsecar line begun from East New York in Brooklyn to 168th Street in Jamaica; Long Island Rail Road opens a stop in Little Neck; *Long Island City Star* newspaper founded in Long Island City

1867 Real estate developer Benjamin W. Hitchcock begins laying out lots in the new village of Woodside on the old John A. Kelley Estate

1868   Railroad line constructed from Flushing through College Point to Whitestone by Conrad Poppenhusen; Poppenhusen gives land and money to the village of College Point for the Poppenhusen Institute; John Schooley lays out a settlement he calls Glendale

1869   Albon P. Man, a Manhattan lawyer and investor, and a landscape architect named Edward Richardson begin laying out Richmond Hill

1870   A hamlet begins to grow in Fosters Meadow near a newly opened Long Island Rail Road station (named Rosedale in 1892); a free kindergarten for the children of College Point opened at the Poppenhusen Institute: based on German models, it is the first of its kind in the United States; Scheutzen Park, a picnic ground and German beer garden, opens near the intersection of the current Steinway Street and Broadway; the New York State legislature creates Long Island City, which includes the former villages of Astoria, Ravenswood, Hunters Point, Dutch Kills, and Blissville

1870–72   The Steinway Company builds a piano factory and factory village on a 400-acre site in the northern section of Long Island City; around the same time, the Steinways purchase the Benjamin Pike mansion near the factory that will serve as the family's summer residence: the area becomes known as Steinway (now part of Astoria)

1871   The Nichols brothers take over the Laurel Hill Chemical Works (opened 1866) and turn the plant into a major producer of various types of acids (it later becomes a copper refinery; Phelps-Dodge takes over the plant in the 1920s)

1873   Hoffman Boulevard is developed from Newtown to what is now Kew Gardens (the road eventually becomes part of Queens Boulevard); Creedmoor Rifle Range opens on what was the Creed farm in the Queens Village area: it becomes nationally famous as the site of shooting contests

1874   Queens County Courthouse holds its first session in Long Island City after moving from Mineola in present-day Nassau County (new courthouse completed in 1876)

1875   Flushing High School, the first state-chartered public high school in what is now New York City, opens its doors

1876   Army engineers detonate an enormous explosion beneath the Hell Gate Channel to destroy some of the largest submerged rocks; Long Island Rail Road opens a new stop called Douglaston about a mile east of the Little Neck stop

1878   William Trist Bailey builds a large hotel and cottages in a new Far Rockaway community he calls Bayswater

1880   Railway trestle over Jamaica Bay to the Rockaways is completed

1882   Ozone Park laid out by Benjamin W. Hitchcock and Charles C. Denton

1883   Morris Park development is begun just south of Richmond Hill (originally the name of a picnic ground in that area, it was a stop on the Long Island Rail Road)

1884   The city of New York purchases Rikers Island from Long Island City for use as a prison farm

1885   Hollis developed by Frederick W. Dunton in an area previously known as East Jamaica

1886   Ferry service begins between College Point and East 92nd Street in Manhattan; North Beach (known as Bowery Bay Beach before 1891) opens: it becomes the Coney Island of northern Queens (it remains a popular attraction until Prohibition); terra-cotta factory opens in Long Island City

1887   Reporter Jacob Riis moves to Richmond Hill, where he writes *How the Other Half Lives*; Flushing Athletic Club opens one of the first golf courses in the United States in north Flushing; first electric trolley in Queens opens, running from Jamaica Avenue in East New York to 168th Street in Jamaica (second such line in the United States)

1888   Flushing Hospital opens; the Long Island Rail Road builds a station in a Jamaica Bay island fishing community called the Raunt (the site is now part of the Jamaica Bay Wildlife Refuge); Remington Vernam completes a hotel and starts selling nearby lots in new Rockaway community called Arverne

1889   Hinsdale renamed Floral Park in honor of John Lewis Childs, who had settled there and developed an immense mail-order nursery business; the Long Island Rail Road opens the Murray Hill station in Flushing, about a mile east of Main Street; Frederick Dunton starts selling building plots on land he purchased near the station's site

1890   Jamaica Hospital opens; the Long Island Land Improvement Company, a subsidiary of the Long Island Rail Road, begins developing Rockaway Park

1891   St. John's Hospital established in Long Island City (later moves to Elmhurst)

1892   Frederick J. Lancaster develops a new Rockaway community called Edgemere, advertised as "the New Venice"; building lots for the community of St. Albans laid out on farmland formerly owned by a W. Francis (Long Island Rail Road opens a nearby station in 1898); St. Adalbert's, a Polish Catholic church, opens in Elmhurst, a sign of the growing diversification of Queens population; work begins on the Steinway Tunnel beneath the East River, but a terrible explosion stops it on December 28 (the Interborough Rapid Transit takes control of the unfinished tunnel in 1905, and after many delays the tunnel opens for subway traffic in 1915)

1893   Louis Tiffany opens the Tiffany Studio in Corona; Public School 1 opens in Long Island City (its completion is long delayed by the corruption of the local political machine headed by Mayor Patrick "Battle-Ax" Gleason)

1894   Jamaica Racetrack opens and quickly becomes a major thoroughbred track (closes in 1959); Aqueduct Racetrack opens in Ozone Park; an advisory vote is held to determine whether the towns of the western half of Queens County should become part of New York City: Long Island City, Newtown, and Jamaica vote yes, Flushing votes no

1895   Villages of Richmond Hill, Morris Park, and Clarenceville (an older village just west of Richmond Hill) incorporated as the village of Richmond Hill; a tornado strikes Woodhaven, causing extensive damage

1896   The New York State legislature passes a bill creating the consolidated New York City, which includes the townships of western Queens; the Oakland Golf Club organized in Bayside; three libraries combine to form the Long Island City Public Library (around the turn of the century other libraries join the system and its name is changed to the Queens Borough Public Library, now the Queens Library); at the urging of real estate developer Cord Meyer the federal government changes the name of Newtown to Elmhurst

1897   A state normal (teacher training) college opens in Jamaica (closed in 1933) on the site of the current Hillcrest High School, which is bordered by a street called Normal Street

1898   The consolidation of western Queens with New York City takes effect on January 1: the first Queens borough president is Frederick Bowley of Long Island City, the first Borough Hall is, very briefly, the former Long Island City city hall; as part of the consolidation the Rockaways are removed from the town of Hempstead and made part of the borough of Queens; President Bowley moves the borough government into a new "temporary" home, the Hackett building on Jackson Avenue in Long Island City (it remains until 1916); the Fire Department of the City of New York (FDNY) takes over firefighting duties from the Long Island City Fire Department, becoming the only professional fire department in Queens

1899   The state creates Nassau County, consisting of the townships of eastern Queens: Hempstead, North Hempstead, and Oyster Bay; Jamaica and Flushing are connected by trolley line

1900   The U.S. Census puts the population of Queens at 152,999; George Tillyou, of Coney Island fame, opens a Steeplechase Park in the Rockaways near Beach 100th Street; a new state law outlaws separate public schools for blacks, abolishing "colored" public schools in Flushing and Jamaica; Newtown High School opens in Elmhurst

1901   Auburndale is laid out by the New England Development and Improvement Company on the old Thomas Willets farm in Flushing; the Long Island Rail Road opens a new station near what is now the intersection of 39th Avenue and 192nd Street; construction begins on the Queensboro Bridge

1903   St. Leo Roman Catholic Church founded as a mission to the growing Italian population in Corona

1904   An excursion boat, the *General Slocum*, catches fire in the East River, and

1,021 passengers are killed, mostly women and children, many of whom are buried in the Lutheran Cemetery in Middle Village, where a monument is erected: the tragedy causes the breakup of the German community on the Lower East Side, and many of its residents move to German communities in Queens, such as Middle Village; Carnegie-funded libraries open in Astoria, College Point, Far Rockaway (the College Point library is called the Poppenhusen Branch because most of the collection was previously housed in the Poppenhusen Institute)

1905   East Elmhurst laid out; the Long Island Rail Road begins electrifying lines in Queens; Temple Derech Emunoh built in Arverne, one of the first synagogues in Queens; Holliswood development opens

1906   Shore Realty Corporation begins laying out Beechhurst in the northeastern corner of Whitestone (first lots put on the market the following year); Cord Meyer begins developing Forest Hills; the Douglas Manor Company begins promoting part of the Douglaston peninsula as a residential area; a real estate development called Westmoreland laid out near the Little Neck Railroad Station; the G. X. Mathews company builds its first three-story, six-family row houses (Mathews Flats) in Ridgewood; first houses put up for sale in Queensboro Hill, a new development south of the village of Flushing

1907   First sections of Belle Harbor developed; Laurelton Land Company sells its first lots in Laurelton; a development called Briarwood begun in the area north of Hillside Avenue in Jamaica

1908   The FDNY takes over firefighting duties from the local Flushing fire companies; first houses built in Malba; the Russell Sage Foundation purchases the future site of a planned community called Forest Hills Gardens from Cord Meyer; development of Jamaica Estates begins; borough president Joseph Bermel (elected 1906) resigns as a result of scandals

1909   Queensboro Bridge opens to traffic; Daniel Leahy starts selling homes in South Ozone Park; a new, larger courthouse built in Long Island City to replace the 1876 building, which was destroyed by fire; the Neponsit Realty Corporation starts laying out a new community in the Rockaways; a New York City school for truant boys opens on the site of the future Queens College; the Hillcrest development in Jamaica, north of Hillside Avenue and east of 164th Street, laid out by developer William Wyckoff

1910   An extension of Bellerose in Nassau County opened for development in Queens; Penn Central opens the Sunnyside Yards to rail traffic; the Pennsylvania Railroad Tunnel under the East River opens, offering electrified railroad service directly to Manhattan; Frogtown School, on Astoria Boulevard near 90th Street, the last remaining one-room schoolhouse in Queens, closed by the Board of Education

1911   Forest Hills Gardens, designed by Grosvenor Atterbury, architect, and Frederick Law Olmsted, Jr., landscape architect, opens for sales; Howard Beach developed by William R. Howard; Queens Chamber of Commerce incorporated

1912   A new state mental hospital opens on the old site of the Creedmoor Rifle Range; the development of Kew Gardens begins; the FDNY takes over firefighting duties from the Newtown Fire Department

1913   The Sage Foundation sells land in Forest Hills Gardens to the West Side Tennis Club, which relocates from Manhattan to Queens; a trolley line opens on Queens Boulevard

1914   The Queensboro Corporation builds its first apartment buildings in Jackson Heights; the FDNY takes over firefighting duties from the Jamaica volunteer fire companies; the Loose-Wiles Company (maker of Sunshine Biscuits) opens a plant in the Degnon Terminal, a state-of-the-art industrial park in Long Island City: other well-known companies follow, including Adams Chewing Gum and the Packard Motor Company (Loose-Wiles is soon employing 2,500 people, making it for many years the largest employer in Queens)

1915   Fulton Street elevated line extended beyond the city line along Liberty Avenue to Lefferts Street; West Side Tennis Club hosts the Nationals (now called the U.S. Open) at the Forest Hills Tennis Stadium; the Interborough Rapid Transit (IRT) opens service to the intersection of Vernon Boulevard and Jackson Avenue in Long Island City; the elevated line to Metropolitan Avenue in Ridgewood opens

1916   The Queens borough president's office moves from the Hackett Building to a new home in the Queens Plaza area (until 1940); New York City declares Jamaica Bay too polluted for fishing; the IRT reaches Queensboro Plaza

1917   New York Connecting Railroad, including the Hell Gate Bridge, opened to traffic across the East River; IRT reaches Corona; Margaret Sanger arrested for distributing information about contraceptives and sentenced to thirty days in the Queens County Penitentiary in Long Island City; the U.S. government completes the construction of Fort Tilden in the Rockaways, part of the World War I coastal defense system

1918   The Brooklyn-Manhattan Transit (BMT) elevated line reaches 168th Street in Jamaica

1919   The Queensboro Corporation, headed by Edward McDougall, opens Linden Court, the first garden co-operative apartment in Jackson Heights; Famous Players–Lasky Studio (later Paramount Studio) opens in Astoria

ca. 1920   A large number of African Americans start settling in the area south of Jamaica Avenue (South Jamaica), coming from the South, Harlem, and the West Indies

1920   The Pomonok Golf Course organized by members of the Flushing Country Club; Cambria Heights development begun

1922   A new state law makes it legal for insurance companies to invest in development and gives a tax break to the builders of apartment buildings: Metropolitan Life builds its first Queens housing development in Astoria; Max Rosner and Nat Strong purchase Dexter Park in Woodhaven and build a popular modern semi-pro ballpark, the home field of Rosner's team, the Bushwicks; extensive building of one-family homes in what comes to be known as the Baisley Park development; fire in Arverne destroys many of the summer cottages

1923   Rego Park developed by the Real Good Construction Company; Fresh Meadows Golf Club opens

1924   City Housing Corporation, a private philanthropic group, begins building Sunnyside Gardens, a garden apartment complex that is widely admired for its architecture and abundance of open space (completed in 1929)

1925   Cross Bay Boulevard completed, connecting the Rockaway Peninsula and southern Queens; F. Scott Fitzgerald's *Great Gatsby* published: partially set in Flushing and Corona, it refers to the Corona dump heaps as "the valley of ashes"

1927   Ruth Snyder of Queens Village and her lover Judd Gray murder Snyder's husband: they are tried at the Long Island City Courthouse in one of the most sensational media trials of its day; Addisleigh Park development in St. Albans opens; St. Demetrius Greek Orthodox Church established in Astoria; the Flushing Oratorio Society (now the Oratorio Society of Queens) performs its first concerts; Jamaica High School (founded 1892) opens new building in Jamaica Hills

1928   Rockaways' Playland opens on the site of the old Steeplechase Park in the Rockaways; the RKO Keith's movie palace opens on the site of the old Flushing Hotel; IRT extended to Main Street, Flushing; Louis Latimer dies in Flushing: the African American scientist had worked with Thomas Edison on the development of the lightbulb

1929   Artist Joseph Cornell moves into a house on Utopia Parkway in Flushing (he lives there until his death in 1971); the Loews Valencia in Jamaica, Queens's largest movie palace, opens; Glenn Curtiss Airfield built at North Beach on the site of the old amusement park

1930   According to the U.S. Census, the population of Queens passes the million mark (1,079,129); Joseph Cullen opens King Kullen, the nation's first supermarket, on Jamaica Avenue near 173rd Street, just east of downtown Jamaica; the Queens Borough Public Library Central Library Building opened in Jamaica; the seventeenth-century Moore Homestead in Elmhurst torn down to make way for the Independent (IND) subway line; the first night baseball game played at Dexter Park

1931   Triboro Theatre opens in Astoria

1932   The city erects a men's prison on Rikers Island to replace the one on Black-well's Island (Roosevelt Island); Tiffany Studio goes bankrupt; golfing great Gene Sarazen wins the U.S. Open at Fresh Meadows; a rent strike in Sunny-side Gardens attracts national attention

1933   Grand Central Parkway opens from Kew Gardens to the Nassau County line; the IND subway opens to Roosevelt Avenue in Jackson Heights

1935   Queens General Hospital, the first municipal hospital in Queens, opens in Jamaica

1936   Boulevard Gardens development opens in Woodside: it is privately built but funded by the federal government; Triborough Bridge opens to traffic; work begins to turn Flushing Meadows into the site of the upcoming World's Fair: two artificial lakes—Meadows Lake and Willow Lake—are created and the Grand Central Parkway Extension from Kew Gardens to the Triborough Bridge is completed; final voyage of ferry from 92nd Street in Manhattan to Long Island City

1937   Mayor Fiorello La Guardia uses the Chisolm mansion in College Point as his summer city hall; Briarwood Estates built; a number of trolley lines in Queens shut down, including the lines that ran along Northern Boulevard and Queens Boulevard; Queens College opens

1938   Chester Carlson invents what he called an electrophotographic machine (better known as the Xerox machine) in his makeshift laboratory on 37th Street in Astoria (it takes him many years to find a manufacturer for it)

1939   Queensbridge Houses open in Long Island City, the first New York City Hous-ing Authority project in Queens (a second, the South Jamaica Houses, opens in 1940); the ferry between College Point and the Bronx closed down; General Courthouse on Sutphin Boulevard in Jamaica dedicated (now the New York State Supreme Courthouse); La Guardia Airport opens on the site of the old Glenn Curtiss Field; Meeker Avenue Bridge over Newtown Creek opened (re-named Kosciuszko Bridge in 1940); the Cross Bay Bridge, connecting Howard Beach and the Rockaways, opens; the Bronx-Whitestone Bridge opens the day before President Franklin D. Roosevelt opens the World's Fair, with the motto "Building the World of Tomorrow," in Flushing Meadows

1940   After four years of construction the Queens-Midtown Tunnel opens to traffic; a permanent Queens Borough Hall opens in Kew Gardens; the Belt Parkway opens; Pan American Airways initiates clipper service from the Marine Air Terminal at La Guardia Airport

1942   Louis Armstrong moves to Corona (he lives there until his death in 1971; the house is now a New York City landmark); the U.S. Army Signal Corps takes over the old Paramount Studio in Astoria

1945   Bowne House turned over to the Bowne House Historical Society and opened as a museum; African Americans, many of them World War II veterans, start moving into St. Albans; several famous black entertainers, including Count Basie, start buying homes in Addisleigh Park

1946 New York Life Insurance Company begins construction of a housing development in Fresh Meadows on the site of the old golf course (opens in 1949)

1947 United Nations builds Parkway Village in the Briarwood area of Queens as housing for its employees; U.N. General Assembly, meeting at the old New York City building on the World's Fair grounds in what is now Flushing Meadows–Corona Park, orders the partition of Palestine; the first tenants, mostly veterans, begin moving into the new Glen Oaks garden apartments

1948 President Harry S Truman and Governor Thomas Dewey help dedicate New York International Airport, more commonly known as Idlewild

1949 Pomonok Golf Course sold; Pomonok Houses, a low- and middle-income housing development, and Electchester, a cooperative apartment complex financed by the Electricians Union, slated for development on the site

1950 Long Island Rail Road train accident in Richmond Hill kills seventy-nine people, the worst accident in the railroad's history; the IND subway reaches Jamaica; the Van Wyck Expressway completed

1951 The first public housing project in the Rockaways, the Arverne Houses, opens

1953 Consolidated Edison opens its power plant in Astoria; Jamaica Bay Wildlife Refuge opened; Queens Symphony Orchestra, founded by conductor David Katz, performs its first concerts

1954 Fire destroys Long Island Rail Road trestle across Jamaica Bay (city rebuilds it and makes it part of the subway system)

1955 St. John's University opens its Queens campus on the site of the old Hillcrest Golf Course; Dexter Park in Woodhaven torn down

1957 Last trolley line in Queens ends with the closing down of the trolley over the Queensboro Bridge; Long Island Expressway opened to the Nassau County line; celebration of the three-hundredth anniversary of the Flushing Remonstrance (it was signed on December 27, 1657)

1958 IND subway reaches Mott Avenue in Far Rockaway

1959 The New York Racing Association reopens Aqueduct Racetrack at the border of Ozone Park and South Ozone Park

1961 Throgs Neck Bridge, connecting Bayside and the Bronx, opened to traffic

1962 The Trans World Airlines Terminal opens at Idlewild Airport: designed by Eero Saarinen, it is now a New York City landmark

1963 Rochdale Village, the largest privately owned apartment development in the country, opens in South Jamaica on the site of Jamaica Racetrack; Big Six cooperative apartment complex opens in Woodside, financed by Local Six of the Typographical Unions; Oakland Gardens community built on site of old

Oakland Golf Course; to prepare for the upcoming World's Fair, the Queens Botanical Gardens moves from its site on the fair grounds to its new home on Main Street in Flushing

1964   President Lyndon B. Johnson opens the 1964 World's Fair in Flushing Meadows–Corona Park; Mets play (and lose) their first game at Shea Stadium; the brutal murder of Kitty Genovese in Kew Gardens and the apparent indifference of many residents who witnessed the crime makes national headlines

1965   National Immigration Act abolishes quotas based on national origin (the law takes full effect in 1969); Pope Paul VI visits the World's Fair; Westinghouse Time Capsule buried next to the capsule from the first World's Fair; Macy's opens a branch on Queens Boulevard in Elmhurst: the new circular store is widely admired for its architecture; the Kingsland Homestead (ca. 1785) is the first site in Queens to be declared a New York City landmark

1966   The new Queens Borough Central Library building on Merrick Boulevard in Jamaica opens; bridge connecting Rikers Island and Astoria is completed

1967   Robert Moses, president of the World's Fair Corporation, turns Flushing Meadows–Corona Park over to the Parks Department

1968   Queens Zoo opens in Flushing Meadows–Corona Park; Queens Historical Society organized; *Long Island Star Journal*, a major daily newspaper established in 1938 as a result of a merger of the *Long Island City Star* and the *North Shore Journal*, closes down

1969   An unknown law professor named Mario Cuomo leads the fight to prevent the city from displacing Corona residents with a new high school; Mets win World Series over the Orioles, four games to one; New York Jets win Super Bowl III

1971   *All in the Family*, the first of many television shows set in Queens, premieres on CBS: the opening credits show homes on Cooper Avenue in Glendale and its main character, Archie Bunker, epitomizes Queens residents for many; La Guardia Community College begins classes in Long Island City at one of the old Degnon Terminal buildings; York College begins classes at its downtown Jamaica campus; a Sikh gurdwara (temple) is established in Richmond Hill, which today has the largest Sikh community outside India

1972   The city's attempt to build a low-income housing development in middle-class Forest Hills causes a community uproar: Mario Cuomo works out a compromise between the opposing groups; Jamaica Bay and Breezy Point included in the new Gateway National Park (as part of a compromise with local residents, the property of the Breezy Point Cooperative is excluded from the park)

1973   The Queens Museum of Art opens in the old New York City building on the World's Fair grounds

1974   The army abandons Fort Tilden on the Rockaway Peninsula, and it becomes part of the Gateway National Park

1975   The North Shore Towers apartment complex opens on the site of the Glen Oaks Golf Club

1976   P.S.1 in Long Island City opens as a museum of contemporary art

1977   David Berkowitz, alias Son of Sam, is arrested after a killing spree that terrorizes neighborhoods throughout Queens and the Bronx; The *Long Island Press*, the last major daily newspaper in Queens, closes down; Hindus consecrate the first Hindu temple in North America on Bowne Street in Flushing

1978   The U.S. Open tennis championship is moved from Forest Hills to the Louis Armstrong Stadium in Flushing Meadows–Corona Park; film production resumes at the old Astoria Studios (renamed Kaufman Astoria Studios in 1982)

1979   Pope John Paul II bids farewell to America with an appearance at Shea Stadium

1982   City allows Broad Channel residents to purchase their property, ending a more than four-decade dispute; Mario Cuomo of Holliswood elected governor of New York

1983   A new film and television studio opens up in Long Island City at the old Silvercup factory; New York Jets announce they will leave Shea Stadium for the Meadowlands in New Jersey; Queens County Farm Museum opens to the public; Phelps-Dodge Corporation closes the old Laurel Hill refining factory (the area remains a dangerous toxic site in need of a very expensive clean-up)

1984   Democratic Congresswoman Geraldine Ferraro of Forest Hills becomes the first woman selected as a vice presidential candidate by a major party; the state authorizes the construction of the Queens West redevelopment project along the East River in Hunters Point; the first episode of *The Cosby Show* is filmed at Kaufman Astoria Studios

1985   The Isamu Noguchi Museum, in the artist's former Long Island City studio, opens to the public

1986   Donald Manes resigns as borough president amid scandals; Deputy Borough President Claire Shulman becomes the new borough president; in July a special election is held to replace the late congressman Joseph Addabbo in which the Reverend Floyd Flake of the Allen African Methodist Episcopal Church in South Jamaica narrowly loses to Alton Waldon but defeats him in the November election: the two are the first African Americans elected to Congress from Queens; Rockaways' Playland demolished; Socrates Sculpture Park opens in Long Island City; Mets win second World Series title

1988   Museum of the Moving Image in Astoria dedicated

1990   Paul Simon and Art Garfunkel inducted into the Rock and Roll Hall of Fame; Citicorp opens a fifty-story skyscraper in Long Island City; the U.S. Census shows the population of Queens at 1,951,000

1992   The U.S. Department of the Census declares Queens to be the most ethnically diverse county in the United States

1996   The city tears down the Aquacade building in Flushing Meadows–Corona Park; the dissident Russian poet Yevgeny Yevtushenko joins the Queens College faculty

1997   The new Allen African Methodist Episcopal Cathedral in South Jamaica, which seats 2,500 people, dedicated; first tenants move into City Lights, a 44-story apartment building in Long Island City on the East River and the first of the nineteen proposed Queens West towers that will transform the decaying waterfront

1998   Borough president Claire Shulman withdraws her support for the erection of a large statue honoring Catherine of Braganza in Long Island City because of widespread opposition from African Americans and other groups; Parks Commissioner Henry Stern presides over a memorial service for Flushing's Weeping Beech Tree, a New York City landmark

1999   At a press conference in College Point, Mayor Rudolph Giuliani and health officials inform the city about the West Nile virus for the first time: College Point is the first area sprayed with insecticide, causing widespread concern; the Flushing Remonstrance is brought down from the state archives and exhibited at the newly opened Flushing branch of the Queens Borough Public Library

2000   U.S. Census shows the population of Queens at more than 2 million persons (2,230,000: 17.5 percent Asian; 19 percent African American; 25 percent Hispanic); in the first "subway series" since 1956, the Yankees defeat the Mets in five games

2001   John Liu of Flushing becomes the first Asian American elected to the New York City Council; Helen Marshall becomes the first African American elected Queens borough president; in the attack on the World Trade Center, Queens loses at least 283 residents, including 19 firemen from a Maspeth firehouse, which suffers the greatest loss of any single firehouse in New York City; an American Airlines jet bound for Santo Domingo crashes in Belle Harbor, killing 260 passengers and crew and 5 people on the ground

2002   Museum of Modern Art relocates to Queens while its Manhattan site is being renovated

2003   Plans are submitted to bring the 2012 Summer Olympics to New York City: Flushing Meadows–Corona Park would host many of the events (the bid goes to London)

2006   Groundbreaking ceremony for a new Mets baseball stadium, to be built next to Shea Stadium and named Citi Field for sponsor Citicorp; Flushing State Assemblyman Brian McLoughlin, the head of the New York City Labor Council, is indicted by the federal government on forty-three racketeering charges

2007   State Comptroller Alan Hevesi of Forest Hills, Queens's most powerful statewide politician, is forced to resign because his wife used a state employee as her personal servant

Characteristics from the 2000 U.S. Census Bureau

TIMOTHY CALABRESE, GEOGRAPHER, POPULATION DIVISION,

NEW YORK CITY DEPARTMENT OF CITY PLANNING

Neighborhood populations change as people move into and out of the area. The data items presented in this section were taken from the 2000 Census Summary Files 1 and 3. Data from the Summary Files are available for a variety of geographic areas throughout the nation, such as states, counties, and census tracts. New York City has 2,217 census tracts, small geographic areas that usually contain between three and five thousand persons. Census tracts were aggregated to approximate the boundaries of neighborhoods, as defined by the maps presented in this book. Census tract boundaries and neighborhood boundaries, while sometimes similar, are never exactly the same. Therefore, the data presented here are meant to give a general picture of the size and characteristics of neighborhoods. In addition, numbers have been rounded to the hundreds, so some items with small values will round to zero, some numbers will not sum exactly, and some percentages will not add up to 100. For more complete small area data, please visit the Department of City Planning's website at www.nyc.gov/planning or the U.S. Census Bureau's website at www.census.gov.

Some data item descriptions were generalized in the tables. "Median age" represents the average of median age for census tracts in a neighborhood. Similarly, "Median household income" was calculated as the average of median household income for census tracts in a neighborhood and is in 1999 U.S. dollars. *Mutually Exclusive Race and Hispanic Origin* combines Hispanics (an ethnic group) as a separate additive category to create a combined race and Hispanic origin distribution. This is done by subtracting Hispanics from each race group to create "White, Non-Hispanic," "Black or African American, Non-Hispanic," "Asian and Pacific Islander, Non-Hispanic," and "Some other race, Non-Hispanic," and then including Hispanics as a single additive category. Also, changes in 2000 permitted respondents to enter more than one race. As a result, each of the major race groups is for single responses only and a separate, "Two or more races, Non-Hispanic" category is included. Finally, in the *Region of Birth of Foreign Born,* "Latin America" includes Central American countries, South American countries (including Brazil and a category called "Other South American Countries," which combines Suriname with Paraguay and Uruguay), Mexico, Cuba, and the Dominican Republic. "Non-Hispanic Caribbean" includes the following categories: Barbados, Jamaica, Haiti, Trinidad and Tobago, Guyana (which, although not a Caribbean island, has significant ethnic and linguistic similarities with other countries in this category), and "Other Caribbean." Oceania was not included given the very small numbers in that category.

ASTORIA

	Number	Percentage
Total Population	147,000	100.0
Age		
Under 18 years	27,400	18.6
65 years and over	16,800	11.4
Median age (years)	33.6	—
Mutually Exclusive Race and Hispanic Origin		
White, Non-Hispanic	72,000	49.0
Black or African American, Non-Hispanic	4,300	2.9
Asian and Pacific Islander, Non-Hispanic	19,800	13.5
Some other race, Non-Hispanic	2,100	1.4
Two or more races, Non-Hispanic	9,500	6.5
Hispanic (of any race)	39,200	26.7
Marital Status		
Population 15 years and over	123,800	100.0
Never married	46,900	37.9
Now married, except separated	50,400	40.7
Separated, widowed, or divorced	26,500	21.4
Housing		
Occupied units	58,700	100.0
Owner-occupied	11,600	19.8
Renter-occupied	47,100	80.2
Education		
Population 25 years and over	103,100	100.0
High school graduate or higher	73,300	71.1
Bachelors degree or higher	26,900	26.1
Region of Birth of Foreign Born		
Total foreign born	76,900	100.0
Europe	25,000	32.5
Asia	19,900	25.9
Africa	3,000	3.9
Latin America	26,800	34.9
Non-Hispanic Caribbean	1,700	2.2
Northern America	400	0.5
Language Spoken at Home		
Population 5 years and over	138,500	100.0
English only	43,900	31.7
Language other than English	94,500	68.2
Household Income		
Median household income (dollars)	37,000	—

BAYSIDE AND BAY TERRACE

	Number	Percentage
Total Population	85,900	100.0
Age		
Under 18 years	16,300	19.0
65 years and over	15,700	18.3
Median age (years)	44.0	—
Mutually Exclusive Race and Hispanic Origin		
White, Non-Hispanic	52,500	61.1
Black or African American, Non-Hispanic	1,800	2.1
Asian and Pacific Islander, Non-Hispanic	21,800	25.4
Some other race, Non-Hispanic	200	0.2
Two or more races, Non-Hispanic	1,900	2.2
Hispanic (of any race)	7,600	8.8
Marital Status		
Population 15 years and over	72,400	100.0
Never married	18,800	26.0
Now married, except separated	39,400	54.4
Separated, widowed, or divorced	14,300	19.8
Housing		
Occupied units	34,600	100.0
Owner-occupied	22,000	63.6
Renter-occupied	12,700	36.7
Education		
Population 25 years and over	64,100	100.0
High school graduate or higher	55,100	86.0
Bachelors degree or higher	24,300	37.9
Region of Birth of Foreign Born		
Total foreign born	29,000	100.0
Europe	6,800	23.4
Asia	17,500	60.3
Africa	400	1.4
Latin America	3,200	11.0
Non-Hispanic Caribbean	700	2.4
Northern America	200	0.7
Language Spoken at Home		
Population 5 years and over	81,700	100.0
English only	44,100	54.0
Language other than English	37,700	46.1
Household Income		
Median household income (dollars)	57,000	—

	Number	Percentage
Total Population	28,500	100.0
Age		
Under 18 years	6,400	22.4
65 years and over	4,900	17.3
Median age (years)	41.4	—
Mutually Exclusive Race and Hispanic Origin		
White, Non-Hispanic	14,300	50.4
Black or African American, Non-Hispanic	2,000	7.2
Asian and Pacific Islander, Non-Hispanic	7,300	25.7
Some other race, Non-Hispanic	200	0.9
Two or more races, Non-Hispanic	700	2.6
Hispanic (of any race)	3,800	13.3
Marital Status		
Population 15 years and over	23,200	100.0
Never married	6,400	27.6
Now married, except separated	12,200	52.6
Separated, widowed, or divorced	4,600	19.9
Housing		
Occupied units	9,800	100.0
Owner-occupied	7,400	75.2
Renter-occupied	2,400	24.8
Education		
Population 25 years and over	20,000	100.0
High school graduate or higher	16,300	81.9
Bachelors degree or higher	5,700	28.4
Region of Birth of Foreign Born		
Total foreign born	9,300	100.0
Europe	1,300	13.9
Asia	5,000	54.1
Africa	100	1.3
Latin America	1,400	15.2
Non-Hispanic Caribbean	1,400	14.7
Northern America	100	0.7
Language Spoken at Home		
Population 5 years and over	26,900	100.0
English only	15,900	59.2
Language other than English	11,000	40.8
Household Income		
Median household income (dollars)	48,100	—

	Number	Percentage
Total Population	26,400	100.0
Age		
Under 18 years	5,600	21.2
65 years and over	3,100	11.7
Median age (years)	35.3	—
Mutually Exclusive Race and Hispanic Origin		
White, Non-Hispanic	7,800	29.5
Black or African American, Non-Hispanic	3,000	11.4
Asian and Pacific Islander, Non-Hispanic	6,600	25.0
Some other race, Non-Hispanic	600	2.3
Two or more races, Non-Hispanic	1,700	6.4
Hispanic (of any race)	6,700	25.4
Marital Status		
Population 15 years and over	21,500	100.0
Never married	6,900	32.1
Now married, except separated	9,800	45.6
Separated, widowed, or divorced	4,900	22.8
Housing		
Occupied units	9,600	100.0
Owner-occupied	3,100	32.3
Renter-occupied	6,500	67.7
Education		
Population 25 years and over	18,700	100.0
High school graduate or higher	14,900	79.7
Bachelors degree or higher	5,700	30.5
Region of Birth of Foreign Born		
Total foreign born	14,900	100.0
Europe	2,200	14.8
Asia	6,200	41.6
Africa	200	1.3
Latin America	3,800	25.5
Non-Hispanic Caribbean	2,500	16.8
Northern America	—	0.0
Language Spoken at Home		
Population 5 years and over	24,800	100.0
English only	8,800	35.5
Language other than English	15,900	64.1
Household Income		
Median household income (dollars)	44,300	—

CAMBRIA HEIGHTS

	Number	Percentage
Total Population	21,200	100.0
Age		
Under 18 years	5,000	23.6
65 years and over	2,700	12.7
Median age (years)	38.5	—
Mutually Exclusive Race and Hispanic Origin		
White, Non-Hispanic	500	2.4
Black or African American, Non-Hispanic	19,200	90.6
Asian and Pacific Islander, Non-Hispanic	100	0.5
Some other race, Non-Hispanic	100	0.5
Two or more races, Non-Hispanic	500	2.4
Hispanic (of any race)	900	4.2
Marital Status		
Population 15 years and over	17,000	100.0
Never married	6,000	35.3
Now married, except separated	7,200	42.4
Separated, widowed, or divorced	3,900	22.9
Housing		
Occupied units	6,700	100.0
Owner-occupied	5,600	83.6
Renter-occupied	1,100	16.4
Education		
Population 25 years and over	14,300	100.0
High school graduate or higher	12,100	84.6
Bachelors degree or higher	3,500	24.5
Region of Birth of Foreign Born		
Total foreign born	7,800	100.0
Europe	300	3.8
Asia	—	0.0
Africa	200	2.6
Latin America	500	6.4
Non-Hispanic Caribbean	6,700	85.9
Northern America	—	0.0
Language Spoken at Home		
Population 5 years and over	20,000	100.0
English only	15,900	79.5
Language other than English	4,100	20.5
Household Income		
Median household income (dollars)	62,900	—

COLLEGE POINT

	Number	Percentage
Total Population	25,600	100.0
Age		
Under 18 years	5,800	22.7
65 years and over	3,500	13.7
Median age (years)	36.4	—
Mutually Exclusive Race and Hispanic Origin		
White, Non-Hispanic	14,300	55.9
Black or African American, Non-Hispanic	400	1.6
Asian and Pacific Islander, Non-Hispanic	4,300	16.8
Some other race, Non-Hispanic	100	0.4
Two or more races, Non-Hispanic	600	2.3
Hispanic (of any race)	5,800	22.7
Marital Status		
Population 15 years and over	20,500	100.0
Never married	5,600	27.3
Now married, except separated	10,500	51.2
Separated, widowed, or divorced	4,400	21.5
Housing		
Occupied units	8,800	100.0
Owner-occupied	4,800	54.5
Renter-occupied	4,000	45.5
Education		
Population 25 years and over	17,600	100.0
High school graduate or higher	14,000	79.5
Bachelors degree or higher	3,700	21.0
Region of Birth of Foreign Born		
Total foreign born	8,800	100.0
Europe	2,100	23.9
Asia	3,300	37.5
Africa	200	2.3
Latin America	2,900	33.0
Non-Hispanic Caribbean	100	1.1
Northern America	100	1.1
Language Spoken at Home		
Population 5 years and over	24,000	100.0
English only	12,200	50.8
Language other than English	11,800	49.2
Household Income		
Median household income (dollars)	49,900	—

	Number	Percentage
Total Population	99,100	100.0
Age		
Under 18 years	26,500	26.7
65 years and over	7,200	7.3
Median age (years)	29.6	—
Mutually Exclusive Race and Hispanic Origin		
White, Non-Hispanic	7,800	7.9
Black or African American, Non-Hispanic	14,400	14.5
Asian and Pacific Islander, Non-Hispanic	10,300	10.4
Some other race, Non-Hispanic	500	0.5
Two or more races, Non-Hispanic	1,800	1.8
Hispanic (of any race)	64,200	64.8
Marital Status		
Population 15 years and over	76,900	100.0
Never married	27,400	35.6
Now married, except separated	28,700	37.3
Separated, widowed, or divorced	20,800	27.0
Housing		
Occupied units	27,700	100.0
Owner-occupied	5,800	20.9
Renter-occupied	21,900	79.1
Education		
Population 25 years and over	59,200	100.0
High school graduate or higher	33,200	56.1
Bachelors degree or higher	6,800	11.5
Region of Birth of Foreign Born		
Total foreign born	61,700	100.0
Europe	2,500	4.1
Asia	9,800	15.9
Africa	1,900	3.1
Latin America	44,000	71.3
Non-Hispanic Caribbean	3,600	5.8
Northern America	—	0.0
Language Spoken at Home		
Population 5 years and over	91,300	100.0
English only	18,200	19.9
Language other than English	73,000	80.0
Household Income		
Median household income (dollars)	34,900	—

	Number	Percentage
Total Population	16,200	100.0
Age		
Under 18 years	3,200	19.8
65 years and over	2,700	16.7
Median age (years)	42.5	—
Mutually Exclusive Race and Hispanic Origin		
White, Non-Hispanic	10,400	64.2
Black or African American, Non-Hispanic	200	1.2
Asian and Pacific Islander, Non-Hispanic	4,100	25.3
Some other race, Non-Hispanic	—	0.0
Two or more races, Non-Hispanic	300	1.9
Hispanic (of any race)	1,100	6.8
Marital Status		
Population 15 years and over	13,600	100.0
Never married	3,400	25.0
Now married, except separated	7,800	57.4
Separated, widowed, or divorced	2,400	17.6
Housing		
Occupied units	6,300	100.0
Owner-occupied	4,600	73.0
Renter-occupied	1,700	27.0
Education		
Population 25 years and over	11,900	100.0
High school graduate or higher	10,600	89.1
Bachelors degree or higher	5,300	44.5
Region of Birth of Foreign Born		
Total foreign born	5,400	100.0
Europe	1,500	27.8
Asia	3,200	59.3
Africa	—	0.0
Latin America	600	11.1
Non-Hispanic Caribbean	100	1.9
Northern America	100	1.9
Language Spoken at Home		
Population 5 years and over	15,500	100.0
English only	8,300	53.5
Language other than English	7,200	46.5
Household Income		
Median household income (dollars)	69,900	—

EAST ELMHURST

	Number	Percentage
Total Population	68,700	100.0
Age		
Under 18 years	17,100	24.9
65 years and over	7,800	11.4
Median age (years)	34.0	—
Mutually Exclusive Race and Hispanic Origin		
White, Non-Hispanic	13,900	20.2
Black or African American, Non-Hispanic	11,600	16.9
Asian and Pacific Islander, Non-Hispanic	9,600	14.0
Some other race, Non-Hispanic	500	0.7
Two or more races, Non-Hispanic	2,000	2.9
Hispanic (of any race)	31,100	45.3
Marital Status		
Population 15 years and over	54,200	100.0
Never married	17,300	31.9
Now married, except separated	23,300	43.0
Separated, widowed, or divorced	13,500	24.9
Housing		
Occupied units	21,900	100.0
Owner-occupied	10,500	47.9
Renter-occupied	11,400	52.1
Education		
Population 25 years and over	45,000	100.0
High school graduate or higher	31,500	70.0
Bachelors degree or higher	7,900	17.6
Region of Birth of Foreign Born		
Total foreign born	36,600	100.0
Europe	4,500	12.3
Asia	7,600	20.8
Africa	600	1.6
Latin America	20,600	56.3
Non-Hispanic Caribbean	3,300	9.0
Northern America	100	0.3
Language Spoken at Home		
Population 5 years and over	63,900	100.0
English only	19,800	31.0
Language other than English	44,000	68.9
Household Income		
Median household income (dollars)	41,400	—

ELMHURST

	Number	Percentage
Total Population	104,100	100.0
Age		
Under 18 years	21,900	21.0
65 years and over	9,700	9.3
Median age (years)	34.5	—
Mutually Exclusive Race and Hispanic Origin		
White, Non-Hispanic	14,600	14.0
Black or African American, Non-Hispanic	1,500	1.4
Asian and Pacific Islander, Non-Hispanic	39,500	37.9
Some other race, Non-Hispanic	700	0.7
Two or more races, Non-Hispanic	2,500	2.4
Hispanic (of any race)	45,400	43.6
Marital Status		
Population 15 years and over	85,600	100.0
Never married	29,400	34.3
Now married, except separated	35,100	41.0
Separated, widowed, or divorced	21,100	24.6
Housing		
Occupied units	32,600	100.0
Owner-occupied	8,600	26.4
Renter-occupied	24,000	73.6
Education		
Population 25 years and over	70,200	100.0
High school graduate or higher	47,600	67.8
Bachelors degree or higher	16,200	23.1
Region of Birth of Foreign Born		
Total foreign born	73,100	100.0
Europe	4,000	5.5
Asia	33,800	46.2
Africa	500	0.7
Latin America	33,400	45.7
Non-Hispanic Caribbean	1,300	1.8
Northern America	100	0.1
Language Spoken at Home		
Population 5 years and over	97,600	100.0
English only	15,400	15.8
Language other than English	82,300	84.3
Household Income		
Median household income (dollars)	40,000	—

	Number	Percentage
Total Population	12,300	100.0
Age		
Under 18 years	2,600	21.1
65 years and over	2,600	21.1
Median age (years)	42.0	—
Mutually Exclusive Race and Hispanic Origin		
White, Non-Hispanic	7,200	58.5
Black or African American, Non-Hispanic	100	0.8
Asian and Pacific Islander, Non-Hispanic	3,900	31.7
Some other race, Non-Hispanic	100	0.8
Two or more races, Non-Hispanic	300	2.4
Hispanic (of any race)	800	6.5
Marital Status		
Population 15 years and over	10,200	100.0
Never married	2,400	23.5
Now married, except separated	5,900	57.8
Separated, widowed, or divorced	1,800	17.6
Housing		
Occupied units	4,400	100.0
Owner-occupied	3,600	81.8
Renter-occupied	800	18.2
Education		
Population 25 years and over	9,000	100.0
High school graduate or higher	7,700	85.6
Bachelors degree or higher	3,000	33.3
Region of Birth of Foreign Born		
Total foreign born	4,100	100.0
Europe	800	19.5
Asia	2,700	65.9
Africa	100	2.4
Latin America	300	7.3
Non-Hispanic Caribbean	200	4.9
Northern America	—	0.0
Language Spoken at Home		
Population 5 years and over	11,700	100.0
English only	6,700	57.3
Language other than English	5,000	42.7
Household Income		
Median household income (dollars)	58,700	—

	Number	Percentage
Total Population	214,000	100.0
Age		
Under 18 years	43,500	20.3
65 years and over	31,600	14.8
Median age (years)	37.8	—
Mutually Exclusive Race and Hispanic Origin		
White, Non-Hispanic	69,900	32.7
Black or African American, Non-Hispanic	10,900	5.1
Asian and Pacific Islander, Non-Hispanic	86,600	40.5
Some other race, Non-Hispanic	1,400	0.7
Two or more races, Non-Hispanic	7,000	3.3
Hispanic (of any race)	38,300	17.9
Marital Status		
Population 15 years and over	177,700	100.0
Never married	51,700	29.1
Now married, except separated	86,600	48.7
Separated, widowed, or divorced	39,400	22.2
Housing		
Occupied units	76,900	100.0
Owner-occupied	31,000	40.3
Renter-occupied	45,900	59.7
Education		
Population 25 years and over	151,800	100.0
High school graduate or higher	115,300	76.0
Bachelors degree or higher	42,600	28.1
Region of Birth of Foreign Born		
Total foreign born	116,700	100.0
Europe	14,400	12.3
Asia	75,900	65.0
Africa	800	0.7
Latin America	21,700	18.6
Non-Hispanic Caribbean	3,600	3.1
Northern America	300	0.3
Language Spoken at Home		
Population 5 years and over	201,900	100.0
English only	65,000	32.2
Language other than English	136,900	67.8
Household Income		
Median household income (dollars)	45,200	—

FOREST HILLS

	Number	Percentage
Total Population	52,500	100.0
Age		
Under 18 years	8,000	15.2
65 years and over	10,100	19.2
Median age (years)	41.7	—
Mutually Exclusive Race and Hispanic Origin		
White, Non-Hispanic	33,400	63.6
Black or African American, Non-Hispanic	1,000	1.9
Asian and Pacific Islander, Non-Hispanic	11,000	21.0
Some other race, Non-Hispanic	200	0.4
Two or more races, Non-Hispanic	1,300	2.5
Hispanic (of any race)	5,400	10.3
Marital Status		
Population 15 years and over	45,800	100.0
Never married	12,900	28.2
Now married, except separated	22,800	49.8
Separated, widowed, or divorced	10,100	22.1
Housing		
Occupied units	24,600	100.0
Owner-occupied	11,100	45.1
Renter-occupied	13,500	54.9
Education		
Population 25 years and over	41,000	100.0
High school graduate or higher	36,500	89.0
Bachelors degree or higher	20,300	49.5
Region of Birth of Foreign Born		
Total foreign born	24,700	100.0
Europe	8,300	33.6
Asia	12,200	49.4
Africa	400	1.6
Latin America	3,000	12.1
Non-Hispanic Caribbean	600	2.4
Northern America	200	0.8
Language Spoken at Home		
Population 5 years and over	50,000	100.0
English only	22,800	45.6
Language other than English	27,200	54.4
Household Income		
Median household income (dollars)	66,700	—

FRESH MEADOWS

	Number	Percentage
Total Population	28,200	100.0
Age		
Under 18 years	6,000	21.3
65 years and over	4,600	16.3
Median age (years)	41.8	—
Mutually Exclusive Race and Hispanic Origin		
White, Non-Hispanic	13,600	48.2
Black or African American, Non-Hispanic	2,200	7.8
Asian and Pacific Islander, Non-Hispanic	8,700	30.9
Some other race, Non-Hispanic	100	0.4
Two or more races, Non-Hispanic	1,200	4.3
Hispanic (of any race)	2,400	8.5
Marital Status		
Population 15 years and over	23,200	100.0
Never married	6,000	25.9
Now married, except separated	13,100	56.5
Separated, widowed, or divorced	4,200	18.1
Housing		
Occupied units	10,600	100.0
Owner-occupied	5,800	54.7
Renter-occupied	4,800	45.3
Education		
Population 25 years and over	20,400	100.0
High school graduate or higher	17,700	86.8
Bachelors degree or higher	8,100	39.7
Region of Birth of Foreign Born		
Total foreign born	11,100	100.0
Europe	2,000	18.0
Asia	7,000	63.1
Africa	200	1.8
Latin America	1,100	9.9
Non-Hispanic Caribbean	700	6.3
Northern America	—	0.0
Language Spoken at Home		
Population 5 years and over	26,500	100.0
English only	12,600	47.5
Language other than English	14,000	52.8
Household Income		
Median household income (dollars)	69,600	—

GLENDALE	Number	Percentage
Total Population	33,400	100.0
Age		
Under 18 years	7,700	23.1
65 years and over	5,100	15.3
Median age (years)	36.3	—
Mutually Exclusive Race and Hispanic Origin		
White, Non-Hispanic	24,900	74.6
Black or African American, Non-Hispanic	300	0.9
Asian and Pacific Islander, Non-Hispanic	700	2.1
Some other race, Non-Hispanic	100	0.3
Two or more races, Non-Hispanic	400	1.2
Hispanic (of any race)	6,900	20.7
Marital Status		
Population 15 years and over	26,900	100.0
Never married	7,500	27.9
Now married, except separated	13,700	50.9
Separated, widowed, or divorced	5,700	21.2
Housing		
Occupied units	13,000	100.0
Owner-occupied	6,000	46.2
Renter-occupied	7,000	53.8
Education		
Population 25 years and over	23,200	100.0
High school graduate or higher	17,500	75.4
Bachelors degree or higher	3,600	15.5
Region of Birth of Foreign Born		
Total foreign born	9,000	100.0
Europe	5,900	65.6
Asia	600	6.7
Africa	200	2.2
Latin America	2,100	23.3
Non-Hispanic Caribbean	100	1.1
Northern America	—	0.0
Language Spoken at Home		
Population 5 years and over	31,500	100.0
English only	17,700	56.2
Language other than English	13,800	43.8
Household Income		
Median household income (dollars)	42,800	—

GLEN OAKS	Number	Percentage
Total Population	10,100	100.0
Age		
Under 18 years	1,600	15.8
65 years and over	2,900	28.7
Median age (years)	56.0	—
Mutually Exclusive Race and Hispanic Origin		
White, Non-Hispanic	6,700	66.3
Black or African American, Non-Hispanic	600	5.9
Asian and Pacific Islander, Non-Hispanic	1,900	18.8
Some other race, Non-Hispanic	—	0.0
Two or more races, Non-Hispanic	200	2.0
Hispanic (of any race)	700	6.9
Marital Status		
Population 15 years and over	8,700	100.0
Never married	2,000	23.0
Now married, except separated	4,400	50.6
Separated, widowed, or divorced	2,300	26.4
Housing		
Occupied units	5,000	100.0
Owner-occupied	3,000	60.0
Renter-occupied	2,000	40.0
Education		
Population 25 years and over	8,000	100.0
High school graduate or higher	7,200	90.0
Bachelors degree or higher	3,100	38.8
Region of Birth of Foreign Born		
Total foreign born	2,400	100.0
Europe	500	20.8
Asia	1,500	62.5
Africa	—	0.0
Latin America	300	12.5
Non-Hispanic Caribbean	100	4.2
Northern America	—	0.0
Language Spoken at Home		
Population 5 years and over	9,600	100.0
English only	6,800	70.8
Language other than English	2,800	29.2
Household Income		
Median household income (dollars)	53,200	—

HOLLIS

	Number	Percentage
Total Population	23,900	100.0
Age		
Under 18 years	6,500	27.2
65 years and over	2,500	10.5
Median age (years)	34.2	—
Mutually Exclusive Race and Hispanic Origin		
White, Non-Hispanic	1,000	4.2
Black or African American, Non-Hispanic	12,500	52.3
Asian and Pacific Islander, Non-Hispanic	3,800	15.9
Some other race, Non-Hispanic	1,100	4.6
Two or more races, Non-Hispanic	1,800	7.5
Hispanic (of any race)	3,700	15.5
Marital Status		
Population 15 years and over	18,700	100.0
Never married	6,800	36.4
Now married, except separated	7,200	38.5
Separated, widowed, or divorced	4,700	25.1
Housing		
Occupied units	7,000	100.0
Owner-occupied	3,800	54.3
Renter-occupied	3,200	45.7
Education		
Population 25 years and over	15,100	100.0
High school graduate or higher	11,100	73.5
Bachelors degree or higher	2,600	17.2
Region of Birth of Foreign Born		
Total foreign born	11,000	100.0
Europe	300	2.7
Asia	1,800	16.4
Africa	100	0.9
Latin America	1,900	17.3
Non-Hispanic Caribbean	6,900	62.7
Northern America	—	0.0
Language Spoken at Home		
Population 5 years and over	22,300	100.0
English only	14,100	63.2
Language other than English	8,200	36.8
Household Income		
Median household income (dollars)	47,500	—

HOLLIS HILLS

	Number	Percentage
Total Population	3,200	100.0
Age		
Under 18 years	700	21.9
65 years and over	700	21.9
Median age (years)	45.8	—
Mutually Exclusive Race and Hispanic Origin		
White, Non-Hispanic	2,300	71.9
Black or African American, Non-Hispanic	—	0.0
Asian and Pacific Islander, Non-Hispanic	600	18.8
Some other race, Non-Hispanic	—	0.0
Two or more races, Non-Hispanic	100	3.1
Hispanic (of any race)	200	6.3
Marital Status		
Population 15 years and over	2,700	100.0
Never married	500	18.5
Now married, except separated	1,800	66.7
Separated, widowed, or divorced	400	14.8
Housing		
Occupied units	1,200	100.0
Owner-occupied	1,100	91.7
Renter-occupied	100	8.3
Education		
Population 25 years and over	2,400	100.0
High school graduate or higher	2,200	91.7
Bachelors degree or higher	1,300	54.2
Region of Birth of Foreign Born		
Total foreign born	1,100	100.0
Europe	400	36.4
Asia	600	54.5
Africa	—	0.0
Latin America	100	9.1
Non-Hispanic Caribbean	—	0.0
Northern America	—	0.0
Language Spoken at Home		
Population 5 years and over	3,100	100.0
English only	1,700	54.8
Language other than English	1,300	41.9
Household Income		
Median household income (dollars)	69,500	—

	Number	Percentage
Total Population	7,000	100.0
Age		
Under 18 years	1,500	21.4
65 years and over	1,100	15.7
Median age (years)	40.0	—
Mutually Exclusive Race and Hispanic Origin		
White, Non-Hispanic	2,200	31.4
Black or African American, Non-Hispanic	2,000	28.6
Asian and Pacific Islander, Non-Hispanic	1,300	18.6
Some other race, Non-Hispanic	200	2.9
Two or more races, Non-Hispanic	400	5.7
Hispanic (of any race)	1,100	15.7
Marital Status		
Population 15 years and over	5,900	100.0
Never married	1,600	27.1
Now married, except separated	2,900	49.2
Separated, widowed, or divorced	1,300	22.0
Housing		
Occupied units	2,600	100.0
Owner-occupied	1,900	73.1
Renter-occupied	700	26.9
Education		
Population 25 years and over	5,100	100.0
High school graduate or higher	4,400	86.3
Bachelors degree or higher	2,000	39.2
Region of Birth of Foreign Born		
Total foreign born	3,200	100.0
Europe	400	12.5
Asia	800	25.0
Africa	100	3.1
Latin America	700	21.9
Non-Hispanic Caribbean	1,200	37.5
Northern America	—	0.0
Language Spoken at Home		
Population 5 years and over	6,700	100.0
English only	3,800	56.7
Language other than English	2,900	43.3
Household Income		
Median household income (dollars)	69,800	—

	Number	Percentage
Total Population	28,100	100.0
Age		
Under 18 years	5,000	17.8
65 years and over	6,000	21.4
Median age (years)	41.9	—
Mutually Exclusive Race and Hispanic Origin		
White, Non-Hispanic	24,000	85.4
Black or African American, Non-Hispanic	300	1.1
Asian and Pacific Islander, Non-Hispanic	900	3.2
Some other race, Non-Hispanic	100	0.4
Two or more races, Non-Hispanic	200	0.7
Hispanic (of any race)	2,600	9.3
Marital Status		
Population 15 years and over	23,900	100.0
Never married	6,400	26.8
Now married, except separated	12,400	51.9
Separated, widowed, or divorced	5,000	20.9
Housing		
Occupied units	11,300	100.0
Owner-occupied	7,900	69.9
Renter-occupied	3,400	30.1
Education		
Population 25 years and over	21,100	100.0
High school graduate or higher	16,700	79.1
Bachelors degree or higher	4,100	19.4
Region of Birth of Foreign Born		
Total foreign born	3,900	100.0
Europe	2,100	53.8
Asia	800	20.5
Africa	100	2.6
Latin America	800	20.5
Non-Hispanic Caribbean	100	2.6
Northern America	100	2.6
Language Spoken at Home		
Population 5 years and over	26,700	100.0
English only	20,100	75.3
Language other than English	6,700	25.1
Household Income		
Median household income (dollars)	50,400	—

JACKSON HEIGHTS

	Number	Percentage
Total Population	71,200	100.0
Age		
Under 18 years	14,700	20.6
65 years and over	8,000	11.2
Median age (years)	35.5	—
Mutually Exclusive Race and Hispanic Origin		
White, Non-Hispanic	15,300	21.5
Black or African American, Non-Hispanic	1,300	1.8
Asian and Pacific Islander, Non-Hispanic	12,200	17.1
Some other race, Non-Hispanic	700	1.0
Two or more races, Non-Hispanic	1,800	2.5
Hispanic (of any race)	39,900	56.0
Marital Status		
Population 15 years and over	58,700	100.0
Never married	19,900	33.9
Now married, except separated	22,900	39.0
Separated, widowed, or divorced	15,900	27.1
Housing		
Occupied units	24,900	100.0
Owner-occupied	6,700	26.9
Renter-occupied	18,200	73.1
Education		
Population 25 years and over	48,900	100.0
High school graduate or higher	34,000	69.5
Bachelors degree or higher	11,600	23.7
Region of Birth of Foreign Born		
Total foreign born	47,000	100.0
Europe	5,100	10.9
Asia	11,200	23.8
Africa	500	1.1
Latin America	29,200	62.1
Non-Hispanic Caribbean	900	1.9
Northern America	100	0.2
Language Spoken at Home		
Population 5 years and over	66,800	100.0
English only	13,300	19.9
Language other than English	53,500	80.1
Household Income		
Median household income (dollars)	39,700	—

JAMAICA

	Number	Percentage
Total Population	132,800	100.0
Age		
Under 18 years	37,100	27.9
65 years and over	13,800	10.4
Median age (years)	33.4	—
Mutually Exclusive Race and Hispanic Origin		
White, Non-Hispanic	3,100	2.3
Black or African American, Non-Hispanic	89,700	67.5
Asian and Pacific Islander, Non-Hispanic	6,700	5.0
Some other race, Non-Hispanic	3,400	2.6
Two or more races, Non-Hispanic	6,300	4.7
Hispanic (of any race)	23,600	17.8
Marital Status		
Population 15 years and over	102,000	100.0
Never married	39,800	39.0
Now married, except separated	32,500	31.9
Separated, widowed, or divorced	29,700	29.1
Housing		
Occupied units	42,700	100.0
Owner-occupied	17,500	41.0
Renter-occupied	25,200	59.0
Education		
Population 25 years and over	81,800	100.0
High school graduate or higher	55,000	67.2
Bachelors degree or higher	10,700	13.1
Region of Birth of Foreign Born		
Total foreign born	46,800	100.0
Europe	1,200	2.6
Asia	3,400	7.3
Africa	2,000	4.3
Latin America	14,200	30.3
Non-Hispanic Caribbean	26,100	55.8
Northern America	100	0.2
Language Spoken at Home		
Population 5 years and over	123,300	100.0
English only	89,800	72.8
Language other than English	33,400	27.1
Household Income		
Median household income (dollars)	37,100	—

	Number	Percentage
Total Population	13,600	100.0
Age		
Under 18 years	2,900	21.3
65 years and over	2,200	16.2
Median age (years)	39.6	—
Mutually Exclusive Race and Hispanic Origin		
White, Non-Hispanic	5,200	38.2
Black or African American, Non-Hispanic	2,500	18.4
Asian and Pacific Islander, Non-Hispanic	3,700	27.2
Some other race, Non-Hispanic	100	0.7
Two or more races, Non-Hispanic	500	3.7
Hispanic (of any race)	1,700	12.5
Marital Status		
Population 15 years and over	11,200	100.0
Never married	3,300	29.5
Now married, except separated	5,300	47.3
Separated, widowed, or divorced	2,600	23.2
Housing		
Occupied units	5,000	100.0
Owner-occupied	2,500	50.0
Renter-occupied	2,400	48.0
Education		
Population 25 years and over	9,800	100.0
High school graduate or higher	8,400	85.7
Bachelors degree or higher	5,000	51.0
Region of Birth of Foreign Born		
Total foreign born	6,100	100.0
Europe	1,000	16.4
Asia	3,000	49.2
Africa	100	1.6
Latin America	700	11.5
Non-Hispanic Caribbean	1,200	19.7
Northern America	—	0.0
Language Spoken at Home		
Population 5 years and over	12,900	100.0
English only	6,100	47.3
Language other than English	6,800	52.7
Household Income		
Median household income (dollars)	63,900	—

	Number	Percentage
Total Population	16,000	100.0
Age		
Under 18 years	3,300	20.6
65 years and over	1,900	11.9
Median age (years)	35.4	—
Mutually Exclusive Race and Hispanic Origin		
White, Non-Hispanic	3,600	22.5
Black or African American, Non-Hispanic	2,200	13.8
Asian and Pacific Islander, Non-Hispanic	6,400	40.0
Some other race, Non-Hispanic	400	2.5
Two or more races, Non-Hispanic	1,000	6.3
Hispanic (of any race)	2,300	14.4
Marital Status		
Population 15 years and over	13,200	100.0
Never married	4,100	31.1
Now married, except separated	5,500	41.7
Separated, widowed, or divorced	3,600	27.3
Housing		
Occupied units	4,700	100.0
Owner-occupied	2,400	51.1
Renter-occupied	2,300	48.9
Education		
Population 25 years and over	10,400	100.0
High school graduate or higher	8,100	77.9
Bachelors degree or higher	3,500	33.7
Region of Birth of Foreign Born		
Total foreign born	8,900	100.0
Europe	800	9.0
Asia	4,900	55.1
Africa	200	2.2
Latin America	1,300	14.6
Non-Hispanic Caribbean	1,700	19.1
Northern America	—	0.0
Language Spoken at Home		
Population 5 years and over	15,100	100.0
English only	6,000	39.7
Language other than English	9,200	60.9
Household Income		
Median household income (dollars)	51,600	—

KEW GARDENS

	Number	Percentage
Total Population	25,900	100.0
Age		
Under 18 years	5,400	20.8
65 years and over	3,100	12.0
Median age (years)	35.6	—
Mutually Exclusive Race and Hispanic Origin		
White, Non-Hispanic	13,300	51.4
Black or African American, Non-Hispanic	1,700	6.6
Asian and Pacific Islander, Non-Hispanic	3,500	13.5
Some other race, Non-Hispanic	400	1.5
Two or more races, Non-Hispanic	1,300	5.0
Hispanic (of any race)	5,700	22.0
Marital Status		
Population 15 years and over	21,500	100.0
Never married	7,500	34.9
Now married, except separated	8,900	41.4
Separated, widowed, or divorced	5,200	24.2
Housing		
Occupied units	10,300	100.0
Owner-occupied	2,500	24.3
Renter-occupied	7,800	75.7
Education		
Population 25 years and over	18,200	100.0
High school graduate or higher	14,800	81.3
Bachelors degree or higher	7,000	38.5
Region of Birth of Foreign Born		
Total foreign born	12,600	100.0
Europe	3,700	29.4
Asia	4,600	36.5
Africa	200	1.6
Latin America	3,000	23.8
Non-Hispanic Caribbean	1,000	7.9
Northern America	100	0.8
Language Spoken at Home		
Population 5 years and over	24,200	100.0
English only	10,200	42.1
Language other than English	14,000	57.9
Household Income		
Median household income (dollars)	48,100	—

KEW GARDENS HILLS

	Number	Percentage
Total Population	26,500	100.0
Age		
Under 18 years	6,600	24.9
65 years and over	3,400	12.8
Median age (years)	35.8	—
Mutually Exclusive Race and Hispanic Origin		
White, Non-Hispanic	14,400	54.3
Black or African American, Non-Hispanic	2,100	7.9
Asian and Pacific Islander, Non-Hispanic	4,200	15.8
Some other race, Non-Hispanic	300	1.1
Two or more races, Non-Hispanic	1,600	6.0
Hispanic (of any race)	3,900	14.7
Marital Status		
Population 15 years and over	21,000	100.0
Never married	6,200	29.5
Now married, except separated	11,000	52.4
Separated, widowed, or divorced	3,900	18.6
Housing		
Occupied units	9,800	100.0
Owner-occupied	4,300	43.9
Renter-occupied	5,600	57.1
Education		
Population 25 years and over	17,300	100.0
High school graduate or higher	14,600	84.4
Bachelors degree or higher	6,700	38.7
Region of Birth of Foreign Born		
Total foreign born	11,500	100.0
Europe	3,100	27.0
Asia	5,600	48.7
Africa	300	2.6
Latin America	1,800	15.7
Non-Hispanic Caribbean	600	5.2
Northern America	100	0.9
Language Spoken at Home		
Population 5 years and over	24,500	100.0
English only	10,900	44.5
Language other than English	13,600	55.5
Household Income		
Median household income (dollars)	50,500	—

	Number	Percentage
Total Population	22,600	100.0
Age		
Under 18 years	5,400	23.9
65 years and over	2,400	10.6
Median age (years)	37.1	—
Mutually Exclusive Race and Hispanic Origin		
White, Non-Hispanic	500	2.2
Black or African American, Non-Hispanic	20,000	88.5
Asian and Pacific Islander, Non-Hispanic	100	0.4
Some other race, Non-Hispanic	100	0.4
Two or more races, Non-Hispanic	700	3.1
Hispanic (of any race)	1,200	5.3
Marital Status		
Population 15 years and over	18,100	100.0
Never married	6,300	34.8
Now married, except separated	7,300	40.3
Separated, widowed, or divorced	4,500	24.9
Housing		
Occupied units	7,100	100.0
Owner-occupied	5,600	78.9
Renter-occupied	1,400	19.7
Education		
Population 25 years and over	15,000	100.0
High school graduate or higher	12,500	83.3
Bachelors degree or higher	3,500	23.3
Region of Birth of Foreign Born		
Total foreign born	7,300	100.0
Europe	200	2.7
Asia	100	1.4
Africa	300	4.1
Latin America	600	8.2
Non-Hispanic Caribbean	6,100	83.6
Northern America	—	0.0
Language Spoken at Home		
Population 5 years and over	21,400	100.0
English only	18,000	84.1
Language other than English	3,400	15.9
Household Income		
Median household income (dollars)	59,900	—

	Number	Percentage
Total Population	8,200	100.0
Age		
Under 18 years	1,500	18.3
65 years and over	2,000	24.4
Median age (years)	45.5	—
Mutually Exclusive Race and Hispanic Origin		
White, Non-Hispanic	5,900	72.0
Black or African American, Non-Hispanic	—	0.0
Asian and Pacific Islander, Non-Hispanic	1,600	19.5
Some other race, Non-Hispanic	—	0.0
Two or more races, Non-Hispanic	200	2.4
Hispanic (of any race)	500	6.1
Marital Status		
Population 15 years and over	7,000	100.0
Never married	1,500	21.4
Now married, except separated	4,100	58.6
Separated, widowed, or divorced	1,400	20.0
Housing		
Occupied units	3,400	100.0
Owner-occupied	2,900	85.3
Renter-occupied	500	14.7
Education		
Population 25 years and over	6,200	100.0
High school graduate or higher	5,500	88.7
Bachelors degree or higher	2,600	41.9
Region of Birth of Foreign Born		
Total foreign born	2,400	100.0
Europe	600	25.0
Asia	1,400	58.3
Africa	—	0.0
Latin America	400	16.7
Non-Hispanic Caribbean	—	0.0
Northern America	—	0.0
Language Spoken at Home		
Population 5 years and over	7,900	100.0
English only	4,900	62.0
Language other than English	3,000	38.0
Household Income		
Median household income (dollars)	58,300	—

LONG ISLAND CITY

	Number	Percentage
Total Population	41,800	100.0
Age		
Under 18 years	10,000	23.9
65 years and over	4,700	11.2
Median age (years)	32.8	—
Mutually Exclusive Race and Hispanic Origin		
White, Non-Hispanic	11,500	27.5
Black or African American, Non-Hispanic	8,100	19.4
Asian and Pacific Islander, Non-Hispanic	5,700	13.6
Some other race, Non-Hispanic	1,000	2.4
Two or more races, Non-Hispanic	1,800	4.3
Hispanic (of any race)	13,600	32.5
Marital Status		
Population 15 years and over	33,400	100.0
Never married	13,000	38.9
Now married, except separated	11,400	34.1
Separated, widowed, or divorced	9,000	26.9
Housing		
Occupied units	16,400	100.0
Owner-occupied	3,100	18.9
Renter-occupied	13,300	81.1
Education		
Population 25 years and over	27,500	100.0
High school graduate or higher	18,900	68.7
Bachelors degree or higher	6,300	22.9
Region of Birth of Foreign Born		
Total foreign born	16,800	100.0
Europe	2,700	16.1
Asia	5,000	29.8
Africa	500	3.0
Latin America	7,800	46.4
Non-Hispanic Caribbean	600	3.6
Northern America	100	0.6
Language Spoken at Home		
Population 5 years and over	39,100	100.0
English only	17,200	44.0
Language other than English	21,900	56.0
Household Income		
Median household income (dollars)	36,000	—

MASPETH

	Number	Percentage
Total Population	42,400	100.0
Age		
Under 18 years	8,600	20.3
65 years and over	6,800	16.0
Median age (years)	37.2	—
Mutually Exclusive Race and Hispanic Origin		
White, Non-Hispanic	27,500	64.9
Black or African American, Non-Hispanic	400	0.9
Asian and Pacific Islander, Non-Hispanic	4,700	11.1
Some other race, Non-Hispanic	100	0.2
Two or more races, Non-Hispanic	900	2.1
Hispanic (of any race)	8,700	20.5
Marital Status		
Population 15 years and over	35,200	100.0
Never married	10,500	29.8
Now married, except separated	17,200	48.9
Separated, widowed, or divorced	7,500	21.3
Housing		
Occupied units	16,400	100.0
Owner-occupied	8,000	48.8
Renter-occupied	8,400	51.2
Education		
Population 25 years and over	30,400	100.0
High school graduate or higher	22,900	75.3
Bachelors degree or higher	5,200	17.1
Region of Birth of Foreign Born		
Total foreign born	15,700	100.0
Europe	7,400	47.1
Asia	3,800	24.2
Africa	100	0.6
Latin America	4,100	26.1
Non-Hispanic Caribbean	200	1.3
Northern America	100	0.6
Language Spoken at Home		
Population 5 years and over	40,000	100.0
English only	20,300	50.8
Language other than English	19,700	49.3
Household Income		
Median household income (dollars)	44,500	—

MIDDLE VILLAGE	Number	Percentage
Total Population	29,200	100.0
Age		
Under 18 years	5,300	18.2
65 years and over	5,700	19.5
Median age (years)	41.4	—
Mutually Exclusive Race and Hispanic Origin		
White, Non-Hispanic	24,400	83.6
Black or African American, Non-Hispanic	100	0.3
Asian and Pacific Islander, Non-Hispanic	1,300	4.5
Some other race, Non-Hispanic	100	0.3
Two or more races, Non-Hispanic	600	2.1
Hispanic (of any race)	2,800	9.6
Marital Status		
Population 15 years and over	24,700	100.0
Never married	7,000	28.3
Now married, except separated	12,400	50.2
Separated, widowed, or divorced	5,400	21.9
Housing		
Occupied units	11,800	100.0
Owner-occupied	6,700	56.8
Renter-occupied	5,100	43.2
Education		
Population 25 years and over	21,800	100.0
High school graduate or higher	17,200	78.9
Bachelors degree or higher	4,400	20.2
Region of Birth of Foreign Born		
Total foreign born	7,800	100.0
Europe	5,100	65.4
Asia	1,100	14.1
Africa	100	1.3
Latin America	1,300	16.7
Non-Hispanic Caribbean	100	1.3
Northern America	—	0.0
Language Spoken at Home		
Population 5 years and over	27,700	100.0
English only	17,400	62.8
Language other than English	10,400	37.5
Household Income		
Median household income (dollars)	51,800	—

OZONE PARK	Number	Percentage
Total Population	49,100	100.0
Age		
Under 18 years	13,000	26.5
65 years and over	5,100	10.4
Median age (years)	32.8	—
Mutually Exclusive Race and Hispanic Origin		
White, Non-Hispanic	17,000	34.6
Black or African American, Non-Hispanic	2,500	5.1
Asian and Pacific Islander, Non-Hispanic	6,500	13.2
Some other race, Non-Hispanic	1,900	3.9
Two or more races, Non-Hispanic	4,300	8.8
Hispanic (of any race)	16,800	34.2
Marital Status		
Population 15 years and over	38,000	100.0
Never married	11,600	30.5
Now married, except separated	18,500	48.7
Separated, widowed, or divorced	8,000	21.1
Housing		
Occupied units	15,900	100.0
Owner-occupied	7,900	49.7
Renter-occupied	7,900	49.7
Education		
Population 25 years and over	31,200	100.0
High school graduate or higher	21,100	67.6
Bachelors degree or higher	3,400	10.9
Region of Birth of Foreign Born		
Total foreign born	19,000	100.0
Europe	2,700	14.2
Asia	3,700	19.5
Africa	200	1.1
Latin America	6,500	34.2
Non-Hispanic Caribbean	6,000	31.6
Northern America	—	0.0
Language Spoken at Home		
Population 5 years and over	45,400	100.0
English only	23,500	51.8
Language other than English	21,900	48.2
Household Income		
Median household income (dollars)	40,300	—

	Number	Percentage
Total Population	61,400	100.0
Age		
Under 18 years	16,500	26.9
65 years and over	5,800	9.4
Median age (years)	34.2	—
Mutually Exclusive Race and Hispanic Origin		
White, Non-Hispanic	5,800	9.4
Black or African American, Non-Hispanic	32,300	52.6
Asian and Pacific Islander, Non-Hispanic	7,400	12.1
Some other race, Non-Hispanic	1,800	2.9
Two or more races, Non-Hispanic	3,900	6.4
Hispanic (of any race)	10,200	16.6
Marital Status		
Population 15 years and over	47,800	100.0
Never married	16,700	34.9
Now married, except separated	21,000	43.9
Separated, widowed, or divorced	10,100	21.1
Housing		
Occupied units	17,900	100.0
Owner-occupied	11,500	64.2
Renter-occupied	6,400	35.8
Education		
Population 25 years and over	39,300	100.0
High school graduate or higher	29,800	75.8
Bachelors degree or higher	7,800	19.8
Region of Birth of Foreign Born		
Total foreign born	28,200	100.0
Europe	1,000	3.5
Asia	4,100	14.5
Africa	700	2.5
Latin America	4,600	16.3
Non-Hispanic Caribbean	17,800	63.1
Northern America	100	0.4
Language Spoken at Home		
Population 5 years and over	57,400	100.0
English only	34,700	60.5
Language other than English	22,700	39.5
Household Income		
Median household income (dollars)	55,100	—

REGO PARK

	Number	Percentage
Total Population	60,900	100.0
Age		
Under 18 years	10,100	16.6
65 years and over	11,200	18.4
Median age (years)	40.1	—
Mutually Exclusive Race and Hispanic Origin		
White, Non-Hispanic	36,600	60.1
Black or African American, Non-Hispanic	1,200	2.0
Asian and Pacific Islander, Non-Hispanic	13,500	22.2
Some other race, Non-Hispanic	300	0.5
Two or more races, Non-Hispanic	1,800	3.0
Hispanic (of any race)	7,500	12.3
Marital Status		
Population 15 years and over	52,600	100.0
Never married	15,300	29.1
Now married, except separated	25,600	48.7
Separated, widowed, or divorced	11,700	22.2
Housing		
Occupied units	27,800	100.0
Owner-occupied	9,000	32.4
Renter-occupied	18,800	67.6
Education		
Population 25 years and over	46,300	100.0
High school graduate or higher	39,500	85.3
Bachelors degree or higher	19,900	43.0
Region of Birth of Foreign Born		
Total foreign born	34,400	100.0
Europe	12,000	34.9
Asia	16,700	48.5
Africa	800	2.3
Latin America	4,200	12.2
Non-Hispanic Caribbean	500	1.5
Northern America	100	0.3
Language Spoken at Home		
Population 5 years and over	58,100	100.0
English only	19,800	34.1
Language other than English	38,300	65.9
Household Income		
Median household income (dollars)	42,800	—

	Number	Percentage
Total Population	101,200	100.0
Age		
Under 18 years	27,400	27.1
65 years and over	7,500	7.4
Median age (years)	32.2	—
Mutually Exclusive Race and Hispanic Origin		
White, Non-Hispanic	14,000	13.8
Black or African American, Non-Hispanic	13,700	13.5
Asian and Pacific Islander, Non-Hispanic	21,400	21.1
Some other race, Non-Hispanic	7,200	7.1
Two or more races, Non-Hispanic	16,000	15.8
Hispanic (of any race)	29,000	28.7
Marital Status		
Population 15 years and over	78,200	100.0
Never married	25,100	32.1
Now married, except separated	36,200	46.3
Separated, widowed, or divorced	16,800	21.5
Housing		
Occupied units	28,600	100.0
Owner-occupied	14,500	50.7
Renter-occupied	14,100	49.3
Education		
Population 25 years and over	62,900	100.0
High school graduate or higher	40,600	64.5
Bachelors degree or higher	8,600	13.7
Region of Birth of Foreign Born		
Total foreign born	57,200	100.0
Europe	2,700	4.7
Asia	9,500	16.6
Africa	300	0.5
Latin America	13,700	24.0
Non-Hispanic Caribbean	30,900	54.0
Northern America	200	0.3
Language Spoken at Home		
Population 5 years and over	93,800	100.0
English only	52,700	56.2
Language other than English	41,100	43.8
Household Income		
Median household income (dollars)	42,600	—

	Number	Percentage
Total Population	67,000	100.0
Age		
Under 18 years	18,000	26.9
65 years and over	6,000	9.0
Median age (years)	31.5	—
Mutually Exclusive Race and Hispanic Origin		
White, Non-Hispanic	27,300	40.7
Black or African American, Non-Hispanic	1,100	1.6
Asian and Pacific Islander, Non-Hispanic	5,500	8.2
Some other race, Non-Hispanic	300	0.4
Two or more races, Non-Hispanic	1,500	2.2
Hispanic (of any race)	31,400	46.9
Marital Status		
Population 15 years and over	51,500	100.0
Never married	16,500	32.0
Now married, except separated	23,000	44.7
Separated, widowed, or divorced	12,000	23.3
Housing		
Occupied units	22,800	100.0
Owner-occupied	5,100	22.4
Renter-occupied	17,800	78.1
Education		
Population 25 years and over	41,900	100.0
High school graduate or higher	26,100	62.3
Bachelors degree or higher	5,600	13.4
Region of Birth of Foreign Born		
Total foreign born	30,800	100.0
Europe	12,900	41.9
Asia	4,900	15.9
Africa	400	1.3
Latin America	12,100	39.3
Non-Hispanic Caribbean	500	1.6
Northern America	—	0.0
Language Spoken at Home		
Population 5 years and over	61,900	100.0
English only	16,400	26.5
Language other than English	45,500	73.5
Household Income		
Median household income (dollars)	33,700	—

THE ROCKAWAYS

	Number	Percentage
Total Population	109,300	100.0
Age		
Under 18 years	31,300	28.6
65 years and over	15,400	14.1
Median age (years)	34.5	—
Mutually Exclusive Race and Hispanic Origin		
White, Non-Hispanic	40,300	36.9
Black or African American, Non-Hispanic	43,400	39.7
Asian and Pacific Islander, Non-Hispanic	1,900	1.7
Some other race, Non-Hispanic	1,200	1.1
Two or more races, Non-Hispanic	3,200	2.9
Hispanic (of any race)	19,500	17.8
Marital Status		
Population 15 years and over	82,800	100.0
Never married	29,100	35.3
Now married, except separated	29,600	35.9
Separated, widowed, or divorced	24,100	29.2
Housing		
Occupied units	37,900	100.0
Owner-occupied	13,100	34.5
Renter-occupied	24,800	64.7
Education		
Population 25 years and over	68,300	100.0
High school graduate or higher	49,100	71.9
Bachelors degree or higher	13,800	20.2
Region of Birth of Foreign Born		
Total foreign born	27,000	100.0
Europe	5,200	19.3
Asia	1,800	6.7
Africa	1,100	4.1
Latin America	7,800	28.9
Non-Hispanic Caribbean	11,200	41.5
Northern America	200	0.7
Language Spoken at Home		
Population 5 years and over	100,800	100.0
English only	73,200	72.5
Language other than English	27,600	27.4
Household Income		
Median household income (dollars)	34,100	—

ROSEDALE

	Number	Percentage
Total Population	25,400	100.0
Age		
Under 18 years	7,300	28.7
65 years and over	2,100	8.3
Median age (years)	34.3	—
Mutually Exclusive Race and Hispanic Origin		
White, Non-Hispanic	2,900	11.4
Black or African American, Non-Hispanic	17,600	69.3
Asian and Pacific Islander, Non-Hispanic	900	3.5
Some other race, Non-Hispanic	300	1.2
Two or more races, Non-Hispanic	1,300	5.1
Hispanic (of any race)	2,300	9.1
Marital Status		
Population 15 years and over	19,300	100.0
Never married	6,800	35.2
Now married, except separated	8,400	43.5
Separated, widowed, or divorced	4,100	21.2
Housing		
Occupied units	7,800	100.0
Owner-occupied	5,200	66.7
Renter-occupied	2,500	32.1
Education		
Population 25 years and over	15,700	100.0
High school graduate or higher	13,000	82.8
Bachelors degree or higher	3,200	20.4
Region of Birth of Foreign Born		
Total foreign born	11,400	100.0
Europe	400	3.5
Asia	600	5.3
Africa	700	6.1
Latin America	1,100	9.6
Non-Hispanic Caribbean	8,600	75.4
Northern America	—	0.0
Language Spoken at Home		
Population 5 years and over	23,600	100.0
English only	16,200	68.6
Language other than English	7,400	31.4
Household Income		
Median household income (dollars)	59,200	—

SOUTH OZONE PARK	Number	Percentage
Total Population	36,900	100.0
Age		
Under 18 years	10,200	27.6
65 years and over	3,600	9.8
Median age (years)	32.6	—
Mutually Exclusive Race and Hispanic Origin		
White, Non-Hispanic	4,000	10.8
Black or African American, Non-Hispanic	17,200	46.6
Asian and Pacific Islander, Non-Hispanic	2,900	7.9
Some other race, Non-Hispanic	2,000	5.4
Two or more races, Non-Hispanic	3,400	9.2
Hispanic (of any race)	7,300	19.8
Marital Status		
Population 15 years and over	28,300	100.0
Never married	9,700	34.3
Now married, except separated	12,100	42.8
Separated, widowed, or divorced	6,500	23.0
Housing		
Occupied units	10,900	100.0
Owner-occupied	7,200	66.1
Renter-occupied	3,700	33.9
Education		
Population 25 years and over	22,900	100.0
High school graduate or higher	16,800	73.4
Bachelors degree or higher	3,000	13.1
Region of Birth of Foreign Born		
Total foreign born	13,200	100.0
Europe	600	4.5
Asia	900	6.8
Africa	200	1.5
Latin America	2,600	19.7
Non-Hispanic Caribbean	8,900	67.4
Northern America	—	0.0
Language Spoken at Home		
Population 5 years and over	34,300	100.0
English only	24,500	71.4
Language other than English	9,800	28.6
Household Income		
Median household income (dollars)	47,200	—

SPRINGFIELD GARDENS	Number	Percentage
Total Population	31,500	100.0
Age		
Under 18 years	8,700	27.6
65 years and over	3,000	9.5
Median age (years)	33.8	—
Mutually Exclusive Race and Hispanic Origin		
White, Non-Hispanic	800	2.5
Black or African American, Non-Hispanic	26,500	84.1
Asian and Pacific Islander, Non-Hispanic	700	2.2
Some other race, Non-Hispanic	300	1.0
Two or more races, Non-Hispanic	1,200	3.8
Hispanic (of any race)	2,100	6.7
Marital Status		
Population 15 years and over	24,200	100.0
Never married	9,100	37.6
Now married, except separated	8,800	36.4
Separated, widowed, or divorced	6,300	26.0
Housing		
Occupied units	9,200	100.0
Owner-occupied	6,300	68.5
Renter-occupied	2,900	31.5
Education		
Population 25 years and over	19,800	100.0
High school graduate or higher	15,300	77.3
Bachelors degree or higher	4,000	20.2
Region of Birth of Foreign Born		
Total foreign born	10,800	100.0
Europe	200	1.9
Asia	300	2.8
Africa	400	3.7
Latin America	700	6.5
Non-Hispanic Caribbean	8,900	82.4
Northern America	100	0.9
Language Spoken at Home		
Population 5 years and over	29,200	100.0
English only	23,900	81.8
Language other than English	5,300	18.2
Household Income		
Median household income (dollars)	50,500	—

ST. ALBANS

	Number	Percentage
Total Population	49,000	100.0
Age		
Under 18 years	12,600	25.7
65 years and over	7,000	14.3
Median age (years)	37.4	—
Mutually Exclusive Race and Hispanic Origin		
White, Non-Hispanic	600	1.2
Black or African American, Non-Hispanic	44,900	91.6
Asian and Pacific Islander, Non-Hispanic	400	0.8
Some other race, Non-Hispanic	300	0.6
Two or more races, Non-Hispanic	1,100	2.2
Hispanic (of any race)	1,700	3.5
Marital Status		
Population 15 years and over	38,500	100.0
Never married	14,700	38.2
Now married, except separated	12,300	31.9
Separated, widowed, or divorced	11,500	29.9
Housing		
Occupied units	15,100	100.0
Owner-occupied	11,000	72.8
Renter-occupied	4,100	27.2
Education		
Population 25 years and over	31,600	100.0
High school graduate or higher	24,800	78.5
Bachelors degree or higher	5,700	18.0
Region of Birth of Foreign Born		
Total foreign born	13,300	100.0
Europe	400	3.0
Asia	300	2.3
Africa	500	3.8
Latin America	1,100	8.3
Non-Hispanic Caribbean	11,000	82.7
Northern America	100	0.8
Language Spoken at Home		
Population 5 years and over	45,800	100.0
English only	40,000	87.3
Language other than English	5,700	12.4
Household Income		
Median household income (dollars)	49,800	—

SUNNYSIDE

	Number	Percentage
Total Population	54,600	100.0
Age		
Under 18 years	10,400	19.0
65 years and over	5,700	10.4
Median age (years)	34.4	—
Mutually Exclusive Race and Hispanic Origin		
White, Non-Hispanic	17,800	32.6
Black or African American, Non-Hispanic	1,300	2.4
Asian and Pacific Islander, Non-Hispanic	12,000	22.0
Some other race, Non-Hispanic	300	0.5
Two or more races, Non-Hispanic	1,900	3.5
Hispanic (of any race)	21,300	39.0
Marital Status		
Population 15 years and over	45,800	100.0
Never married	16,600	36.2
Now married, except separated	17,600	38.4
Separated, widowed, or divorced	11,600	25.3
Housing		
Occupied units	21,200	100.0
Owner-occupied	3,500	16.5
Renter-occupied	17,700	83.5
Education		
Population 25 years and over	38,900	100.0
High school graduate or higher	27,900	71.7
Bachelors degree or higher	9,700	24.9
Region of Birth of Foreign Born		
Total foreign born	33,000	100.0
Europe	5,300	16.1
Asia	11,600	35.2
Africa	600	1.8
Latin America	14,800	44.8
Non-Hispanic Caribbean	600	1.8
Northern America	100	0.3
Language Spoken at Home		
Population 5 years and over	51,500	100.0
English only	14,000	27.2
Language other than English	37,500	72.8
Household Income		
Median household income (dollars)	34,100	—

WHITESTONE

	Number	Percentage
Total Population	33,100	100.0
Age		
Under 18 years	6,100	18.4
65 years and over	6,700	20.2
Median age (years)	41.5	—
Mutually Exclusive Race and Hispanic Origin		
White, Non-Hispanic	26,000	78.5
Black or African American, Non-Hispanic	100	0.3
Asian and Pacific Islander, Non-Hispanic	4,000	12.1
Some other race, Non-Hispanic	100	0.3
Two or more races, Non-Hispanic	400	1.2
Hispanic (of any race)	2,500	7.6
Marital Status		
Population 15 years and over	27,800	100.0
Never married	6,600	23.7
Now married, except separated	15,700	56.5
Separated, widowed, or divorced	5,500	19.8
Housing		
Occupied units	13,000	100.0
Owner-occupied	9,300	71.5
Renter-occupied	3,600	27.7
Education		
Population 25 years and over	24,800	100.0
High school graduate or higher	20,300	81.9
Bachelors degree or higher	6,800	27.4
Region of Birth of Foreign Born		
Total foreign born	9,400	100.0
Europe	4,600	48.9
Asia	3,200	34.0
Africa	100	1.1
Latin America	1,200	12.8
Non-Hispanic Caribbean	200	2.1
Northern America	100	1.1
Language Spoken at Home		
Population 5 years and over	31,400	100.0
English only	18,500	58.9
Language other than English	12,900	41.1
Household Income		
Median household income (dollars)	54,800	—

WOODHAVEN

	Number	Percentage
Total Population	37,200	100.0
Age		
Under 18 years	9,700	26.1
65 years and over	3,900	10.5
Median age (years)	35.2	—
Mutually Exclusive Race and Hispanic Origin		
White, Non-Hispanic	11,900	32.0
Black or African American, Non-Hispanic	1,300	3.5
Asian and Pacific Islander, Non-Hispanic	5,200	14.0
Some other race, Non-Hispanic	800	2.2
Two or more races, Non-Hispanic	1,700	4.6
Hispanic (of any race)	16,100	43.3
Marital Status		
Population 15 years and over	28,900	100.0
Never married	8,900	30.8
Now married, except separated	14,000	48.4
Separated, widowed, or divorced	6,000	20.8
Housing		
Occupied units	12,100	100.0
Owner-occupied	6,200	51.2
Renter-occupied	5,900	48.8
Education		
Population 25 years and over	24,000	100.0
High school graduate or higher	17,500	72.9
Bachelors degree or higher	4,200	17.5
Region of Birth of Foreign Born		
Total foreign born	15,600	100.0
Europe	2,200	14.1
Asia	3,700	23.7
Africa	100	0.6
Latin America	7,300	46.8
Non-Hispanic Caribbean	2,300	14.7
Northern America	—	0.0
Language Spoken at Home		
Population 5 years and over	34,600	100.0
English only	14,400	41.6
Language other than English	20,300	58.7
Household Income		
Median household income (dollars)	45,700	—

	Number	Percentage
Total Population	52,000	100.0
Age		
Under 18 years	10,300	19.8
65 years and over	5,800	11.2
Median age (years)	34.9	—
Mutually Exclusive Race and Hispanic Origin		
White, Non-Hispanic	11,600	22.3
Black or African American, Non-Hispanic	1,800	3.5
Asian and Pacific Islander, Non-Hispanic	18,600	35.8
Some other race, Non-Hispanic	200	0.4
Two or more races, Non-Hispanic	2,000	3.8
Hispanic (of any race)	17,800	34.2
Marital Status		
Population 15 years and over	43,100	100.0
Never married	14,900	34.6
Now married, except separated	17,500	40.6
Separated, widowed, or divorced	10,700	24.8
Housing		
Occupied units	18,400	100.0
Owner-occupied	4,900	26.6
Renter-occupied	13,500	73.4
Education		
Population 25 years and over	36,100	100.0
High school graduate or higher	25,800	71.5
Bachelors degree or higher	8,800	24.4
Region of Birth of Foreign Born		
Total foreign born	32,600	100.0
Europe	3,200	9.8
Asia	16,300	50.0
Africa	400	1.2
Latin America	12,300	37.7
Non-Hispanic Caribbean	400	1.2
Northern America	—	0.0
Language Spoken at Home		
Population 5 years and over	48,700	100.0
English only	11,900	24.4
Language other than English	36,800	75.6
Household Income		
Median household income (dollars)	37,500	—

Bibliography

Books

Alleman, Richard. *The Movie Lovers' Guide to New York.* New York: Perennial Library, 1988.

Ballenas, Carl, and Nancy Cataldi, with the Richmond Hill Historical Society. *Images of America: Richmond Hill.* Portsmouth, N.H.: Arcadia, 2002.

Blair, Gwenda. *The Trumps: Three Generations That Built an Empire.* New York: Simon and Schuster, 2000.

Bolton, Reginald Pelham. *Indian Life of Long Ago in the City of New York.* 1934. Enlarged ed. New York: Harmony, 1972.

————. *New York City in Indian Possession.* 1920. 2d ed. New York: Museum of the American Indian, 1975.

Burrows, Edwin, and Mike Wallace. *Gotham: A History of New York City to 1898.* New York: Oxford University Press, 1999.

Cantwell, Anne-Marie, and Diane diZerega Wall. *Unearthing Gotham: The Archaeology of New York City.* New Haven: Yale University Press, 2001.

Cohen, Rich. *Tough Jews.* New York: Simon and Schuster, 1998.

Comstock, Sarah. *Old Roads from the Heart of New York: Journeys Today by Ways of Yesterday Within Thirty Miles Around the Battery.* New York: Putnam, 1915.

Disturnell, John, ed. *New York As It Was and As It Is: Giving an Account of the City from its Settlement to the Present Time; Forming a Complete Guide to the Great Metropolis of the Nation Including the City of Brooklyn and the Surrounding Cities and Villages.* New York: Van Nostrand, 1876.

Flanagan, Mary, ed. *Victorian Richmond Hill.* New York: Richmond Hill Chapter of the Queens Historical Society, 1980.

Freeman, Joshua B. *Working-Class New York: Life and Labor Since World War II.* New York: New Press, 2000.

Gregory, Catherine. *Woodside, Queens County, New York: A Historical Perspective, 1652–1994.* New York: Woodside on the Move, 1994.

Groce, Nancy. *New York: Songs of the City.* New York: Billboard/Watson-Guptill, 1999.

Jackson, Kenneth T. *Crabgrass Frontier: The Suburbanization of the United States.* New York: Oxford University Press, 1985.

Jackson, Kenneth T., ed. *The Encyclopedia of New York City.* New Haven: Yale University Press, 1995.

Karatzas, Daniel. *Jackson Heights, a Garden in the City: The History of America's First Garden and Cooperative Apartment Community.* 2d ed. New York: Jackson Heights Beautification Group, 1998.

Kessner, Thomas. *The Golden Door: Italian and Jewish Immigrant Mobility in New York City.* New York: Oxford University Press, 1977.

Kouwenhoven, John A. *The Columbia Historical Portrait of New York.* Garden City, N.Y.: Doubleday, 1953.

Leeds, Mark. *Passport's Guide to Ethnic New York: A Complete Guide to the Many Faces and Cultures of New York.* Lincolnwood, Ill.: Passport, 1996.

Lewis, Barry. *Kew Gardens: Urban Village in the Big City.* New York: Kew Gardens Council for Recreation and the Arts, 1999.

Lieberman, Janet E., and Richard K. Lieberman. *City Limits: A Social History of Queens.* Dubuque, Iowa: Kendall/Hunt Publishing, 1983.

New York City Landmarks Preservation Commission. *Guide to New York City Landmarks.* Entries written by Andrew S. Dolkart. 2d ed. New York: John Wiley and Sons, 1998.

New York Public Library American History Desk Reference. New York: Stonesong/Macmillan, 1997.

Petroski, Henry. *Paperboy: Confessions of a Future Engineer.* New York: Knopf, 2002.

Powell, Charles Underhill, compiler, and Alice H. Meigs, ed. *Private and Family Cemeteries in the Borough of Queens.* Report of the Topographical Bureau of the City of New York, Office of the President of the Borough of Queens. Jamaica, N.Y.: Queens Borough Public Library, Long Island Collection, 1932.

Powell, Colin, and Joseph E. Persico. *My American Journey.* New York: Random House, 1995.

Reichstein, Steve. *Discovering Queens.* New York: H and M Productions, 2000.

Roff, Sandra Shoiock, Anthony M. Cucchiara, and Barbara J. Dunlap. *From the Free Academy to CUNY: Illustrating Public Higher Education in New York City, 1847–1997.* New York: Fordham University Press, 2000.

Seitz, Sharon, and Stuart Miller. *The Other Islands of New York City: A Historical Companion.* Woodstock, Vt.: Countryman, 1996.

Seyfried, Vincent F. *Queens: A Pictorial History.* Virginia Beach, Va.: Donning, 1982.

———. *The Story of Woodhaven and Ozone Park.* New York: Leader-Observer, 1986.

———. *Three Hundred Years of Long Island City, 1630–1930.* New York: Queens Historical Society, 1997.

Seyfried, Vincent F., and William Asadorian. *Old Queens, N.Y., in Early Photographs: 261 Prints.* New York: Dover, 1991.

———. *Old Rockaway, N.Y., in Early Photographs.* New York: Dover, 1999.

Smith, Albert E., and Phil A. Koury. *Two Reels and a Crank: From Nickelodeon to Picture Palaces.* Garden City, N.Y.: Doubleday, 1952.

Sutherland, Cara A. *Bridges of New York City.* Museum of the City of New York: Portraits of America. New York: Barnes and Noble, 2003.

White, Norval, and Elliot Willensky. *AIA Guide to New York City.* 4th ed. New York: Crown, 2000.

Wolfe, Gerald R. *New York, a Guide to the Metropolis: Walking Tours of Architecture and History* 2d ed. New York: McGraw-Hill, 1994.

The WPA Guide to New York City: The Federal Writers' Project Guide to 1930s New York. Ed. William H. Whyte. New York: Pantheon, 1982.

Newspapers

Crain's New York Business

Daily News

Forest Hills Ledger

Glendale Register

Gotham Gazette

Independent Press Association, Irish Echo

Jamaica Times Ledger

New York Post

New York Sun

New York Times

Queens Chronicle

Queens Courier

Queens Tribune

Queens Village Times

Real Estate Weekly

Time Out New York

Village Voice

Western Queens Gazette

Web Sites

arvernebythesea.com

astorialic.org

baysidehistorical.org

bellerosebusiness.org

cinematreasures.org

collegepoint.org

cordmeyer.com

cuny.edu

dlnhs.org

forgotten-ny.com

glenoaksvillage.com

hollisny.com

holliswood.com

home.nyc.gov

howardbeach.com

jhbg.org

junipercivic.com

lihistory.com

littleneck.net

malba.org

nationaltrust.org

nationalregisterofhistoricplaces.com

neighborhoodlink.com/queens

nyc.gov

nycgovparks.org

nyhistory.org

nyra.com

oldkewgardens.com

queenscouncilart.org

queenshistoricalsociety.org

queensnewyork.com

richmondhillhistory.org

ridgewoodhistorical.org

rosedalecivic.org

woodhavenculturalhistory.com

Chambers of Commerce and Civic Associations

Auburndale Improvement Association

Bowne Park Civic Association

Cambria Heights Civic Association
Creedmoor Civic Association
Dunton Block and Civic Association
Greater Ridgewood Restoration Corporation
Hillcrest Estates Civic Association
Holliswood Civic Association
Jamaica Hill Community Association
Little Neck Pines Civic Association
Lost Community Civic Association
Office of the Queens Borough President
Queens Chamber of Commerce
Rosedale Civic Association
Sunnyside Chamber of Commerce
Woodhull Civic Association

Index

Page numbers in *italics* indicate photographs and maps.